ROOFING & SIDING

Other Publications:

AMERICAN COUNTRY

VOYAGE THROUGH THE UNIVERSE

THE THIRD REICH

THE TIME-LIFE GARDENER'S GUIDE

MYSTERIES OF THE UNKNOWN

TIME FRAME

FIX IT YOURSELF

FITNESS, HEALTH & NUTRITION

SUCCESSFUL PARENTING

HEALTHY HOME COOKING

UNDERSTANDING COMPUTERS

LIBRARY OF NATIONS

THE ENCHANTED WORLD

THE KODAK LIBRARY OF CREATIVE PHOTOGRAPHY

GREAT MEALS IN MINUTES

THE CIVIL WAR

PLANET EARTH

COLLECTOR'S LIBRARY OF THE CIVIL WAR

THE EPIC OF FLIGHT

THE GOOD COOK

WORLD WAR II

HOME REPAIR AND IMPROVEMENT

THE OLD WEST

ROOFING & SIDING

TIME-LIFE BOOKS
ALEXANDRIA, VIRGINIA

Fix It Yourself was produced by
ST. REMY PRESS

MANAGING EDITOR	Kenneth Winchester
MANAGING ART DIRECTOR	Pierre Léveillé

Staff for *Roofing & Siding*

Series Editor	Brian Parsons
Editor	Kent J. Farrell
Series Art Director	Diane Denoncourt
Art Director	Philippe Arnoldi
Research Editor	Heather L. Mills
Contributing Editors	Elizabeth Cameron, Elizabeth W. Lewis
Contributing Writers	Andrew Benn, Iris Clendenning, Edward Earle, Stewart Freed, Richard Friedman, Carol Halls, Linda Jarosiewicz, Grant Loewen, Yesim Ternar
Electronic Designer	Maryse Doray
Contributing Illustrators	Gérard Mariscalchi, Jacques Proulx
Technical Illustrators	Nicolas Moumouris, Robert Paquet
Cover	Robert Monté
Index	Christine M. Jacobs
Administrator	Denise Rainville
Administrative Assistant	Natalie Watanabe
Coordinator	Michelle Turbide
Systems Manager	Shirley Grynspan
Systems Analyst	Simon Lapierre
Studio Director	Maryo Proulx
Photographer	Julie Léger

Time-Life Books Inc. is a wholly owned subsidiary of
TIME INCORPORATED

FOUNDER	Henry R. Luce 1898-1967
Editor-in-Chief	Jason McManus
Chairman and Chief Executive Officer	J. Richard Munro
President and Chief Operating Officer	N. J. Nicholas Jr.
Editorial Director	Richard B. Stolley
Executive Vice President, Books	Kelso F. Sutton
Vice President, Books	Paul V. McLaughlin

TIME-LIFE BOOKS INC.

EDITOR	George Constable
Executive Editor	Ellen Phillips
Director of Design	Louis Klein
Director of Editorial Resources	Phyllis K. Wise
Editorial Board	Russell B. Adams Jr., Dale M. Brown, Roberta Conlan, Thomas H. Flaherty, Lee Hassig, Donia Ann Steele, Rosalind Stubenberg
Director of Photography and Research	John Conrad Weiser
Asst. Director of Editorial Resources	Elise Ritter Gibson
PRESIDENT	Christopher T. Linen
Chief Operating Officer	John M. Fahey Jr.
Senior Vice Presidents	Robert M. DeSena, James L. Mercer, Paul R. Stewart
Vice Presidents	Stephen L. Bair, Ralph J. Cuomo, Neal Goff, Stephen L. Goldstein, Juanita T. James, Carol Kaplan, Susan J. Maruyama, Robert H. Smith, Joseph J. Ward
Director of Production Services	Robert J. Passantino
Supervisor of Quality Control	James King

Editorial Operations

Copy Chief	Diane Ullius
Production	Celia Beattie
Library	Louise D. Forstall
Correspondents	Elizabeth Kraemer-Singh (Bonn); Maria Vincenza Aloisi (Paris); Ann Natanson (Rome).

THE CONSULTANTS

Consulting Editor **David L. Harrison** served as an editor for several Time-Life Books do-it-yourself series, including *Home Repair and Improvement*, *The Encyclopedia of Gardening* and *The Art of Sewing*.

Joseph Truini is Shop and Tools Editor of Popular Mechanics magazine and specializes in home improvement articles for do-it-yourselfers. He has worked as a home improvement contractor, carpenter and home remodeler.

Richard Day, a do-it-yourself writer for over a quarter century, is a founder of the National Association of Home and Workshop Writers, and is the author of several home repair books.

Glen Walsh, special consultant for Canada, has been in the construction industry for 20 years and has specialized in roofing for the past 11 years. He is the founder of The Homeowners' Roofing Clinic Program, which informs consumers about quality, properly-installed roofing.

Joseph R. Provey, editor of Practical Homeowner magazine, has also worked as editor of Home Mechanix and Family Handyman magazines. He has roofing and general carpentry experience, and has written hundreds of do-it-yourself articles on home remodeling, repair and maintenance.

Library of Congress Cataloging-in-Publication Data
Roofing & siding.
     p. cm. – (Fix it yourself)
     Includes index.
     ISBN 0-8094-6240-0
     ISBN 0-8094-6241-9(lib. bdg.)
     1. Roofing—Amateur's manuals.
     2. Siding (Building materials)—Amateur's manuals.
     3. Dwellings—Maintenance and repair—Amateur's manuals.
I. Time-Life Books. II. Title:
Roofing and siding. III. Series.
TH2401.R58   1989
695—dc19   88-34860
                             CIP

For information about any Time-Life book, please write:
Reader Information
Time-Life Customer Service
P.O. Box C-32068
Richmond, Virginia
23261-2068

CONTENTS

HOW TO USE THIS BOOK   6

EMERGENCY GUIDE   8

YOUR ROOFING AND SIDING   14

WORKING SAFELY AT HEIGHTS   24

GUTTERS AND DOWNSPOUTS   34

FASCIAS   46

ASPHALT SHINGLES   50

TILE AND SLATE ROOFING   62

TAR AND GRAVEL ROOFING   70

WOOD SHINGLES AND SHAKES   74

WOOD SIDING   86

VINYL AND ALUMINUM SIDING   102

TOOLS & TECHNIQUES   112

INDEX   126

ACKNOWLEDGMENTS   128

HOW TO USE THIS BOOK

Roofing and Siding is divided into three sections. The Emergency Guide on pages 8 to 13 provides information that can be indispensable, even lifesaving, in the event of a household emergency. Take the time to study this section *before* you need the important advice it contains.

The Repairs section — the heart of the book — is a comprehensive approach to troubleshooting and repairing roofing and siding. Shown below are four sample pages from the chapter on gutters and downspouts with captions describing the various features of the book and how they work.

For example, if a gutter is overflowing onto the roofing or down the siding, the Troubleshooting Guide on page 34 will suggest possible causes; if the problem is a bent, broken or missing hanger, you will be directed to page 40 for detailed instructions on how to install a new one. Or, if a gutter section has been damaged by ice and snow, for instance, you will be directed to page 41 to replace a metal gutter section and to page 43 to replace a vinyl gutter section.

Each job has been rated by degree of difficulty and by the average time it will take for a do-it-yourselfer to complete.

Introductory text
Describes the way roofing and siding materials are installed, their most common problems and basic repair approaches.

Troubleshooting Guide
To use this chart, locate the symptom that most closely resembles your roofing or siding problem, review the possible causes in column 2, then follow the recommended procedures in column 3. Simple fixes may be explained on the chart; in most cases you will be directed to an illustrated, step-by-step repair sequence.

Anatomy diagrams
Locate and describe the various components of the roofing or siding material.

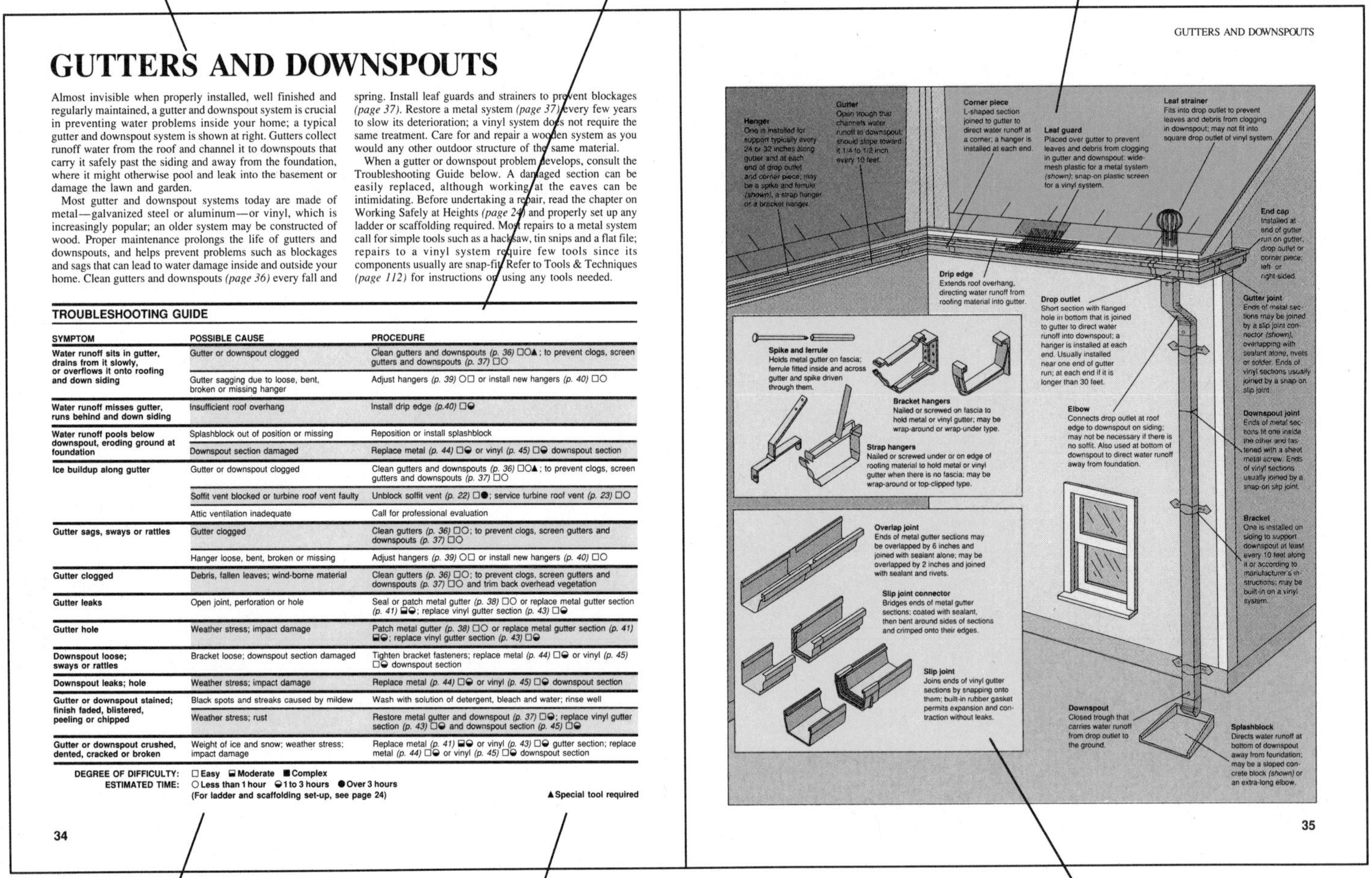

Degree of difficulty and time
Rate the complexity of each repair and how much time the job should take for a homeowner with average do-it-yourself skills.

Special tool required
Some repairs call for a specialized tool; in this example, a trap-and-drain auger is required to unblock a badly clogged downspout.

Variations
Differences in roofing and siding materials are described throughout the book, particularly if a repair procedure varies from one type of material to another.

Keep in mind that this rating is only a suggestion and does not include ladder or scaffolding set-up. Before deciding whether you should attempt a repair, read all the instructions carefully and consult the Working Safely at Heights chapter *(page 24)* for details on using ladders and scaffolding. Then be guided by your own confidence, and the tools and time available to you. For more complex or time-consuming repairs, such as improving attic or wall ventilation, you may wish to call for a professional evaluation. You will still have saved time and money by diagnosing the problem yourself.

Most repairs in *Roofing and Siding* can be made with basic carpentry and metal-working tools such as hammers, pry bars, tin snips, trowels, caulking guns, saws, chisels, and drills. Any special tool required is indicated in the Troubleshooting Guide. The proper way to use tools along with information on sealants and adhesives, fasteners, and finishes is presented in the Tools & Techniques section starting on page 112. If you are a novice at home repair, read this chapter before starting a job. Repairing roofing and siding can be easy and worry-free if you work logically and follow all safety precautions.

Tools and techniques
General information on using tools properly is covered in the Tools & Techniques section *(page 112)*. When a specific tool or method is required for a job, it is described within the step-by-step repair.

Name of repair
You will be referred by the Troubleshooting Guide to the first page of a specific repair job.

Step-by-step procedures
Bold lead-ins summarize each step or highlight the key action pictured. Follow the numbered repair sequence carefully. Depending on the result of each step, you may be directed to a later step, or to another part of the book, to complete the repair.

GUTTERS AND DOWNSPOUTS

INSTALLING A GUTTER HANGER

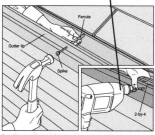

Installing a spike and ferrule. If the gutter is vinyl or there is no fascia, install strap hangers *(step right)*. Otherwise, prepare to work safely on the gutter *(page 24)*. To correct a gutter sag, remove as many spikes and ferrules as necessary *(page 39)*. For each additional spike and ferrule to be installed, drill a hole *(page 121)* in the gutter lip *(inset)*, placing a 2-by-4 as a brace inside the gutter; if possible, position the hole at a rafter, usually located every 12 or 16 inches behind the fascia. To install a spike and ferrule, fit the ferrule inside the gutter over the hole and tap the spike into it; holding the ferrule steady, position the gutter and drive the spike through it *(above)*, into the fascia and rafter behind it. Use the same procedure to install at least one spike and ferrule every 24 or 32 inches along the gutter.

Installing a strap hanger. If the gutter is metal and there is a fascia, install spikes and ferrules *(step left)*. Otherwise, prepare to work safely on the gutter *(page 24)*. To correct a gutter sag, remove as many strap or bracket hangers as necessary *(page 39)*. Install strap hangers of a type that fits the gutter, following the manufacturer's instructions. For the type of strap hanger shown, snap the clips onto the gutter edges. Position the strap on or under the edge of the roofing material, adjusting it until the gutter is in position, and drive roofing nails *(page 121)* into it *(above)*. Apply roofing cement *(page 115)* on each nail head. Use the same procedure to install at least one strap hanger every 24 or 32 inches along the gutter.

INSTALLING A DRIP EDGE

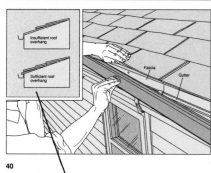

Insufficient roof overhang

Sufficient roof overhang

Fascia   Gutter

Putting up a drip edge. Prepare to work safely along the roof edge *(page 24)* and install a drip edge if the roofing material does not overhang the roof edge by at least 1 inch *(inset)*. Buy drip edge equal to the length of the roof edge at a building supply center. If necessary, cut the drip edge to length using a hacksaw or tin snips *(page 120)* or assemble it in sections following the manufacturer's instructions; the sections of the vinyl drip edge shown are spliced to interlock. Remove burrs from a cut metal edge and smooth rough spots off a cut vinyl edge with a flat file *(page 123)*. To install the drip edge, fit one side between the roofing material and the building paper along the roof edge *(left)*, pushing until the other side is aligned along the inside gutter edge and overhanging it by at least 1 inch. Following the manufacturer's instructions, install any fasteners *(page 121)* required to secure the drip edge; the drip edge shown is held in place by the roofing material and requires no fasteners.

40

REPLACING A METAL GUTTER SECTION

GUTTERS AND DOWNSPOUTS

Board

Tin snips

1 Removing the damaged section. Prepare to work safely along the gutter *(page 24)*, having a helper on hand. Remove any downspout assembly from the damaged section *(page 44)*. Mark a cutting line on the gutter at one end of the damaged section and wedge a board at it between the gutter and the roof edge. Wearing work gloves and safety goggles, use a hacksaw *(page 120)* to cut off the damaged section *(left)*; remove any hangers in the way *(page 39)*. If necessary, use tin snips *(page 120)* to finish the cut *(inset)*. Repeat the procedure at the other end of the damaged section. Take off the damaged section by removing its spikes and ferrules or releasing it from its strap or bracket hangers; if necessary, remove them along with it. Lower the damaged section to the ground. Use a chalkline *(page 117)* to mark the position of a replacement section along the roof edge, ensuring a gutter slope of about 1/16 inch per foot toward the downspout.

2 Measuring and cutting a replacement section. Calculate the length of gutter needed, adding a few feet for waste, and determine the number of end caps, corner pieces, drop outlets, and hangers required; if there is a fascia, using spikes and ferrules to replace any strap or bracket hangers removed is easiest. For each joint, using a sealant *(page 115)* and a slip joint connector is easiest; or, use a sealant alone or, if you live in a region of heavy rainfall or snow, with rivets *(page 121)*. Buy components for a replacement section at a building supply center.

Mark off the replacement gutter: equal in length to the damaged section if you are using a slip joint connector at each joint; long enough for about 6 inches of overlap at each joint if you are using a sealant alone; long enough for about 2 inches of overlap at each joint if you are using rivets. Wearing work gloves and safety goggles, cut the gutter to length: use a hacksaw *(page 120)* if it is unpainted *(far left)*, placing a 2-by-4 as a brace inside it; use tin snips *(page 120)* if it is prefinished *(near left)*. Remove burrs from the cut edges with a flat file *(page 123)*. If more than one gutter length is needed, mark off and cut each one the same way; then, assemble the gutter lengths *(step 3)*. If only one gutter length is needed, add any end cap, corner piece and drop outlet required *(step 4)*; otherwise, prepare the replacement section for installation *(step 5)*.

41

Insets
Provide close-up views of specific steps and illustrate variations in techniques.

Cross-references
Direct you to important information elsewhere in the book, including alternative techniques and disassembly steps.

EMERGENCY GUIDE

Preventing problems in roofing and siding repairs. The exterior of your home, while designed to be attractive and inviting, provides you with the functional security of having a roof over your head. Built to withstand the rigors of the outdoors, exterior roofing and siding requires special care and maintenance to ensure that your home can withstand the relentless attack of the sun, wind, rain, snow and ice.

Regularly inspect your roofing and siding system *(page 14)*—and undertake repairs *before* an emergency situation arises. The list of safety tips at right covers basic guidelines for the repair of roofing and siding; consult the particular chapter for more specific advice. Before beginning any repair, methodically prepare all your tools and materials on the ground and safely set up and use any ladders or scaffolding required for the job *(page 24)*. Review Tools & Techniques *(page 112)*; it provides valuable information on repair procedures and the safe use of tools.

Repairs undertaken high up on the exterior walls or roof of your home need not be any more dangerous than repairs carried out at ground level. Most work accidents arise from carelessness: unsafe work habits at heights, improper use of tools, misuse of electricity outdoors and mishandling of toxic materials. Nonetheless, you should prepare yourself to handle any emergency before one occurs. The Troubleshooting Guide on page 9 places emergency procedures at your fingertips; it provides quick-action steps to take and refers you to the procedures on pages 10 through 13 for detailed instructions.

When a sudden leak in your roof occurs, minimize damage inside your home by containing water in the attic *(page 10)* or by piercing the water-laden ceiling *(page 11)*. When the roof is dry, install a patch over damaged or missing roofing material *(page 11)* to act as a temporary barrier until the roof can be repaired. **Caution:** Do not attempt any repairs on a roof that is wet or laden with snow or ice.

If you must rescue someone who is experiencing an electrical shock, do not touch the person; use a board or a wooden broom handle to knock the victim free of the power source *(page 13)*. Do not move the victim of a fall; call an ambulance immediately, then cover the victim with a blanket to regulate body temperature in case of shock *(page 13)* until medical assistance arrives.

When in doubt about your ability to handle an emergency, do not hesitate to call for help. Post emergency fire, medical and poison control numbers near the telephone; in most areas, dial 911 in the event of a life-threatening emergency. Also seek technical help when you need it. If you are in doubt about the nature or safety of a repair, have it checked by a professional roofing or siding contractor. Even in non-emergency situations, a building inspector in your local community can answer questions concerning the condition of your roofing and siding.

SAFETY TIPS

1. Before beginning any repair in this book, read the entire procedure. Familiarize yourself with the specific safety information presented in each chapter.

2. Use the proper tool for the job. Refer to Tools & Techniques *(page 112)* for the correct use and maintenance of tools. Store tools not in use well out of the reach of children.

3. When working outdoors with power tools, use only heavy-duty, three-prong extension cords rated for outdoor use. Inspect the cord closely; if it is damaged, replace it. Secure the connection between the power tool and extension cord by looping the cords together loosely before plugging in the tool.

4. Plug power tools into GFCI-protected outlets only, and never cut off or bypass the third, or grounding, prong on a power tool plug. A power tool with a two-prong plug must be labeled "double insulated". Do not use any power tool in a damp area.

5. When working in high places, wear rubber- or crepe-soled shoes, preferably with ankle support. To prevent heat exhaustion, wear a hat when working in hot, sunny weather.

6. Wear the proper protective gear for the job: safety goggles when operating power tools or working above your head; work gloves when applying roofing cement or handling fiberglass insulation or metal flashing; rubber gloves when applying cleaning solvents, preservatives and finishing products. Remove watches and jewelry before starting a repair.

7. Follow basic safety rules for ladders and scaffolds *(page 24)*. Work with a helper or within earshot of someone else. To avoid accidents from falling tools or materials, keep people and pets away from the work area.

8. Do not undertake any repair near overhead utility lines.

9. Work only in good weather conditions, never when it is wet or windy. Do not attempt any repairs on a roof if it is wet or laden with snow or ice.

10. Never undertake repairs when you are tired. If you are taking medication, consult your physician. When thirsty, drink a non-alcoholic beverage.

11. Carefully read the label on any paint, solvent, sealant, adhesive or other material used. Follow the manufacturer's instructions and pay special attention to safety precautions, hazard warnings and storage instructions.

12. Do not pour solvents, cleaners or finishing products down a house drain or into a septic system. Consult your municipal authorities on proper disposal procedures in your community.

13. When working with flammable chemicals or power tools, have on hand a portable fire extinguisher rated ABC and know how to use it. Install smoke detectors in your home.

14. Store a roll of building paper or plastic sheeting for use as a temporary water barrier in case of an emergency.

16. Keep a first-aid kit on hand. Stock it with mild antiseptic, sterile gauze dressings and bandages, adhesive tape and scissors, tweezers, and a packet of needles.

17. Post emergency, utility company and repair service numbers near your telephone.

TROUBLESHOOTING GUIDE

SYMPTOM	PROCEDURE
Power line fallen on roof	Call power company, police or fire department
	Treat every downed cable as a live cable. Stay far away from fallen power line and anything it touches. Keep people and pets away from area
Tree fallen on roof	Call power company, police or fire department
	Keep people and pets away from area
Fall from roof, ladder or scaffolding	Call an ambulance immediately; cover victim with blanket to treat for possible shock *(p. 13)*
Sudden leak through ceiling from attic or roof	Minimize interior damage by installing a temporary water barrier in the attic *(p. 10)* or by piercing the water-laden ceiling *(p. 11)*
Icicles overhanging or falling from roof	Break off icicles using a board or wooden broom handle *(p. 12)*
Roofing material damaged or missing	Install a temporary patch *(p. 11)*. **Caution:** Do not attempt any repair on a roof that is wet or laden with snow or ice
Fire in wood, in power tool or outlet, or in cleaning or refinishing product	Call fire department, then use ABC-rated fire extinguisher
Electrical shock	Knock person free of source using a board or wooden broom handle *(p. 13)*
	Check whether victim is breathing and has pulse. If not, have someone call for medical help, and begin artificial resuscitation or cardiopulmonary resuscitation (CPR) only if you are qualified. Otherwise, place victim in recovery position *(p. 13)* and seek medical attention immediately
Spark or shock from power tool	Unplug tool power cord at outlet or shut off power at main service panel *(p. 10)*
	Locate and repair cause of spark or shock before using tool again
Extension cord sparks or is hot to touch	Shut off power at main service panel *(p. 10)*
	Inspect extension cord and replace it with one rated for power tool being used
Cleaning or refinishing product swallowed	Call local poison control center and seek medical attention; follow emergency instructions on product label and take product with you to hospital
Head injury	Check whether victim is breathing and has pulse. If not, have someone call for medical help, and begin artificial resuscitation or cardiopulmonary resuscitation (CPR) only if you are qualified. Otherwise, place victim in recovery position *(p. 13)* and seek medical attention
	If victim loses consciousness, even for only one second, seek medical attention immediately
Large object embedded under skin	Support object in place with loose bandages and seek medical attention immediately. **Caution:** Removing object can cause hemorrhage
Electrical burn	Seek medical attention immediately. **Caution:** Never apply ointment to a burn
Cut or minor wound	Apply pressure to stop bleeding *(p. 12)*
	If bleeding persists or if wound is deep, seek medical attention
Skin scratch or puncture from rusted or dirty fastener or metal flashing	Wash wound using soap and water; seek medical attention concerning need for a tetanus shot
Bruise	Apply ice pack to reduce swelling. If pain does not diminish or swelling persists, seek medical attention
Splinter	Use sterilized needle and tweezers to open wound and pull out splinter *(p. 12)*
	If splinter is lodged deeply or if wound becomes infected, seek medical attention
Sawdust, particle, or cleaning or refinishing product in eye	Do not rub eye; flush eye with water from garden hose *(p. 12)* and seek medical attention
Cleaning or refinishing product on skin	Wash skin thoroughly with soap and water; refer to product label for additional instructions
	If skin irritation develops, seek medical attention and take product with you
Faintness, dizziness, nausea or blurred vision when working in hot sun	Lie down in shade with feet elevated; apply cool, wet cloth to forehead and drink a non-alcoholic beverage
	If symptoms persist, seek medical attention
Strained back	Apply ice pack immediately
	If pain persists, seek medical attention

TURNING OFF ELECTRICAL POWER

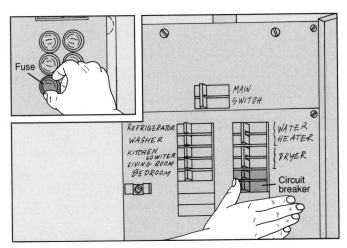

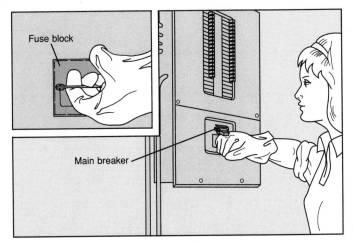

Disconnecting power at a circuit. At the electrical panel, locate the circuit breaker or fuse protecting the circuit. In an emergency, or if the circuit breaker or fuse is not identified, shut down the entire electrical system *(step right)*. Work only in dry conditions, use one hand, and do not touch anything metal with the other hand. At a circuit breaker panel, flip the circuit breaker toggle switch to OFF *(above)*; it may spring back to an intermediate position. To reset the toggle switch, push the toggle to OFF, then to ON. At a fuse panel, grasp the fuse by its insulated rim only and unscrew it *(inset)*. To reset the fuse, screw it back in.

Shutting down the entire electrical system. If the floor around the service panel is wet, stand on a dry board or a rubber mat and wear heavy, dry rubber gloves. Use one hand only; keep the other hand in your pocket or behind your back. At a circuit breaker panel, flip off the main breaker *(above)*—as an added precaution, use your knuckle; any shock will jerk your hand away from the panel. At a fuse panel, remove the main fuse block by gripping its metal handle and pulling it from the box *(inset)*. On a panel with more than one fuse block, remove them all. Some fuse panels have a shutoff lever instead; pull down the lever to turn off power.

MINIMIZING LEAK DAMAGE

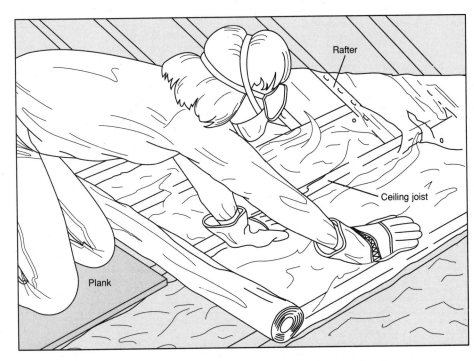

Containing water in an attic. If water from a leak is collecting in an attic, minimize damage by protecting the attic with plastic sheeting. If a large amount of water has collected above the ceiling, release the water *(page 11)*. If the attic has no floor, position planks across the ceiling joists to use as walkways. Wearing safety goggles, work gloves and a dust mask, remove any water-laden insulation between the joists and bag it for disposal; if the attic has little headroom, wear a hard hat. Working across the attic, lay the sheeting across the joists *(left)* or the attic floor. Overlap parallel lengths of sheeting by 12 to 18 inches and seal the seams with duct tape. To minimize water runoff, use a staple gun to staple the outside edges of the sheeting to the rafters and studs along the attic perimeter. As water collects on the sheeting, clean it up with a mop and bucket. When repairs are made, remove the staples and roll up the sheeting, and replace any insulation removed. If repairs cannot be made immediately, install an emergency patch *(page 11)*.

MINIMIZING LEAK DAMAGE (continued)

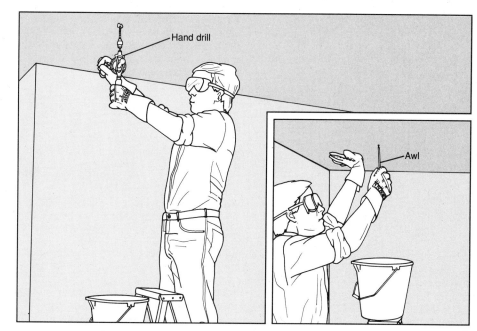

Releasing water from a ceiling. If water from a leak is dripping through a ceiling and the water cannot be contained in the attic *(page 10)*, minimize damage by piercing the ceiling and collecting the water in a bucket. To prevent electrical shock, turn off power to the room or the entire house *(page 10)*. Set up a stepladder *(page 26)* under the wet ceiling with a bucket on it to catch drips. Wearing safety goggles, release water collected above a drywall ceiling by puncturing it with an awl or an ice pick *(inset)*, twisting the tool to enlarge the hole. Pierce a plaster ceiling using a hand drill with a 3/8-inch bit *(left)* or a long nail and a hammer. **Caution:** To avoid electrical shock, do not use a power drill. If necessary, make more than one hole to release all the water. When roofing repairs are made, replace any water-laden insulation and patch the ceiling. If roofing repairs cannot be made immediately, install an emergency patch *(step below)*.

INSTALLING AN EMERGENCY PATCH

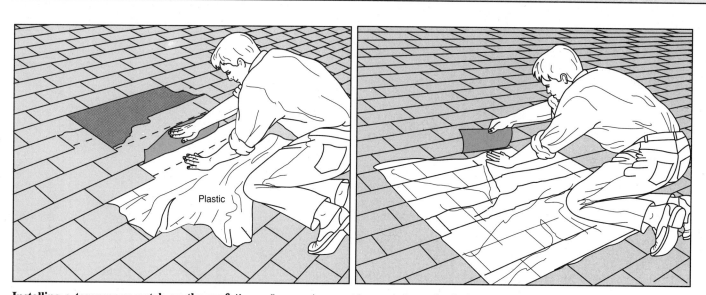

Installing a temporary patch on the roof. If a roofing repair cannot be made immediately, install an emergency patch using building paper or plastic sheeting. Prepare to work safely on the roof *(page 24)*, setting up a ladder near the damaged area. **Caution:** Do not get on the roof if it is wet or laden with snow or ice. Use scissors to cut a patch 4 feet longer and wider than the damaged area. Slip the patch under the first undamaged course of roofing material below the damaged area *(above, left)*, fold it flat over the damaged area, and tuck it under the first course of roofing material above the damaged area *(above, right)*. Position as many patches as necessary to cover the entire damaged area, overlapping them vertically by 12 to 18 inches and sealing the seams with duct tape. Drive nails *(page 121)* through each patch into the damaged area. Apply roofing cement *(page 115)* on the nail heads.

REMOVING OVERHANGING ICICLES

Breaking off icicles. Caution: Always knock icicles off eaves or gutters away from the house and yourself; if you are working outdoors, wear safety goggles and a hard hat. If the icicles can be reached from the ground, knock them off using a board or a wooden broom handle; if the icicles cannot be reached from the ground, try to reach them from a window *(left)*. If the icicles cannot be reached from the ground or a window, clear the ground next to them of snow and ice and set up a ladder safely *(page 24)*; have a helper hold the ladder steady or secure it by tying it to a 2-by-4 stake driven into the ground under it. Brush snow off the ladder and wear boots or sneakers with non-skid rubber soles to climb it. Use a board or a wooden broom handle to knock off the icicles.

PROVIDING MINOR FIRST AID

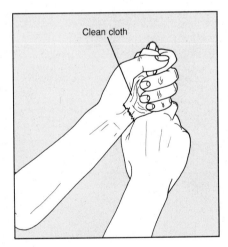

Clean cloth

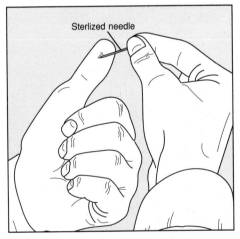

Sterilized needle

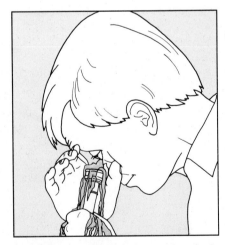

Treating a cut or scratch. To stop bleeding, wrap a clean cloth around the wound and apply direct pressure with your hand, elevating the limb *(above)*. If the cloth becomes blood-soaked, add a second cloth over the first one. Continue applying pressure and elevating the limb until the bleeding stops. Wash a minor wound with soap and water, then bandage it. Seek medical attention if bleeding persists or if the wound is deep.

Treating a splinter. Wash your hands and the area around the wound with soap and water. A metal splinter may require treatment for tetanus; seek medical attention. For other splinters, use the point of a needle that is sterilized in a flame or with alcohol to loosen the splinter *(above)*; pry it up until it can be pulled out with tweezers. Wash the area again with soap and water to prevent infection, then bandage it. If the splinter is lodged too deeply for removal, seek medical attention.

Flushing foreign particles or chemicals from the eye. Immediately hold the eyelids apart and position the injured eye under a steady, gentle flow of cool water from a garden hose to flush the eye for 10 minutes *(above)*. Then, cover the eye with a sterile gauze bandage and seek medical attention immediately.

RESCUING A VICTIM OF ELECTRICAL SHOCK

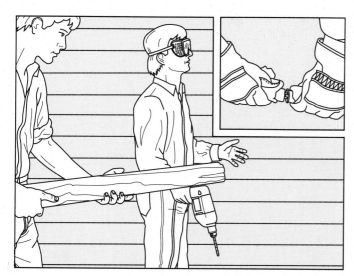

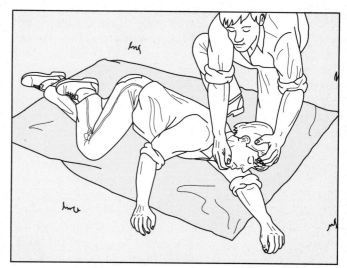

Freeing someone from a live current. Usually a person who contacts live current is thrown back from the source, but sometimes muscles contract involuntarily around a power tool or its cord. Do not touch the victim or the tool. In a dry area only, insulate your hands with heavy work gloves or thick pieces of cloth and unplug the power tool or extension cord *(inset)*; if the area is wet, shut off power at the main service panel *(page 10)*. If the power cannot be cut immediately, use a board, a wooden broom handle or other non-conducting object to separate the victim from the current source *(above)*. Tingling or numbness may indicate an internal injury; seek medical attention immediately.

Handling a victim of electrical shock. Call for help immediately. Check the victim's breathing and heartbeat. If there is no breathing or heartbeat, give mouth-to-mouth resuscitation or cardiopulmonary resuscitation (CPR) only if you are qualified. If the victim is breathing and has not sustained neck or back injuries, place him in the recovery position *(above)*. Tilt the head back with the face to one side and the tongue forward to maintain an open airway. Keep the victim calm and comfortable until help arrives.

TREATING THE VICTIM OF A FALL

Treating the victim of a fall. Call an ambulance immediately, then cover the victim to regulate body temperature in case of shock *(left)*. **Caution:** The victim of a fall should not be moved until qualified medical help arrives, especially if there is pain in the area of the neck or back, or if clear spinal fluid can be seen flowing from the ears or nose. Help the victim to stay calm and keep others from crowding around. When qualified medical help arrives, make sure they are advised of possible spinal cord injury.

YOUR ROOFING AND SIDING

Your roofing and siding are an integral part of your home's structure, adding style and beauty to the exterior and protecting the interior from the elements. Roofing and siding are your home's first and best line of defence against water, wind and temperature extremes. The materials and installation methods used for roofing and siding also permit excess interior moisture, heat and gases to escape to the exterior, keeping you comfortable and safe indoors.

One of the most important functions of your roofing and siding is protection against water penetration. The material of your roofing and siding—asphalt, coal tar, wood, clay, concrete or slate for roofing, and wood, vinyl or aluminum for siding—have all stood the test of time; when properly installed and maintained, they can provide years of defence against water, whether in the form of rain, hail, sleet, snow or ice.

Roofing and siding materials are almost always installed in overlapping patterns, with the material higher up the roof slope or wall lapped over the material installed below it. Water can flow down the lapped materials and is prevented from running back up under them. This method of overlapping is key to ensuring that water does not penetrate your roofing and siding, that it instead is diverted away from the underlying structure and interior of your home, and directed down to the ground and safely away from the foundation.

The roofing and siding installation shown at right demonstrates how the various elements that make up the system work together to provide water and weather protection for your home. On the roof, overlapped roofing material carries water from the ridge to the eave of the house where specially-installed roofing material directs it into the gutter. A slight slope in the gutter ensures that the water runs to a downspout, which in turn carries it safely past the siding and to the ground, away from the foundation.

Any break in the roof surface is fitted with special roofing material or flashing that is in turn lapped with the roofing material to ensure the same downward water flow and keep water from seeping through the joint. Valleys, vents, skylights and chimneys are fitted with flashing, while ridges and hips are fitted with specially-cut roofing material. Flashing damaged by impact, loosened by wind or rusted by exposure to water can cause damage to surrounding roofing material and the underlying house structure.

On the outside walls, overlapped siding material carries water down them. Any break in a wall is fitted with special siding material or flashing to protect against water seepage. Horizontal breaks may be fitted with Z flashing, while vertical breaks may be fitted with special trim and sealed. The siding is protected from water running off the roof by overhanging eaves and rakes and by the gutters and downspouts.

The attic or space between the roofing material and interior ceilings, and the space between the siding material and interior walls, are ventilated to balance humidity levels indoors that result from everyday living activities and outdoors that result from weather changes. Vents in the soffit and the gable or roof allow air circulation through the attic, while unsealed siding

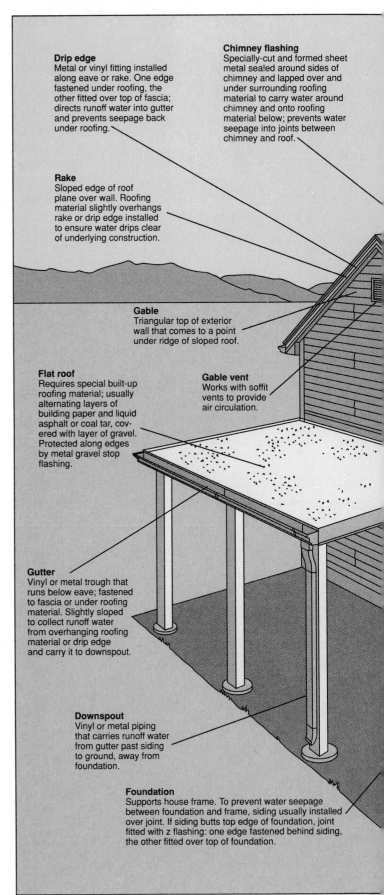

Drip edge
Metal or vinyl fitting installed along eave or rake. One edge fastened under roofing, the other fitted over top of fascia; directs runoff water into gutter and prevents seepage back under roofing.

Chimney flashing
Specially-cut and formed sheet metal sealed around sides of chimney and lapped over and under surrounding roofing material to carry water around chimney and onto roofing material below; prevents water seepage into joints between chimney and roof.

Rake
Sloped edge of roof plane over wall. Roofing material slightly overhangs rake or drip edge installed to ensure water drips clear of underlying construction.

Gable
Triangular top of exterior wall that comes to a point under ridge of sloped roof.

Flat roof
Requires special built-up roofing material; usually alternating layers of building paper and liquid asphalt or coal tar, covered with layer of gravel. Protected along edges by metal gravel stop flashing.

Gable vent
Works with soffit vents to provide air circulation.

Gutter
Vinyl or metal trough that runs below eave; fastened to fascia or under roofing material. Slightly sloped to collect runoff water from overhanging roofing material or drip edge and carry it to downspout.

Downspout
Vinyl or metal piping that carries runoff water from gutter past siding to ground, away from foundation.

Foundation
Supports house frame. To prevent water seepage between foundation and frame, siding usually installed over joint. If siding butts top edge of foundation, joint fitted with z flashing: one edge fastened behind siding, the other fitted over top of foundation.

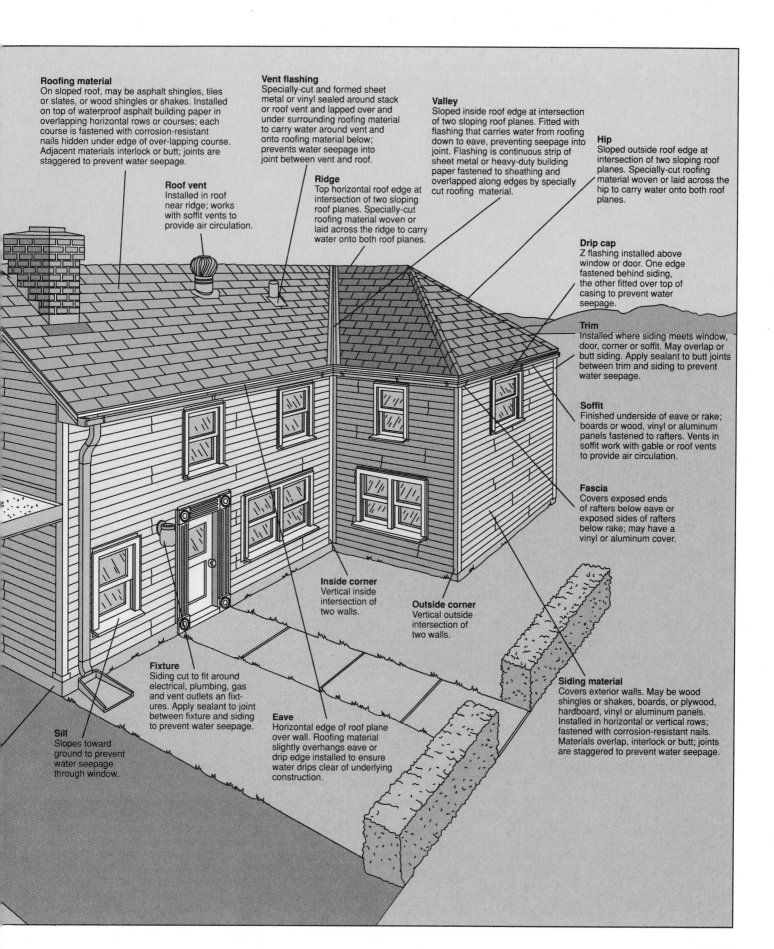

Roofing material
On sloped roof, may be asphalt shingles, tiles or slates, or wood shingles or shakes. Installed on top of waterproof asphalt building paper in overlapping horizontal rows or courses; each course is fastened with corrosion-resistant nails hidden under edge of over-lapping course. Adjacent materials interlock or butt; joints are staggered to prevent water seepage.

Roof vent
Installed in roof near ridge; works with soffit vents to provide air circulation.

Vent flashing
Specially-cut and formed sheet metal or vinyl sealed around stack or roof vent and lapped over and under surrounding roofing material to carry water around vent and onto roofing material below; prevents water seepage into joint between vent and roof.

Ridge
Top horizontal roof edge at intersection of two sloping roof planes. Specially-cut roofing material woven or laid across the ridge to carry water onto both roof planes.

Valley
Sloped inside roof edge at intersection of two sloping roof planes. Fitted with flashing that carries water from roofing down to eave, preventing seepage into joint. Flashing is continuous strip of sheet metal or heavy-duty building paper fastened to sheathing and overlapped along edges by specially cut roofing material.

Hip
Sloped outside roof edge at intersection of two sloping roof planes. Specially-cut roofing material woven or laid across the hip to carry water onto both roof planes.

Drip cap
Z flashing installed above window or door. One edge fastened behind siding, the other fitted over top of casing to prevent water seepage.

Trim
Installed where siding meets window, door, corner or soffit. May overlap or butt siding. Apply sealant to butt joints between trim and siding to prevent water seepage.

Soffit
Finished underside of eave or rake; boards or wood, vinyl or aluminum panels fastened to rafters. Vents in soffit work with gable or roof vents to provide air circulation.

Fascia
Covers exposed ends of rafters below eave or exposed sides of rafters below rake; may have a vinyl or aluminum cover.

Inside corner
Vertical inside intersection of two walls.

Outside corner
Vertical outside intersection of two walls.

Fixture
Siding cut to fit around electrical, plumbing, gas and vent outlets an fixtures. Apply sealant to joint between fixture and siding to prevent water seepage.

Sill
Slopes toward ground to prevent water seepage through window.

Eave
Horizontal edge of roof plane over wall. Roofing material slightly overhangs eave or drip edge installed to ensure water drips clear of underlying construction.

Siding material
Covers exterior walls. May be wood shingles or shakes, boards, or plywood, hardboard, vinyl or aluminum panels. Installed in horizontal or vertical rows; fastened with corrosion-resistant nails. Materials overlap, interlock or butt; joints are staggered to prevent water seepage.

joints permit air circulation behind the siding. Blocked vents or inadequate ventilation can lead to a buildup of condensation in an attic or wall which, over time, can damage the roofing, siding and underlying structure.

Inspect all the elements of your roofing and siding routinely each spring and fall, and the moment an interior leak occurs. Because the elements of your roofing and siding are so carefully integrated, checking and repairing one component alone is no guarantee that a problem will not turn up elsewhere or that you have solved a problem completely. Use the Troubleshooting Guide below as a checklist in examining the elements of your roofing and siding system—the attic, the vents, the siding material, the roofing material, the flashing, the gutters and downspouts, and the fascias. The Troubleshooting Guide will direct you as needed to information in other chapters on repairs for specific roofing and siding materials.

Always begin your inspection in the attic. Check all rafters, beams, joists, studs, sheathing and insulation; pay particular attention to areas along eaves and rakes, under valleys, and around the base of any chimney or vent. Be on the lookout for physical damage, mildew, rot, watermarks or water that are evidence of a leak or a ventilation problem. Check soffit, gable and roof vents for damage, blockage and faulty operation.

Outside, do a walking tour around the house to inspect the siding and roofing. Pay special attention to southern wall and

TROUBLESHOOTING GUIDE

SYMPTOM	POSSIBLE CAUSE	PROCEDURE
INSPECTING THE ATTIC		
Leak into attic or from ceiling	Water penetrating roofing; hole in plumbing	Minimize immediate water damage (p. 10) □○
	Flashing damaged	Patch flashing with metal (p. 19) □○ or with fiberglass (p. 20) □○; repair flashing joints (p. 20) □○; if damage extensive, call for professional evaluation
	Gutter or downspout damaged or faulty	Troubleshoot and repair gutters and downspouts (p. 34)
	Roofing damaged	Troubleshoot and repair: asphalt shingles (p. 50); tile and slate (p. 63); tar and gravel (p. 70); wood shingles and shakes (p. 76)
	Skylight, stack vent or chimney damaged	Call for professional evaluation
Attic damp; condensation or frost in cold weather	Soffit vent blocked or turbine roof vent faulty	Unblock soffit vent (p. 22) □●; service turbine roof vent (p. 23) □○
	Attic ventilation or insulation inadequate	Call for professional evaluation
Soffit vent blocked	Insulation or debris	Unblock soffit vent (p. 22) □●
	Birds nesting	Call for professional evaluation
Gable vent loose or damaged	Weather stress; impact damage	Service gable vent (p. 23) □○
	Birds nesting	Call for professional evaluation
Turbine roof vent noisy or does not operate	Bearings lack lubricant; vent faulty	Service turbine roof vent (p. 23) □○
INSPECTING THE SIDING		
Leak through wall or into basement	Flashing damaged	Patch flashing with metal (p. 19) □○ or with fiberglass (p. 20) □○; repair flashing joints (p. 20) □○; if damage extensive, call for professional evaluation
	Gutter or downspout damaged or faulty	Troubleshoot and repair gutters and downspouts (p. 34)
	Roofing damaged	Troubleshoot and repair: asphalt shingles (p. 50); tile and slate (p. 63); tar and gravel (p. 70); wood shingles and shakes (p. 76)
	Siding damaged	Troubleshoot and repair: wood shingles and shakes (p. 76); wood siding (p. 87); vinyl and aluminum siding (p. 103)
Sealant loose or missing	Weather stress; impact damage	Apply sealant (p. 115) □○
Gable vent loose or damaged	Weather stress; impact damage	Service gable vent (p. 23) □○
	Birds nesting	Call for professional evaluation
Siding loose or damaged	Weather stress; impact damage	Troubleshoot and repair: wood shingles and shakes (p. 76); wood siding (p. 87); vinyl and aluminum siding (p. 103)
	Structural damage	Call for professional evaluation

DEGREE OF DIFFICULTY: □ Easy ◪ Moderate ■ Complex
ESTIMATED TIME: ○ Less than 1 hour ◔ 1 to 3 hours ● Over 3 hours
(For ladder and scaffolding set-up, see page 24)

roof exposures that may be subject to deterioration from sunlight, as well as protected or shaded exposures that may be subject to excess moisture and poor air circulation. Use binoculars to pinpoint any problem high on the exterior walls, under the soffits, along the roof edges or on the roof. If necessary, set up a ladder *(page 24)* to inspect the gutters, roof edges and roofing material more carefully.

On the siding, look for deteriorated or damaged finish and for stains or discoloration that may be a sign of water damage; if left untreated, a more serious and costly problem may develop. Check seams and gaps where the siding material meets trim and fixtures for loose or missing sealant. Look for loose, damaged or missing siding material.

Along the roof edges, look for stains, discoloration or physical damage that might indicate a problem with a soffit or fascia. Check the roofing material for signs of damage. Inspect gutters for blockages and signs of water backup, as well as for corrosion, holes and loose or leaking joints.

On the roof, be on the lookout for debris that may cause damage to the roofing material. Inspect any stains or discoloration that may be evidence of water damage or that, if left untreated, may contribute to further damage. Look for loose, damaged or missing roofing material. Pay special attention to the flashing around chimneys, vents and skylights and in valleys. Look for signs of corrosion, tears, holes and loose or unsealed joints.

TROUBLESHOOTING GUIDE

SYMPTOM	POSSIBLE CAUSE	PROCEDURE
INSPECTING THE GUTTERS AND DOWNSPOUTS		
Water backs up onto roofing; runs down fascia and siding	Gutter or downspout clogged or damaged	Troubleshoot and repair gutters and downspouts *(p. 34)*
Gutter or downspout loose or damaged	Weather stress; impact damage	Troubleshoot and repair gutters and downspouts *(p. 34)*
INSPECTING THE FASCIA AND SOFFIT		
Soffit wet or leaking	Water penetrating roofing	Call for professional evaluation
Fascia loose or damaged	Gutter or downspout damaged or faulty	Troubleshoot and repair gutters and downspouts *(p. 34)*
	Weather stress; impact damage	Troubleshoot and repair fascias *(p. 46)*
	Structural damage	Call for professional evaluation
INSPECTING THE FLASHING		
Flashing tear or hole	Weather stress; impact damage	Patch flashing with metal *(p. 19)* □○ or with fiberglass *(p. 20)* □○; if damage extensive, call for professional evaluation
Flashing joint open	Weather stress; impact damage	Repair flashing joints *(p. 20)* □○; if damage extensive, call for professional evaluation
Flashing rusted or pitted	Weather stress	Restore flashing *(p. 18)* □○
INSPECTING THE ROOFING		
Leak into attic or from ceiling, through wall or into basement	Water penetrating roofing or siding	Minimize immediate water damage *(p. 10)* □○
	Flashing damaged	Patch flashing with metal *(p. 19)* □○ or with fiberglass *(p. 20)* □○; repair flashing joints *(p. 20)* □○; if damage extensive, call for professional evaluation
	Gutter or downspout damaged or faulty	Troubleshoot and repair gutters and downspouts *(p. 34)*
	Roofing damaged	Troubleshoot and repair: asphalt shingles *(p. 50)*; tile and slate *(p. 63)*; tar and gravel *(p. 70)*; wood shingles and shakes *(p. 76)*
	Skylight, stack vent or chimney damaged	Call for professional evaluation
Ice buildup at roof edge, over gutter or under roofing	Soffit vent blocked or turbine roof vent faulty	Unblock soffit vent *(p. 22)* □●; service turbine roof vent *(p. 23)* □○
	Attic ventilation or insulation inadequate	Call for professional evaluation
Turbine roof vent noisy or does not operate	Bearings lack lubricant; vent faulty	Service turbine roof vent *(p. 23)* □○
Roofing loose or damaged	Weather stress; impact damage	Troubleshoot and repair: asphalt shingles *(p. 50)*; tile and slate *(p. 63)*; tar and gravel *(p. 70)*; wood shingles and shakes *(p. 76)*
	Structural damage	Call for professional evaluation

DEGREE OF DIFFICULTY: □ Easy ▤ Moderate ■ Complex
ESTIMATED TIME: ○ Less than 1 hour ◑ 1 to 3 hours ● Over 3 hours
(For ladder and scaffolding set-up, see page 24)

RESTORING FLASHING

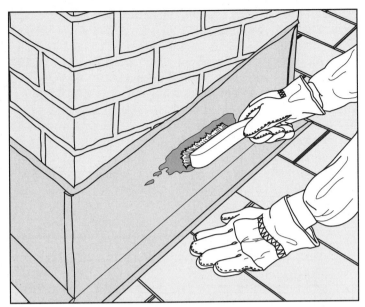

1 **Preparing the surface.** Prepare to work safely on the roof *(page 24)*. If the flashing is extensively corroded or damaged, call for a professional evaluation. Restore flashing that is rusted slightly in spots. Wearing work gloves and safety goggles, use a wire brush to remove loose rust, dirt and old finish *(above)*; then, wipe the surface with a clean, moist rag. Using medium-grit sandpaper, remove any remaining rust, then wipe off the surface with a clean, dry rag. If the surface is pitted or has pinhole perforations, cement it *(step 3)*. Patch any holes with metal *(page 19)* or fiberglass *(page 20)*. Otherwise, paint the flashing *(step 2)*.

2 **Painting the surface.** Buy a metal paint to match other surfaces and, if painting bare metal, a primer *(page 124)*; if painting flashing that is not visible from the ground, you may wish to buy asphalt paint *(page 115)*. Cover nearby roofing material with plastic sheeting and duct tape. Wearing work gloves, use a paintbrush *(page 124)* to apply each coat of primer and paint following the manufacturer's instructions. Working from top to bottom, first apply the primer to any bare metal and allow it to dry. Then, apply the metal paint *(above)* or asphalt paint; if necessary, apply a second coat after the first one dries.

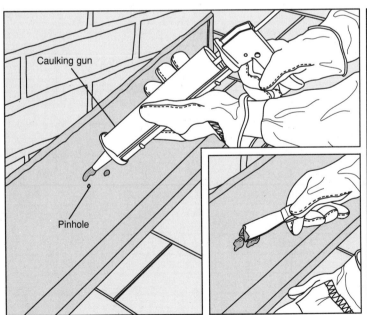

Caulking gun

Pinhole

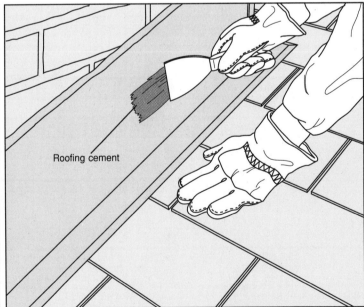

Roofing cement

3 **Cementing the surface.** Cement the surface of chimney, valley or vent flashing if it is pitted or has pinhole perforations; if the flashing is visible from the ground, you may wish to patch it with fiberglass *(page 20)* instead. Cover nearby roofing material with plastic sheeting and duct tape. If the flashing has pinhole perforations, wear work gloves and use a caulking gun loaded with a cartridge of roofing cement *(page 115)* to fill the holes *(above, left)*; then, use a putty knife to smooth extruded cement onto the flashing around the hole *(inset)*. After filling each pinhole, or if the flashing is pitted, apply an even coat of roofing cement on the damaged surface *(above, right)*. Depending on the local climate, the durability of the roofing cement will vary; inspect the flashing periodically and call for a professional evaluation if a problem develops.

PATCHING FLASHING WITH METAL

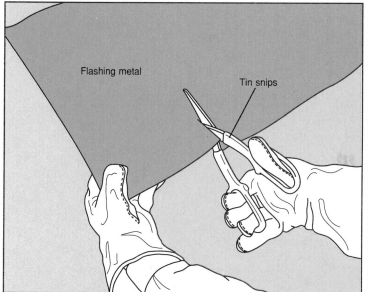

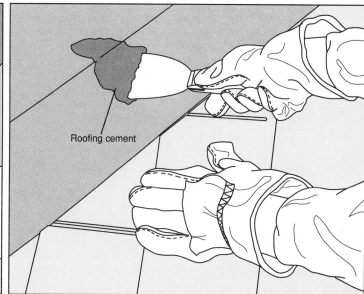

1 **Preparing the patch.** Prepare to work safely on the roof *(page 24)*. To patch the flashing with metal, use sheet metal of the same material (galvanized steel or aluminum) and gauge (thickness) as the flashing. If you cannot match the metal, if you require a flexible patch to fit into an awkward angle or around the edge of chimney or vent flashing, or if the patch will be in a visible area and you wish to paint it to conceal it, apply a fiberglass patch *(page 20)* instead. Otherwise, buy a piece of sheet metal for the patch at a building supply center; if necessary bring a small piece of flashing with you to match it. Wearing work gloves and safety goggles, remove dirt, grit and loose paint from the

damaged surface using a wire brush. Wipe off the surface using a clean, moist rag. Use medium-grit sandpaper to remove rust spots and smooth the surface, then wipe off the surface with a clean, dry rag. Using tin snips *(page 120)*, cut a patch at least 2 inches longer and wider than the damaged surface *(above, left)*; if installing the patch at an open valley, cut it 2 inches wider than the damaged surface and long enough to lap it 1 inch under the roofing material on each side of the valley. Apply an even layer of roofing cement *(page 115)* on the damaged surface using a putty knife *(above, right)* or trowel, covering an area equal to the size of the patch.

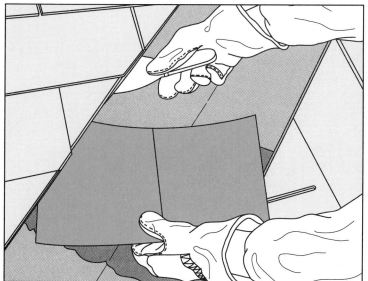

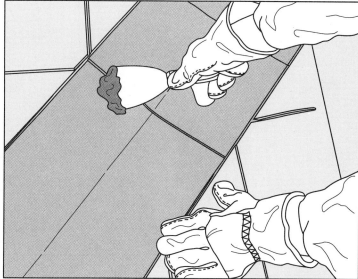

2 **Installing the patch.** If fitting the patch at an open valley, bend it to conform to the valley center line. If there are asphalt shingles sealed to the flashing along the sides of the valley, use a putty knife to break their seal, then lift their edges slightly and slide the patch into position *(above, left)*, ensuring that it laps 1 inch under the shingles on each side of the valley. Center the patch on the damaged surface and press it firmly into place, embedding it in the roofing cement; if necessary, push more roofing cement under the edges and

push down firmly to completely bond the patch. Then, use the putty knife to apply a 2-inch band of roofing cement along each edge of the patch *(above, right)*, completely covering the seams between the patch and the flashing. If you lifted the edges of asphalt shingles to fit the patch at an open valley, apply a small dab of roofing cement under the edges and press down firmly to seal the shingles. Depending on the local climate, the durability of the roofing cement will vary; inspect the flashing periodically and call for a professional evaluation if a problem develops.

PATCHING FLASHING WITH FIBERGLASS

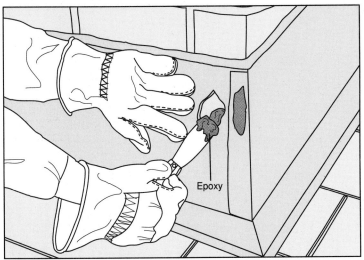

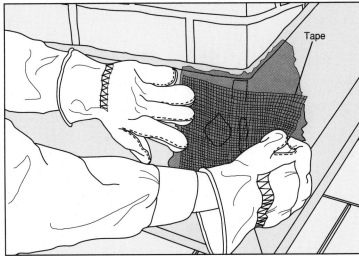

Preparing and installing the patch. Prepare to work safely on the roof *(page 24)*. To patch with fiberglass, buy fiberglass tape and epoxy resin *(page 115)* at a building supply center. Wearing work gloves and safety goggles, clean off the damaged surface with a wire brush and wipe it with a clean, moist rag. Use medium-grit sandpaper to remove rust, then wipe the surface with a clean, dry rag. Using scissors, cut a piece of fiberglass tape 3 inches longer and wider than the damaged surface; for a patch at an open valley, cut the tape 3 inches wider than the damaged surface and long enough to lap 1 inch under the roofing material on each side of the valley. Mix the epoxy following the manufacturer's instructions, then use a putty knife to spread it onto the damaged surface *(above, left)*, covering an area equal to the size pf the patch.

If at an open valley and there are asphalt shingles sealed to the flashing, use the putty knife to break their seal, then lift their edges slightly and slide the patch into position, ensuring that it laps 1 inch under the shingles on each side of the valley. Center the patch on the damaged surface and press it firmly into place *(above, right)*, embedding it in the epoxy. Then, use the putty knife to apply epoxy on the patch, saturating it completely. Let the epoxy cure according to the manufacturer's instructions. If you lifted the edges of asphalt shingles to fit the patch at a valley, apply a dab of roofing cement under the edges and press down firmly to seal the shingles. If necessary, paint the flashing to conceal the patch *(page 18)*. Inspect the flashing periodically and call for a professional evaluation if a problem develops.

REPAIRING FLASHING JOINTS

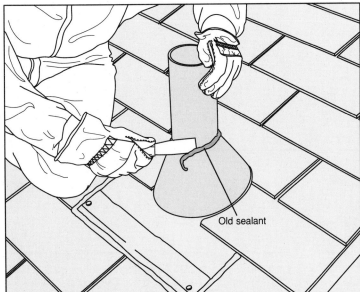

Sealing flashing joints. Prepare to work safely on the roof *(page 24)*. If flashing installed in a mortar joint or flush against a masonry surface is loose, reattach it *(page 21)*. If joints between overlapping pieces of flashing or between flashing and asphalt shingles are open, seal them. Wearing work gloves, use a putty knife to carefully scrape out any remaining old sealant *(above, left)*. Clean off the surface using a wire brush to remove debris, grit and any old finish. Wipe the surface with

a clean, moist rag. Use medium-grit sandpaper to remove any remaining rust, then wipe off the surface with a clean, dry rag. Load a caulking gun with sealant *(page 115)* and apply a continuous bead along the length of the joint *(above, right)*. If necessary, use a putty knife to press the sealant into the joint; wearing a rubber glove, run a wet finger along the joint to smooth and shape it. After the sealant cures, restore the surface of the flashing *(page 18)*, if necessary.

REPAIRING FLASHING JOINTS (continued)

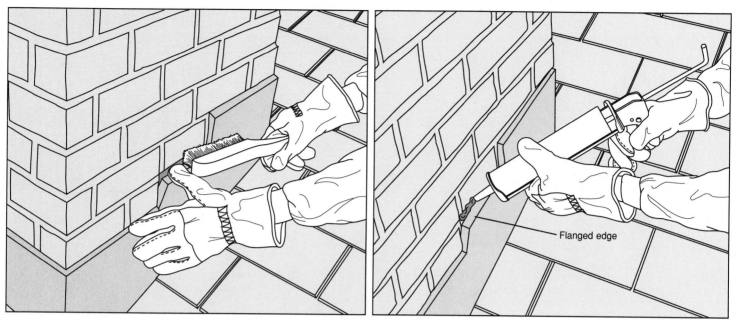

Flanged edge

Reattaching flashing to a mortar joint. Prepare to work safely on the roof *(page 24)*. If flashing installed in a mortar joint is loose, reattach it. Wearing work gloves and safety goggles, carefully pull the flashing away from the mortar joint, freeing its flanged edge. Taking care not to damage the flashing, use an old flat-tipped screwdriver or cold chisel to scrape any large pieces of loose mortar out of the joint; then, use a wire brush to remove any remaining bits of mortar and grit *(above, left)*. Using a caulking gun loaded with roofing cement *(page 115)*, fill the joint *(above, right)*. Then, push the flanged edge of the flashing back into the joint, setting it firmly in the roofing cement. After the roofing cement cures, restore the surface of the flashing *(page 18)*, if necessary.

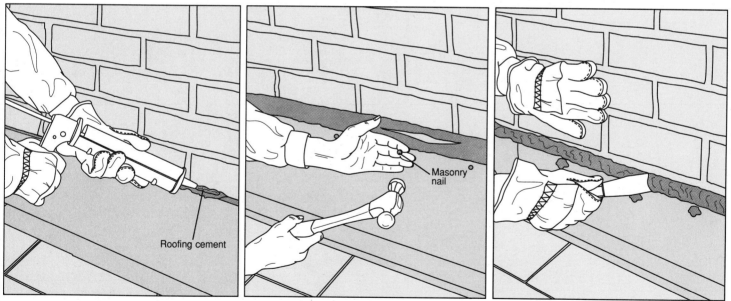

Roofing cement

Masonry nail

Reattaching flashing to a masonry surface. Prepare to work safely on the roof *(page 24)*. If flashing installed flush against a masonry surface is loose, reattach it. Wearing work gloves and safety goggles, carefully pull the flashing away from the masonry surface; use a putty knife to scrape any old sealant out of the joint, then clean the joint with a wire brush. Using a caulking gun loaded with roofing cement *(page 115)*, fill the gap between the flashing and the masonry surface *(above, left)*. Press the flashing firmly against the masonry surface to bond it to the roofing cement. If the flashing is bent and does not sit flush, secure

it with masonry nails *(page 121)*. Drive a nail into the flashing where necessary along it, 1 inch below the edge of it; on a brick wall, into a mortar joint *(above, center)*. Using a putty knife, cover each nail head with a dab of roofing cement. Then, apply a 2-inch band of roofing cement along the edge of the flashing *(above, right)*, covering the joint; on a brick wall, also pack roofing cement into the mortar joints along the edge of the flashing. After the roofing cement cures, restore the surface of the flashing *(page 18)*, if necessary.

UNBLOCKING A SOFFIT VENT

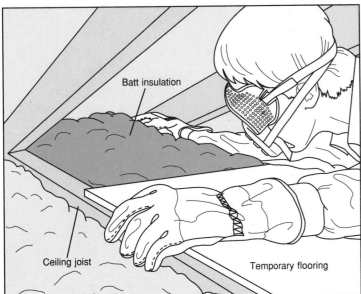

Batt insulation

Ceiling joist

Temporary flooring

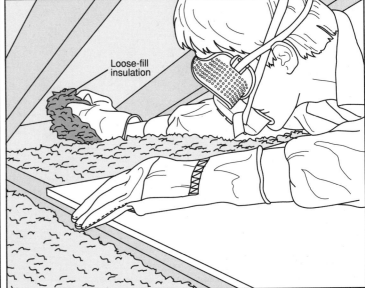

Loose-fill insulation

1 **Clearing away insulation.** If attic insulation or other debris is covering soffit vents, ventilation problems may develop, resulting in excess attic condensation, exterior ice dams, and damage to the roof framing and sheathing and the roofing material. Determine the position of vents from the ground outside, then check and unblock them from inside the attic. Wear work gloves, safety goggles, a dust mask, long sleeves and, if the attic has little head room, a hard hat; if the attic has no floor, lay planks across the ceiling joists as temporary flooring. Locate the vents. If batt insulation covers a vent, lift out the end of it

(above, left). Using a utility knife *(page 120)*, cut off the batt where the ceiling joists end at the eave and bag it for disposal. Repeat the procedure at each soffit vent. To remove remaining particles of insulation clogging the screen or louver of the vent, remove and clean it from outside *(step 3)*. If loose-fill insulation covers a vent, follow the same procedure, scooping it away from the soffit by hand *(above, right)* and bagging it for disposal; then, install a baffle *(step 2)* to prevent remaining loose-fill insulation from falling into the soffit and blocking the vent.

Preformed baffle

2 **Installing a baffle.** Buy styrofoam sheeting or a preformed baffle at a building suppy store. To make a baffle from styrofoam sheeting, use a utility knife *(page 120)* to cut it 2 feet long and equal in width to the distance between the center of the rafters on each side of the vent. To install the baffle, position it against the rafters on each side of the vent and butting the top of the wall; if necessary, notch it to fit around the end of a ceiling joist *(inset)*. Then, use the utility knife to cut off the top of the baffle 1 foot from the end of the insulation. Using a staple gun, staple the edges of the baffle to the rafter *(above)*. Repeat the procedure at each vent. To remove remaining particles of insulation clogging the screen or louver of the vent, remove and clean it from outside *(step 3)*.

Vent

Soffit

3 **Removing and reinstalling the vent.** Prepare to work safely under the soffit *(page 24)*. Wearing safety goggles, remove any screws from the vent *(above)*, then pull down the louver or screen. If the vent is damaged, buy a replacement at a building supply center. Remove any insulation or debris from the vent by hand, then wash it in a bucket of soapy water and let it dry. Reinstall the vent, then use a caulking gun to apply sealant *(page 115)* along its edges.

SERVICING A GABLE VENT

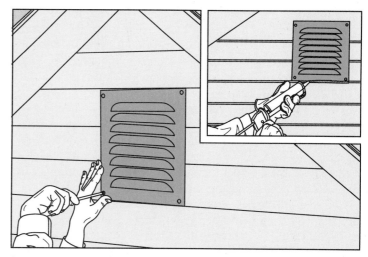

Installing a gable vent screen. If the outside louver of the vent is damaged, loose or missing, replace it *(step right)*; if the inside screen is damaged, leave the vent in place and install a new screen over the back of it in the attic. If the attic has little head room, wear a hard hat; if it has no floor, lay planks across the ceiling joists as temporary flooring. Measure the frame around the vent; then, buy a piece of window screen at a building supply center and use tin snips *(page 120)* or scissors to cut it to fit. Holding the screen taut, in position on the vent, use a staple gun to staple it *(above)* every 4 inches onto the studs and headers.

Securing or replacing a gable vent. Prepare to work safely on the siding *(page 24)*. If the vent is loose, tighten any screws or replace them with longer identical screws *(page 121)*. If the sealant around the vent is loose or missing, use a putty knife to scrape off any remaining old sealant; then, use a caulking gun loaded with sealant *(page 115)* to apply a continuous bead along the edges *(inset)*. If the vent is damaged, re-move any screws holding it in place *(above)* and take it out. Buy a replacement vent at a building supply center. Install the new vent, then use a caulking gun to apply sealant along its edges.

SERVICING A TURBINE ROOF VENT

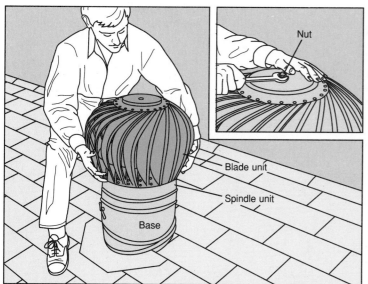

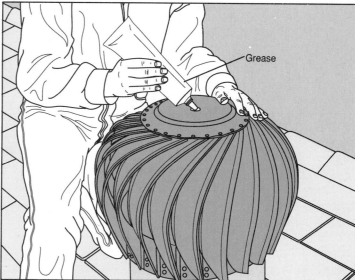

Lubricating or replacing a turbine vent. Prepare to work safely on the roof *(page 24)*. If a turbine vent is faulty, ventilation problems may develop, resulting in attic and roof damage. Check the owner's manual to see if you can lubricate the vent bearings or replace the blade and spindle units; if not, call for a profesional evaluation. If the blade unit does not spin freely, try lubricating the bearings. Follow the manufac-turer's instructions to detach the blade unit from the spindle unit. On the model shown, use a wrench to remove the nut from the protruding end of the spindle unit *(inset)*, then lift the blade unit slightly from the spindle unit *(above, left)*. Tilting the blade unit to one side, insert the

tip of a tube of multipurpose grease into the opening on top of it and apply enough grease to cover the bearings on the end of the spindle unit *(above, right)*. Fit the blade unit back onto the spindle unit and reinstall the nut. If the blade unit still does not spin freely, replace the blade and spin-dle units. Take the blade unit off the spindle unit, then detach the spindle unit from the base; on the model shown, unscrew it. If you cannot detach the spindle unit, call for a professional evaluation. Buy replacement blade and spindle units at a building supply center. Fit the new spindle unit onto the base, then fit the new blade unit onto the spindle unit following the manufacturer's instructions.

WORKING SAFELY AT HEIGHTS

Although most roofing and siding repairs are easy to perform, extreme caution is required at all times when working at heights on a ladder or scaffolding, or on the roof. Avoid injuries by reading this chapter carefully and following the instructions for safe working practices. Never use a ladder or scaffolding or work on the roof in wet, cold or windy weather; wait for optimal weather conditions. Do not set up a ladder or scaffolding near utility lines. Wear footgear with a well-defined heel and a non-slip sole. Stop working when you feel tired and avoid undertaking a repair during the hottest part of the day. Have a helper on hand while you are working, but keep others away from the work area.

A typical stepladder, extension ladder and scaffolding are shown at right. To work safely and comfortably on the siding and stand up to 10 feet from the ground, set up a stepladder *(page 26)*; allow for about 5 to 10 minutes of set-up time. To work safely and comfortably on the siding and stand more than 10 feet from the ground, or to work on the roof, set up an extension ladder *(page 27)*; add about 20 to 30 minutes for setting it up to the estimated time needed for your repair. To work safely and comfortably extensively along the siding at a height you cannot reach from the ground, or along the roofing at an eave, set up scaffolding *(page 31)*; allow about 15 to 20 minutes to assemble each single level.

Before climbing onto your roof, determine its pitch *(page 26)*. If the pitch of your roof is more than 6 in 12, call for a professional evaluation rather than undertake a repair on it yourself. If the pitch of your roof is 4 to 6 in 12, wear a safety harness or belt *(page 30)* while working on it as an added precaution. Roofing of tile or slate breaks easily under pressure and should not be walked on; if you cannot perform a roof repair safely and comfortably from the eave, call for a professional evaluation.

If you need to use a ladder, choose an appropriate type for the job; verify its duty rating, which is the total weight that it is designed to support. There are three grades of ladders: Household, Commercial and Industrial; a Type 1 or 1A Industrial ladder with non-slip rubber shoes is recommended. To work from an extension ladder on the siding, use standoff stabilizers for added lateral stability or to bridge a window; foam or fabric covers are available for the end caps to avoid marring the siding. Store your extension ladder horizontally on hooks. Keep a wooden ladder in a dry area, out of direct sunlight. Never paint a wooden ladder, which could hide defects; apply a clear wood preservative, if necessary.

When ordering scaffolding units, request prefabricated decks; they hook onto the end frames and are stronger and safer than wooden planks. Order extra decks to leave on each intermediate scaffolding level. Make sure you obtain guardrails and toeboards for the working platform, as well as enough frame couplers to secure each level and standoffs to stabilize the scaffolding against the house.

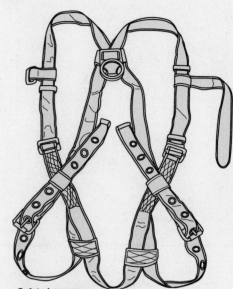

Safety harness
A fully adjustable body harness, usually made of nylon. A metal ring on the back attaches to the fall-arrest system: the lanyard, the rope grab and the fall-arrest rope.

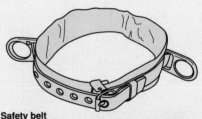

Safety belt
A substitute for the safety harness, usually made of nylon. Worn around the waist with a metal ring over the hip attached to the fall-arrest system: the lanyard, the rope grab and the fall-arrest rope.

Lanyard
A thick rope about 2 feet long with a locking hook on each end; clips onto the safety harness or belt and the rope grab.

Rope grab
Attached to the lanyard and connected to the fall-arrest rope. Designed to allow controlled movement up and down on the rope, but to lock if jerked suddenly. Usually made of stainless steel, with an arrow to indicate the direction of orientation for the rope.

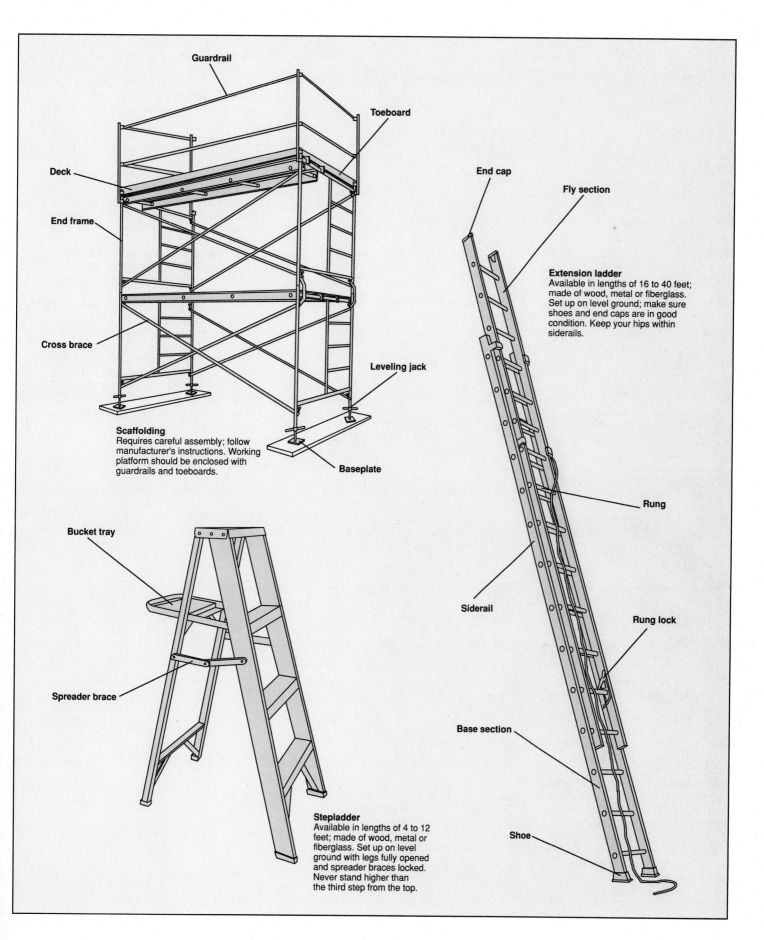

Guardrail

Toeboard

Deck

End cap

Fly section

End frame

Extension ladder
Available in lengths of 16 to 40 feet;
made of wood, metal or fiberglass.
Set up on level ground; make sure
shoes and end caps are in good
condition. Keep your hips within
siderails.

Cross brace

Leveling jack

Scaffolding
Requires careful assembly; follow
manufacturer's instructions. Working
platform should be enclosed with
guardrails and toeboards.

Baseplate

Rung

Bucket tray

Siderail

Rung lock

Spreader brace

Base section

Stepladder
Available in lengths of 4 to 12
feet; made of wood, metal or
fiberglass. Set up on level
ground with legs fully opened
and spreader braces locked.
Never stand higher than
the third step from the top.

Shoe

SETTING UP AND USING A STEPLADDER

Setting up a stepladder. To work safely and comfortably on the siding and stand up to 10 feet from the ground, set up a stepladder; as a rule, use a stepladder at least 2 feet longer than the height at which you need to stand. Inspect the stepladder before using it; do not use it if, for example, a foot is worn, a step is loose or a spreader brace does not open fully. Read the safety instruction label, usually located on a siderail.

Set up the stepladder on firm, level ground, opening its legs completely and locking its spreader braces. If the ground is soft or uneven, place boards under the front and back feet of the stepladder, as shown; dig up the soil with a spade to level them, if necessary, and never use an unanchored object such as a stone to prop them up. Pull down on the bucket tray to open it and place tools and materials on it before climbing the stepladder; or, carry tools in a tool belt.

Wearing footgear with a well-defined heel, face the stepladder to climb up or down it, using both hands to grasp the steps rather than the siderails. While working from the stepladder, lean into it and keep your hips between the siderails *(left)*; do not stand higher than the third step from the top. Never overreach or straddle the space between the stepladder and the siding; instead, climb down from the stepladder and reposition it.

Spreader brace

Siderail

MEASURING ROOF SLOPE

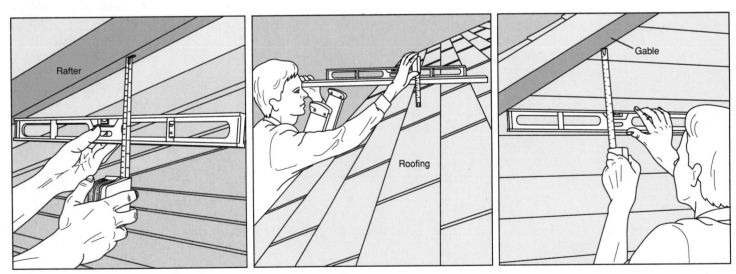

Rafter

Roofing

Gable

Determining roof pitch. A roof's slope, or pitch, is the measurement of its vertical rise in inches every 12 horizontal inches and is expressed as a number in 12. If your roof rises vertically by more than 6 inches every 12 inches horizontally, a pitch greater than 6 in 12, call for a professional evaluation rather than undertake a repair on it yourself. To determine the pitch of your roof, climb to your attic or set up an extension ladder *(page 27)* to reach an eave or a rake. On a carpenter's level or a board, mark a reference line 12 inches from one end. Hold the level or the board with a level on it horizontal, the end of it against a reference structure and the reference line on it facing the roof; then, measure the vertical distance between the reference structure and the reference line. For the reference structure in the attic, use a rafter *(above, left)*; at the eave, use the roofing *(above, center)*; at the rake, use the top of the gable *(above, right)*. The pitch of your roof is this vertical distance, measured in inches, in 12.

SETTING UP AN EXTENSION LADDER

1 **Positioning and raising the ladder.**
To work safely and comfortably on the siding standing more than 10 feet from the ground or on the roof, set up an extension ladder; to work on the roof, determine its pitch *(page 26)* and do not climb onto it if its pitch is more than 6 in 12. To calculate the length of ladder you need, estimate height by multiplying the number of stories you need to reach by the interior ceiling height (usually 8 to 10 feet), adding about 1 foot per floor (usually the distance between it and the ceiling below it) and adding the distance from the ground to the first floor; if you are getting off the ladder onto the roof, add another 3 feet. Inspect the ladder and do not use it if, for example, a shoe is worn or missing, a rung is loose, or a rung lock or the rope and pulley system is faulty. Read the safety instruction label, usually located on a siderail.

Place the unextended ladder on the ground, perpendicular to the wall where it will be positioned, with its fly section on the bottom and its feet out from the wall 1/4 of the height to which it will be raised; to work on the roof, set it up at an eave. To increase side-to-side stability or to bridge a window, attach standoff stabilizers to the ladder following the manufacturer's instructions. With a helper bracing the bottom of the ladder with his feet, use both hands to raise the top of it above your head *(left)*. Walk under the ladder toward the bottom of it, moving your hands along the siderails, until it is upright.

2 **Extending the fly section.** With your helper supporting the ladder, stand slightly to one side of it, bracing the bottom of it with one foot, and pull on the rope to disengage the rung locks and raise the fly section *(left)*. When the fly section is extended to the height desired, gently release pressure on the rope to engage the rung locks. If your ladder does not have a rope and pulley system, keep both feet on the ground against the bottom of the siderails to push the fly section up with your hands; never stand on the ladder to raise the fly section. Carefully rest the ladder against the siding or eave; if the roof is covered with tiles or slates, be careful not to break them. Check that the bottom of the ladder is out from the wall by 1/4 the height of the ladder; if necessary, reposition it. If you installed standoff stabilizers on the ladder, make sure they rest properly against the siding *(inset)*, following the manufacturer's instructions. If you plan to get onto the roof, make sure the ladder extends at least 3 feet, or rungs, above the eave; if necessary, work with your helper to raise the fly section higher.

SETTING UP AN EXTENSION LADDER (continued)

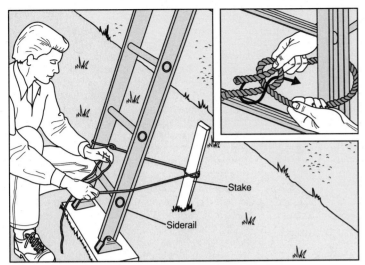

3 **Stabilizing the bottom of the ladder.** Stand on the first rung of the ladder to test its stability. If the ladder does not stand steady on firm, level ground, place a board under the feet, as shown; if necessary, dig up the soil with a spade to level it. To stabilize the bottom of the ladder, drive a wooden stake into the ground between it and the wall, and use 3/8-inch diameter nylon rope to tie each siderail to the stake *(above)* with a slip-proof knot such as the bowline *(inset)*. Make a small loop in the rope about 1 foot from one end; wrap the overlapping end around a siderail and up through the loop, as shown, and then around the overlapped end and down through the original loop. Pull either end of the rope to tighten the knot.

4 **Stabilizing the top of the ladder.** Climb the ladder *(step 1, below)* and work safely from it *(step 2, below)*. If you are working at the eave or plan to get off the ladder onto the roof, stabilize the top of the ladder. If the ladder rests against a gutter at the eave, first fit a 2-by-4 inside the gutter to keep it from crushing under the weight of the ladder. Then, install an eye screw or drive a 3-inch spiral nail *(page 121)* into the fascia near each siderail, just above or below the gutter. Using 3/8-inch diameter nylon rope, tie each siderail of the ladder to the eye screw *(above)* or nail, using a slip-proof knot such as the bowline used to stabilize the bottom of the ladder *(step 3)*.

USING AN EXTENSION LADDER

1 **Climbing the ladder.** Never climb up or down the ladder carrying tools or materials. Carry tools in a tool belt; or, place tools and materials in a bucket and hoist it up with a rope looped over a rung of the ladder. To hold your tools and materials while you are working from the ladder, you may use a tool tray, designed to clip onto the rungs. If necessary, transport tools up to the roof *(page 30)*. Wearing footgear with a well-defined heel, face the ladder to climb up *(above)* or down it, using both hands to grasp the rungs, as shown, rather than the siderails; move only one hand or foot at a time.

2 **Working safely from the ladder.** Never climb higher than the third rung from the top of the ladder; if necessary, get off the ladder onto the roof *(page 29)*. While working from the ladder, hold onto a rung with one hand, if possible *(above)*; lean into the ladder and keep your hips between the siderails. Spread your legs slightly, as shown, keeping your feet against the siderails. Never overreach or straddle the space between the ladder and the siding; instead, climb down from the ladder *(step 1)* and reposition it. Keep others away from the ladder while you are working from it.

GETTING ON AND OFF THE ROOF

1 **Getting onto the roof from the ladder.** Wear a safety harness or belt to work on the roof *(page 30)*, if necessary; never go up onto the roof in wet, cold or windy weather. Climb the ladder *(page 28)* until your feet are on the rung level with or just below the eave. If you tied onto your belt loop a rope for transporting tools and materials or a fall-arrest rope, untie it and tie it to the siderail of the ladder on your left. Holding firmly onto the top of the siderails with your hands, keep your left foot on the rung of the ladder and carefully step onto the roof with your right foot *(above, left)*, without leaning forward onto the top of the ladder. Grasp the right siderail with your left hand, then remove your right hand from the top of it and carefully step onto the roof with your left foot *(above, right)*. When both feet are on the roof, let go of the ladder; untie any rope you tied to the ladder. Work safely on the roof, transporting tools and materials up to it and traversing it as necessary *(page 30)*.

2 **Getting onto the ladder from the roof.** Before getting off the roof, transport any tools and materials neces-sary to the ground *(page 30)*. If you are wearing a safety harness or belt, unclip the lanyard from the rope grab. To get off the roof onto the ladder, stand to the left of the ladder, facing it, and grasp the top of the siderail closest to you with your right hand *(above, left)*. At the same time, swing your left foot onto the center of the rung at the eave and grasp the top of the other siderail with your left hand *(above, center)*, pivoting on your right foot. Then, swing your right foot onto the center of the rung below your left foot, still grasping the siderails with your hands *(above, right)*. Finally, step down one rung with your left foot and spread your legs slightly, keeping your feet against the siderails. Having a helper on the ground brace the bottom of the ladder, untie the rope from the siderails and the eye screws or nails. Remove the eye screws or nails and apply a sealant *(page 115)* to the holes in the fascia; use wood putty for wood or a sealant of a matching color for aluminum or vinyl. Take the 2-by-4 out of the gutter. Lower tools and materials in a bucket tied to a rope looped over a rung of the ladder. Climb down the ladder.

WORKING ON THE ROOF

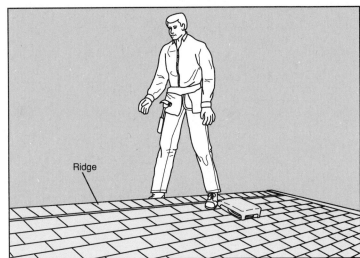

Transporting tools and materials. To raise tools and materials up to the roof, use a bucket and a 3/8-inch diameter nylon rope long enough to reach the roof with a few feet to spare. Tie one end of the rope to the bucket handle, place the tools and materials in the bucket, and tie the other end of the rope to your belt loop; do not overload the bucket. Climb up the ladder *(page 28)* and get onto the roof *(page 29)*. Sitting on the roof next to the ladder with your feet planted flat for stability, pull up the rope to raise the bucket *(above)*. When the bucket reaches the eave, carefully pull it over the gutter or roof overhang and onto the roof; hold the ladder for stability. Work on the roof, traversing it, if necessary *(step right)*. Reverse the procedure to lower tools and materials to the ground. Then, get off the roof onto the ladder *(page 29)*.

Traversing the roof. While working on the roof, avoid walking along the eave or rake. If the roof pitch is 4 or less in 12, you may carefully walk diagonally up the slope. If the roof pitch is higher than 4 in 12 and 6 or less in 12, do not walk diagonally up the slope. Instead, to move from one area to another area, walk carefully straight up from the ladder at the eave to the ridge, bending your knees slightly to maintain a low center of gravity. When you reach the ridge, stand straddling it and walk along it *(above)*, keeping your legs spread and one foot on each side of it, as shown. When you reach the area of the roof desired, carefully walk straight down the slope to it. Reverse the procedure to walk back to the ladder. Then, transport tools and materials to the ground *(step left)* and get off the roof onto the ladder *(page 29)*.

SETTING UP AND USING A SAFETY HARNESS OR BELT

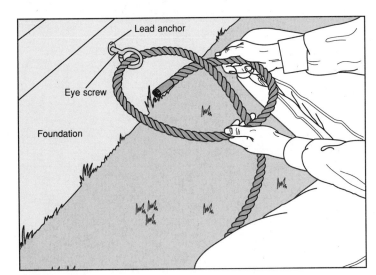

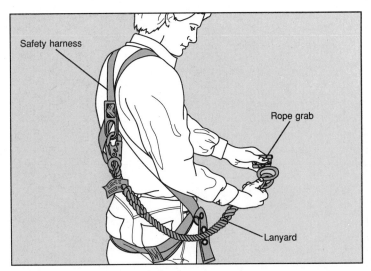

1 **Anchoring the fall-arrest rope.** To work on a roof with a pitch of 4 to 6 in 12, wear a safety harness or belt as an added precaution; a safety harness or belt, rope grab, and lanyard with clips is available at a building supply center or a tool rental agency. Also buy a fall-arrest rope of 5/8-inch diameter polypropylene to tie to a sturdy, fixed object on the side of the house opposite the work area. Tie the rope to a tree or a porch, if possible; or, install a lead anchor and eye screw *(page 121)* in the foundation and tie the rope to it *(above)*, using a slip-proof knot such as the bowline used to stabilize the bottom of the ladder *(page 28)*.

2 **Putting on the safety harness or belt.** If you are using a safety harness, clip one end of the lanyard onto the ring on the back of it. Put on the harness, adjusting the straps to fit it snugly around you without constricting your movement; the ring holding the lanyard should always be centered on your back and never in front of you. If you are using a safety belt, clip one end of the lanyard onto the ring on the side of it and fasten it snugly around your waist, with the ring holding the lanyard over one hip. Clip the other end of the lanyard to the rope grab *(above)*, which will hold the fall-arrest rope.

SETTING UP AND USING A SAFETY HARNESS OR BELT (continued)

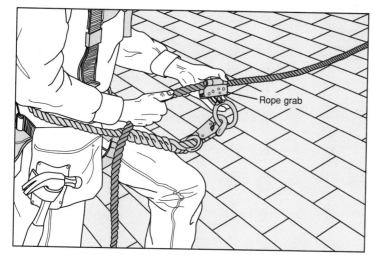

Rope grab

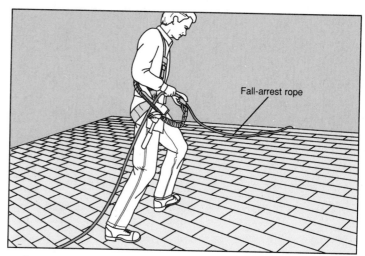

Fall-arrest rope

3 **Hooking up the fall-arrest rope.** With one end of the fall-arrest rope tied securely at ground level and enough slack in the rope to reach the roof, tie the other end of the rope to your tool belt or belt loop. Climb the ladder *(page 28)* and get onto the roof *(page 29)* keeping the rope and lanyard away from your feet. Once on the roof, walk carefully up the slope to the ridge and down the slope on the other side to the work area, feeding out the rope as you go. Insert the rope into the rope grab, following the manufacturer's instructions; make sure the rope is oriented correctly so it will lock when required. Check that the rope will feed through the rope grab *(above)*.

4 **Using the fall-arrest system.** Keep the fall-arrest rope taut, with just enough slack to work comfortably; if you fall, the system will keep you from sliding off the roof. If your model of rope grab has a safety catch, release it to move up or down the roof; set it when you are at the work area. On other models of rope grab, hold the rope grab with one hand and smoothly feed the rope up or down with the other hand *(above)*; do not apply downward pressure on the ring clipped to the lanyard. To move up the roof toward the ridge, walk with your knees slightly bent; to move down toward the eave, turn sideways and walk down carefully, keeping the trailing end of the rope free of your feet. When you have finished working, get off the roof *(page 29)*.

SETTING UP SCAFFOLDING

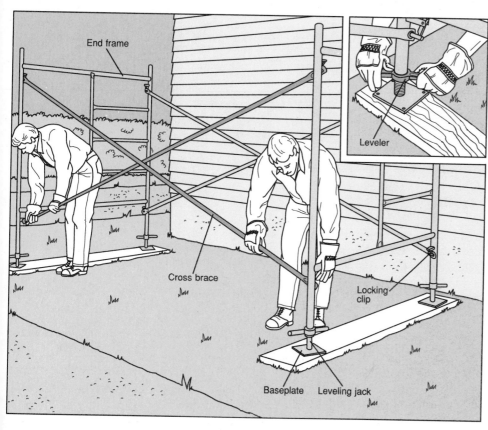

End frame

Leveler

Cross brace

Locking clip

Baseplate   Leveling jack

1 **Assembling the base level.** Rent scaffolding at a tool rental agency, estimating the height at which you will be working and ordering the appropriate number of units—each unit includes end frames, cross braces, frame couplers, baseplates, leveling jacks, prefabricated decks or wooden planks, and guardrails. Inspect the scaffolding and do not use it if, for example, an end frame is rusted or its welds are damaged, a frame coupler is broken, a baseplate is bent, or a deck or plank is cracked or warped. If the ground is soft, use 2-by-6s or -10s under the end frames to support them.

Position the baseplates and leveling jacks. Working with a helper, wear work gloves and slide each end frame onto its leveling jacks. Install cross braces on the locking clips of the end frames *(above)*. Use a carpenter's level to ensure the end frames are vertical and horizontal; if necessary, adjust a leveler *(inset)*. Repeat the procedure, if necessary, adding another end frame for each extra length of scaffolding you need. To work at the height of the scaffolding, set up a full working platform of decks or planks on top of the end frames; if using planks, make sure they overhang each end frame by at least 1 foot and no more than 2 feet. Then, install guardrails *(step 4)*. Otherwise, set up one deck or two planks alongside the climbing bars and assemble additional scaffolding levels *(step 2)*.

SETTING UP SCAFFOLDING (continued)

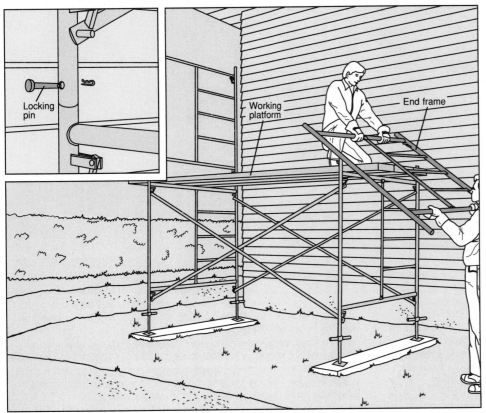

Locking pin

Working platform

End frame

2 **Assembling additional levels.** Kneeling on the working platform, have your helper pass up each end frame for the next level *(above)*, then slide it onto one of the end frames for the level below it; align its climbing bars with those on the end frame below it, as shown. Install cross braces as you did for the base level *(step 1)*. Then, install a frame coupler at the bottom of each foot on the end frames to anchor it to the top of the end frame below it; depending on your scaffolding model, the frame coupler is a type of locking arm or pin *(inset)*. To work at the height of the scaffolding, set up a full working platform of decks or planks on top of the end frames; if using planks, make sure they overhang each end frame by at least 1 foot and no more than 2 feet. Then, install guardrails *(step 4)*. Otherwise, set up one deck or two planks alongside the climbing bars and assemble an additional scaffolding level. If necessary, pull up each component from the ground using a 3/8-inch diameter nylon rope; tie the rope using a non-slip knot such as the bowline as you would to stabilize the bottom of a ladder *(page 28)*. After assembling an additional scaffolding level above each story of the house, secure it to the wall *(step 3)*.

Eye screw

Pipe

Clamp

3 **Securing the scaffolding to the wall.** Secure every second end frame of the scaffolding to the wall at each story above the first story of the house; reposition a deck or two planks as close to the wall as possible, if necessary, for a working platform. To prevent the scaffolding from falling away from the house, install an eye screw in the wall and tie the end frame to it using 5/8-inch diameter nylon rope *(above left)* or 1/4-inch diameter cable; locate a wall stud for the eye screw or, if the wall is masonry, first install a lead anchor *(page 121)*. To prevent the scaffolding from falling against the house, install a standoff following the manufacturer's instructions; the type shown consists of a metal pipe and adjustable swivel clamp. Fit the clamp onto the end frame and slide the pipe through the clamp until its end is 1 inch away from the wall. Using an adjustable wrench, tighten the bolts on the clamp to secure the pipe *(above, right)*.

SETTING UP SCAFFOLDING (continued)

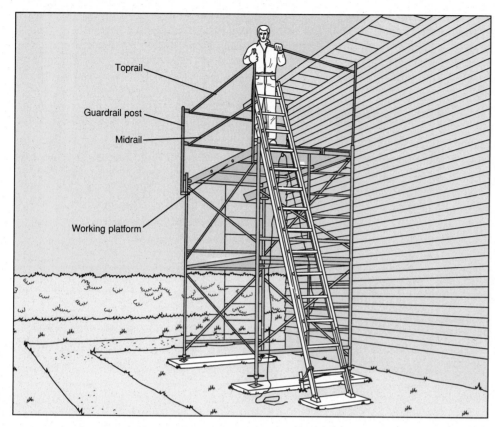

Toprail

Guardrail post

Midrail

Working platform

4 Installing guardrails. After assembling the number of scaffolding levels you need, set up an extension ladder *(page 27)* at one end of the scaffolding, if necessary, for easy access to the working platform; tie the top of it to the end frame as you would at the eave. Then, enclose the working platform with a guardrail along each open side of it and a toeboard along each side at the bottom of it. Have your helper on the ground pass up each component or pull it up from the ground using a 3/8-inch diameter nylon rope; tie the rope to it using a non-slip knot such as the bowline used to stabilize the bottom of the ladder *(page 28)*. Slide a guardrail post onto the top of each end of the end frames and secure it with a locking pin. Attach the toprails and midrails onto the locking pins on the posts; on the end with the ladder, install only a toprail *(left)*, omitting a midrail, and be careful getting on and off the ladder. Attach each toeboard to the guardposts following the manufacturer's instructions.

DISMANTLING SCAFFOLDING

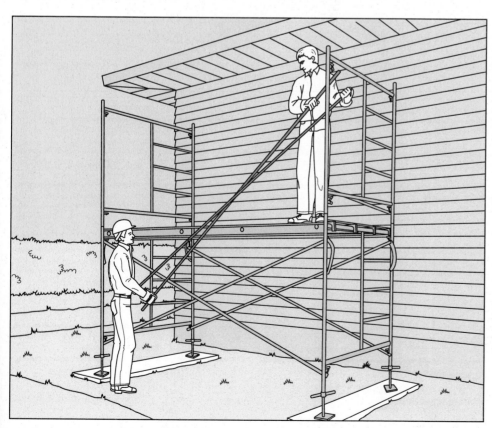

Lowering the components to the ground. Take down each level of the scaffolding, reversing the procedure you used to assemble it, working with a helper on the ground. Take off the toeboards, the guardrails and guardrail posts, and pass them down one at a time to your helper; or, tie each component in turn to a 3/8-inch diameter nylon rope and carefully lower it to the ground. Remove any standoffs and untie any rope or cable used to secure the scaffolding to the wall; take out each eye screw and apply a sealant *(page 115)* to the hole in the siding, using wood putty for wood or a sealant of a matching color for aluminum or vinyl. Untie and take down the ladder, if you used one. Then, use the climbing bars on an end frame to move down to the next scaffolding level and take off the decks or planks of the working platform, working with your helper. Remove each cross brace from the scaffolding level and pass it to your helper on the ground *(above)* or use the rope to lower it, if necessary. Take off any frame coupler, then lift off each end frame and lower it to the ground. Continue the procedure until the entire scaffolding is disassembled, stacking the components on the ground.

GUTTERS AND DOWNSPOUTS

Almost invisible when properly installed, well finished and regularly maintained, a gutter and downspout system is crucial in preventing water problems inside your home; a typical gutter and downspout system is shown at right. Gutters collect runoff water from the roof and channel it to downspouts that carry it safely past the siding and away from the foundation, where it might otherwise pool and leak into the basement or damage the lawn and garden.

Most gutter and downspout systems today are made of metal—galvanized steel or aluminum—or vinyl, which is increasingly popular; an older system may be constructed of wood. Proper maintenance prolongs the life of gutters and downspouts, and helps prevent problems such as blockages and sags that can lead to water damage inside and outside your home. Clean gutters and downspouts *(page 36)* every fall and spring. Install leaf guards and strainers to prevent blockages *(page 37)*. Restore a metal system *(page 37)* every few years to slow its deterioration; a vinyl system does not require the same treatment. Care for and repair a wooden system as you would any other outdoor structure of the same material.

When a gutter or downspout problem develops, consult the Troubleshooting Guide below. A damaged section can be easily replaced, although working at the eaves can be intimidating. Before undertaking a repair, read the chapter on Working Safely at Heights *(page 24)* and properly set up any ladder or scaffolding required. Most repairs to a metal system call for simple tools such as a hacksaw, tin snips and a flat file; repairs to a vinyl system require few tools since its components usually are snap-fit. Refer to Tools & Techniques *(page 112)* for instructions on using any tools needed.

TROUBLESHOOTING GUIDE

SYMPTOM	POSSIBLE CAUSE	PROCEDURE
Water runoff sits in gutter, drains from it slowly, or overflows it onto roofing and down siding	Gutter or downspout clogged	Clean gutters and downspouts *(p. 36)* □○▲; to prevent clogs, screen gutters and downspouts *(p. 37)* □○
	Gutter sagging due to loose, bent, broken or missing hanger	Adjust hangers *(p. 39)* ○□ or install new hangers *(p. 40)* □○
Water runoff misses gutter, runs behind and down siding	Insufficient roof overhang	Install drip edge *(p.40)* □◕
Water runoff pools below downspout, eroding ground at foundation	Splashblock out of position or missing	Reposition or install splashblock
	Downspout section damaged	Replace metal *(p. 44)* □◕ or vinyl *(p. 45)* □◕ downspout section
Ice buildup along gutter	Gutter or downspout clogged	Clean gutters and downspouts *(p. 36)* □○▲; to prevent clogs, screen gutters and downspouts *(p. 37)* □○
	Soffit vent blocked or turbine roof vent faulty	Unblock soffit vent *(p. 22)* □●; service turbine roof vent *(p. 23)* □○
	Attic ventilation inadequate	Call for professional evaluation
Gutter sags, sways or rattles	Gutter clogged	Clean gutters *(p. 36)* □○; to prevent clogs, screen gutters and downspouts *(p. 37)* □○
	Hanger loose, bent, broken or missing	Adjust hangers *(p. 39)* ○□ or install new hangers *(p. 40)* □○
Gutter clogged	Debris, fallen leaves; wind-borne material	Clean gutters and downspouts *(p. 36)* □○ and trim back overhead vegetation
Gutter leaks	Open joint, perforation or hole	Seal or patch metal gutter *(p. 38)* □○ or replace metal gutter section *(p. 41)* ◨◕; replace vinyl gutter section *(p. 43)* □◕
Gutter hole	Weather stress; impact damage	Patch metal gutter *(p. 38)* □○ or replace metal gutter section *(p. 41)* ◨◕; replace vinyl gutter section *(p. 43)* □◕
Downspout loose; sways or rattles	Bracket loose; downspout section damaged	Tighten bracket fasteners; replace metal *(p. 44)* □◕ or vinyl *(p. 45)* □◕ downspout section
Downspout leaks; hole	Weather stress; impact damage	Replace metal *(p. 44)* □◕ or vinyl *(p. 45)* □◕ downspout section
Gutter or downspout stained; finish faded, blistered, peeling or chipped	Black spots and streaks caused by mildew	Wash with solution of detergent, bleach and water; rinse well
	Weather stress; rust	Restore metal gutter and downspout *(p. 37)* □◕; replace vinyl gutter section *(p. 43)* □◕ and downspout section *(p. 45)* □◕
Gutter or downspout crushed, dented, cracked or broken	Weight of ice and snow; weather stress; impact damage	Replace metal *(p. 41)* ◨◕ or vinyl *(p. 43)* □◕ gutter section; replace metal *(p. 44)* □◕ or vinyl *(p. 45)* □◕ downspout section

DEGREE OF DIFFICULTY: □ Easy ◨ Moderate ■ Complex
ESTIMATED TIME: ○ Less than 1 hour ◕ 1 to 3 hours ● Over 3 hours
(For ladder and scaffolding set-up, see page 24)

▲ Special tool required

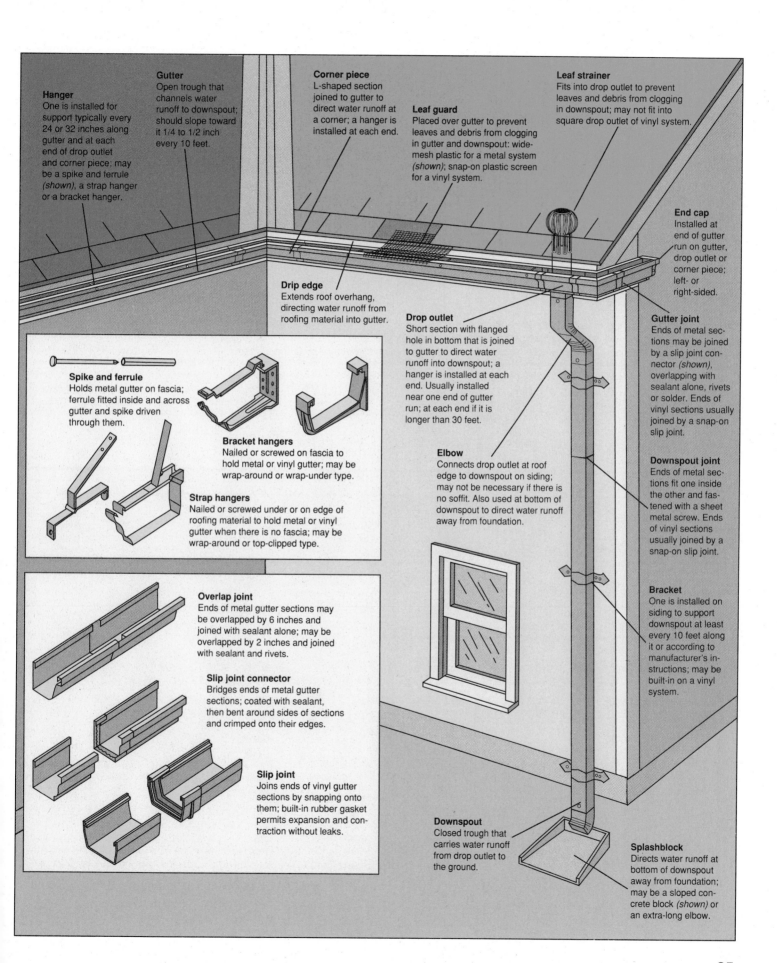

Hanger
One is installed for support typically every 24 or 32 inches along gutter and at each end of drop outlet and corner piece; may be a spike and ferrule *(shown)*, a strap hanger or a bracket hanger.

Gutter
Open trough that channels water runoff to downspout; should slope toward it 1/4 to 1/2 inch every 10 feet.

Corner piece
L-shaped section joined to gutter to direct water runoff at a corner; a hanger is installed at each end.

Leaf guard
Placed over gutter to prevent leaves and debris from clogging in gutter and downspout: wide-mesh plastic for a metal system *(shown)*; snap-on plastic screen for a vinyl system.

Leaf strainer
Fits into drop outlet to prevent leaves and debris from clogging in downspout; may not fit into square drop outlet of vinyl system.

End cap
Installed at end of gutter run on gutter, drop outlet or corner piece; left- or right-sided.

Drip edge
Extends roof overhang, directing water runoff from roofing material into gutter.

Drop outlet
Short section with flanged hole in bottom that is joined to gutter to direct water runoff into downspout; a hanger is installed at each end. Usually installed near one end of gutter run; at each end if it is longer than 30 feet.

Gutter joint
Ends of metal sections may be joined by a slip joint connector *(shown)*, overlapping with sealant alone, rivets or solder. Ends of vinyl sections usually joined by a snap-on slip joint.

Spike and ferrule
Holds metal gutter on fascia; ferrule fitted inside and across gutter and spike driven through them.

Bracket hangers
Nailed or screwed on fascia to hold metal or vinyl gutter; may be wrap-around or wrap-under type.

Strap hangers
Nailed or screwed under or on edge of roofing material to hold metal or vinyl gutter when there is no fascia; may be wrap-around or top-clipped type.

Elbow
Connects drop outlet at roof edge to downspout on siding; may not be necessary if there is no soffit. Also used at bottom of downspout to direct water runoff away from foundation.

Downspout joint
Ends of metal sections fit one inside the other and fastened with a sheet metal screw. Ends of vinyl sections usually joined by a snap-on slip joint.

Overlap joint
Ends of metal gutter sections may be overlapped by 6 inches and joined with sealant alone; may be overlapped by 2 inches and joined with sealant and rivets.

Slip joint connector
Bridges ends of metal gutter sections; coated with sealant, then bent around sides of sections and crimped onto their edges.

Slip joint
Joins ends of vinyl gutter sections by snapping onto them; built-in rubber gasket permits expansion and contraction without leaks.

Bracket
One is installed on siding to support downspout at least every 10 feet along it or according to manufacturer's instructions; may be built-in on a vinyl system.

Downspout
Closed trough that carries water runoff from drop outlet to the ground.

Splashblock
Directs water runoff at bottom of downspout away from foundation; may be a sloped concrete block *(shown)* or an extra-long elbow.

CLEANING A GUTTER

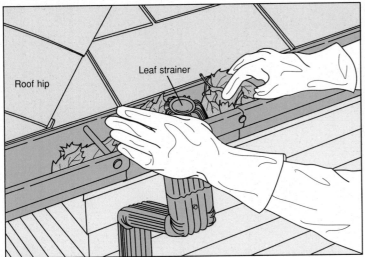

Flushing a gutter. Prepare to work safely along the gutter *(page 24)*. Wearing rubber gloves, handpick *(above, left)* and bag any leaves, twigs and other debris at the roof edge, leaf guards, open gutters and leaf strainers; work from one end to the other end of the gutter. To flush dirt and grit out of the gutter, start at the end without a downspout, or, if there is a downspout at each end, at the center. If the gutter has a leaf guard, remove it. Have a helper pass up a garden hose and turn on the water. Wash dirt and grit off the gutter, brushing it ahead toward the downspout with a whisk broom *(above, right)*. Use a small putty knife, if necessary, to carefully dislodge material adhering to the gutter. Continue the procedure until you reach the downspout, inspecting the gutter as you go; then, have your helper turn off the water and take the hose. If the water in the gutter drains slowly or not at all, clean the downspout *(step below)*. If a metal gutter is rusted, restore it *(page 37)*; if it leaks, repair the holes or cracks *(page 38)* or replace the damaged section *(page 41)*. If a vinyl gutter leaks, replace the damaged section *(page 43)*. If water pools in the gutter because of a sag in it, adjust the hangers *(page 39)* or install extra hangers *(page 40)* to raise it. Otherwise, reinstall any leaf guard removed *(page 37)*.

CLEANING A DOWNSPOUT

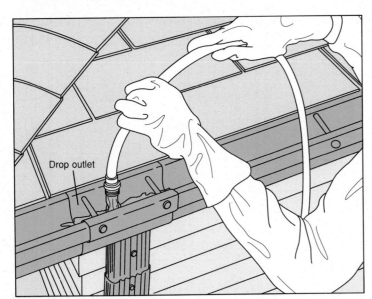

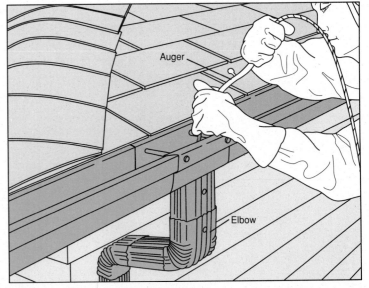

1 **Flushing a downspout.** Prepare to work safely at the downspout *(page 24)*. Wearing rubber gloves, reach down the drop outlet and pull out as much debris as possible. Have a helper pass up a garden hose. Aiming the hose into the drop outlet *(above)*, flush debris through the elbow and out the bottom of the downspout, having the helper turn the water on full. If the downspout is not cleared by flushing it, unclog it *(step 2)*. To prevent a blockage in the future, install a leaf strainer in the downspout or a leaf guard in the gutter *(page 37)*.

2 **Unclogging a downspout.** To unclog a downspout, use a trap-and-drain auger (plumber's snake), available at a building supply center. Wearing rubber gloves, push the auger coil into the drop outlet and as far as possible through the elbow, then lock the handle. Slowly turn the handle clockwise *(above)*. When the handle moves easily, stop turning it, feed in more coil and repeat the procedure. Continue until the downspout is unclogged, then remove the coil and flush the downspout *(step 1)*. If necessary, work from the bottom of the downspout to unclog it. To prevent a blockage in the future, install a leaf strainer in the downspout or a leaf guard in the gutter *(page 37)*.

SCREENING GUTTERS AND DOWNSPOUTS

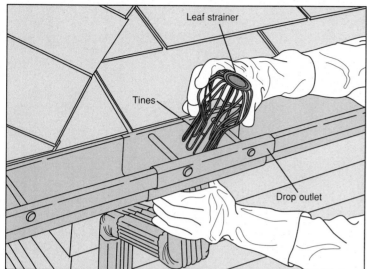

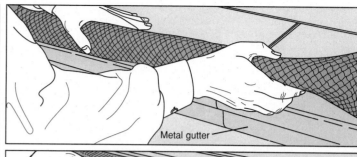

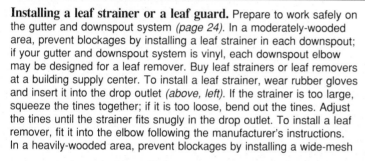

Installing a leaf strainer or a leaf guard. Prepare to work safely on the gutter and downspout system *(page 24)*. In a moderately-wooded area, prevent blockages by installing a leaf strainer in each downspout; if your gutter and downspout system is vinyl, each downspout elbow may be designed for a leaf remover. Buy leaf strainers or leaf removers at a building supply center. To install a leaf strainer, wear rubber gloves and insert it into the drop outlet *(above, left)*. If the strainer is too large, squeeze the tines together; if it is too loose, bend out the tines. Adjust the tines until the strainer fits snugly in the drop outlet. To install a leaf remover, fit it into the elbow following the manufacturer's instructions. In a heavily-wooded area, prevent blockages by installing a wide-mesh

plastic leaf guard in the gutter. Buy a roll of leaf guard at a building supply center; if your gutter and downspout system is vinyl, buy a type to fit your model. Use scissors to cut off a strip of leaf guard as long as the gutter; at a corner or if more than one strip is necessary, overlap the ends by at least 1 inch. To install each strip, fit one side between the roofing material and the building paper along the roof edge, pushing until the other side is aligned along the outside gutter edge. If the roofing material cannot be lifted, roll the leaf guard and sit it in the gutter *(above right, top)*, notching it to fit over the hangers. To install a snap-on leaf guard along a vinyl gutter, press it into place under the hanger edges *(above right, bottom)*.

RESTORING METAL GUTTERS AND DOWNSPOUTS

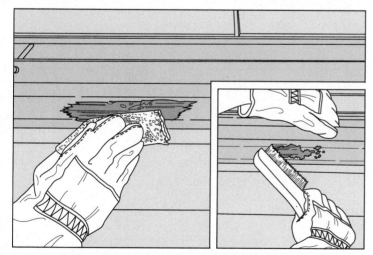

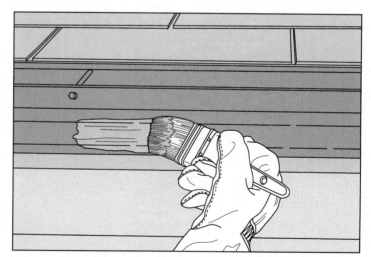

1 **Preparing the surface.** Repaint a metal gutter and downspout system every two years as the finish deteriorates and when rust or pitting appears; work only when it is dry. Prepare to work safely along the gutter and downspout system *(page 24)*, first to clean it *(page 36)*. Wearing work gloves and safety goggles, remove dirt, grit and loose paint using a wire brush *(inset)* or a small putty knife. Wipe off the inside of the gutter using a clean rag dampened with paint thinner. Using medium-grit sandpaper, remove rust spots and smooth the surfaces *(above)*, then wipe them off with a clean, dry rag. Seal or patch any open joints, perforations and holes *(page 38)*.

2 **Applying paint.** Buy asphalt paint, a metal paint to match other surfaces, and, if painting bare metal, a primer *(page 124)* at a building supply center. Cover nearby vegetation and surfaces not to be coated with plastic sheeting and duct tape. Wearing work gloves, use a paintbrush *(page 124)* to apply each coat of paint and primer, following the manufacturer's instructions. Starting on the inside of the gutter, apply an even coat of the asphalt paint on the trough to protect it against further deterioration; allow it to dry. Then, apply the primer on any bare metal on the outside of each gutter and downspout. Finally, when the primer is dry, apply the metal paint *(above)*; if necessary, apply a second coat after the first one dries.

SEALING AND PATCHING A METAL GUTTER

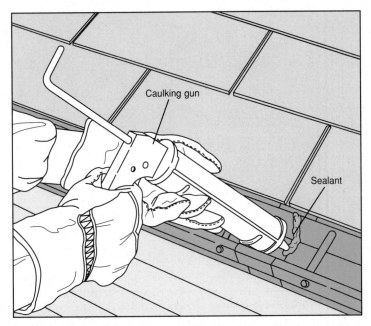

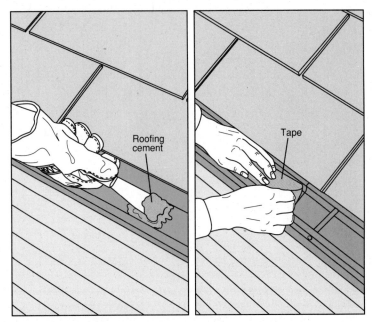

Sealing an open joint. If a gutter joint separates and begins to leak, reseal it when the gutter is dry. Prepare to work safely on the gutter *(page 24)*. Wearing work gloves, use a clean, damp rag to wipe dirt and grit off the inside of the gutter along the joint. Load a caulking gun with sealant *(page 115)* and apply a continuous bead of it along the joint *(above)*; use a small putty knife to smooth the sealant, forcing it into the joint. If the joint leaks again, patch the gutter *(step below)*.

Sealing perforations and small holes. Prepare to work safely on the gutter *(page 24)* when it is dry. Wearing work gloves, use a clean, damp rag to wipe dirt and grit off the damaged surface inside the gutter. Using coarse-grit sandpaper, remove any rust and roughen the surface, then wipe it with a clean, dry rag. To seal perforations, apply a layer of roofing cement *(page 115)* using a small putty knife *(above, left)*, smoothing the edges. To seal a hole less than 1/4 inch in diameter, cut a piece of adhesive-backed aluminum repair tape several inches larger than the hole with scissors and remove the backing. Center the tape over the hole and press it firmly into place *(above, right)*.

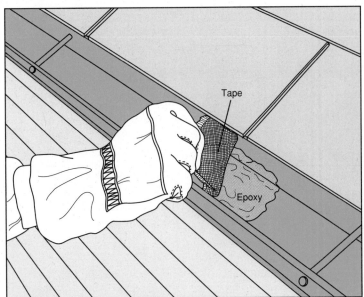

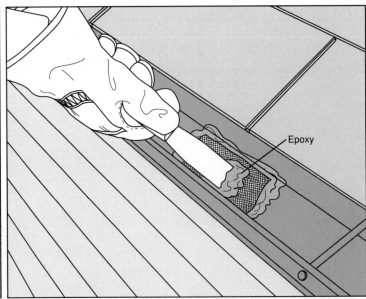

Patching a large hole. Prepare to work safely on the gutter *(page 24)* when it is dry. Wearing work gloves and safety goggles, remove dirt, grit and loose paint around the hole inside the gutter using a wire brush or a small putty knife. Wipe off the surface using a clean rag dampened with paint thinner. Use coarse-grit sandpaper to remove rust spots and smooth the surface, then wipe it with a clean, dry rag. Cut a piece of fiberglass tape at least 1 inch longer and wider than the hole with scissors. Mix

a small amount of epoxy *(page 115)* following the manufacturer's instructions and use a small putty knife to spread it around the hole edges. Center the tape over the hole and press it firmly into place *(above, left)*, embedding it in the epoxy. Then, use the putty knife to apply a coat of epoxy on the patch *(above, right)*, saturating it completely. Let the epoxy cure according to the manufacturer's instructions.

ADJUSTING GUTTER HANGERS

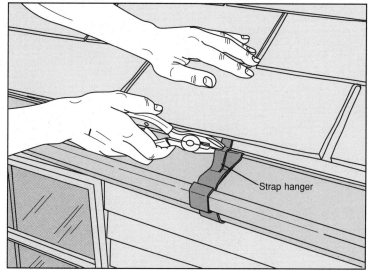

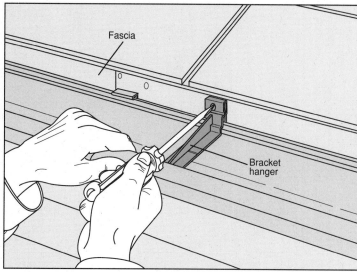

Repositioning a strap or bracket hanger. Prepare to work safely on the gutter *(page 24)*. Test the fascia for rot and patch minor damage *(page 116)*; if the damage is extensive, replace the fascia *(page 47)*. To test the fascia behind a vinyl or an aluminum fascia cover and repair or replace it, remove the fascia cover *(page 48)*. If the sheathing under a strap hanger has rotted, call for a professional evaluation. To correct a gutter sag caused by loose spikes and ferrules, install additional ones *(page 40)*. To correct a gutter sag caused by loose strap or bracket hangers, try adjusting them.

To adjust a strap hanger, use pliers to make a slight upward bend in the strap *(above, left)*; if the hanger nails or screws are accessible, remove them, adjust the hanger position and install new fasteners *(page 121)*. To adjust a bracket hanger, remove its fasteners, adjust its position and screw it back onto the fascia *(above, right)*. If the hanger fasteners are not accessible, install an additional strap hanger *(page 40)*. Adjust other hangers the same way, if necessary, to correct the gutter sag; if the gutter still sags, install additional strap hangers.

REMOVING A GUTTER HANGER

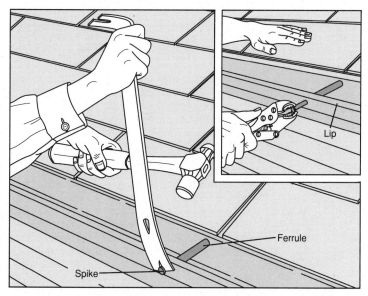

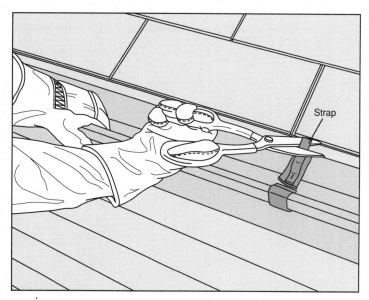

Removing a spike and ferrule. Prepare to work safely on the gutter *(page 24)*. To loosen the spike from a ferrule, slip the notched end of a pry bar behind the head of the spike and strike the pry bar with a ball-peen hammer *(above)*. Using locking pliers, grasp the head of the spike and pull it out *(inset)*. Lift the ferrule out of the gutter, angling it if necessary to clear the gutter lip. To reposition or take off a gutter section, remove as many spikes and ferrules as necessary the same way.

Cutting off a strap or bracket hanger. Prepare to work safely on the gutter *(page 24)*. Wearing work gloves and safety goggles, use tin snips *(page 120)* to cut off a strap hanger at the roof edge *(above)*. Leaving in place the end of the hanger fastened to the roof edge, cut off or unclip the end of the hanger attached to the gutter. Remove a bracket hanger the same way, unscrewing it from the roof edge first if its fasteners are accessible. To reposition or take off a gutter section, remove as many hangers as necessary using the same procedure.

INSTALLING A GUTTER HANGER

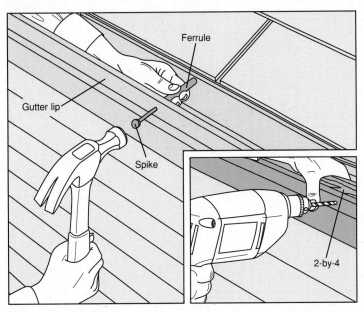

Installing a spike and ferrule. If the gutter is vinyl or there is no fascia, install strap hangers (*step right*). Otherwise, prepare to work safely on the gutter (*page 24*). To correct a gutter sag, remove as many spikes and ferrules as necessary (*page 39*). For each additional spike and ferrule to be installed, drill a hole (*page 121*) in the gutter lip (*inset*), placing a 2-by-4 as a brace inside the gutter; if possible, position the hole at a rafter, usually located every 12 or 16 inches behind the fascia. To install a spike and ferrule, fit the ferrule inside the gutter over the hole and tap the spike into it; holding the ferrule steady, position the gutter and drive the spike through it (*above*), into the fascia and rafter behind it. Use the same procedure to install at least one spike and ferrule every 24 or 32 inches along the gutter.

Installing a strap hanger. If the gutter is metal and there is a fascia, install spikes and ferrules (*step left*). Otherwise, prepare to work safely on the gutter (*page 24*). To correct a gutter sag, remove as many strap or bracket hangers as necessary (*page 39*). Install strap hangers of a type that fits the gutter, following the manufacturer's instructions. For the type of strap hanger shown, snap the clips onto the gutter edges. Position the strap on or under the edge of the roofing material, adjusting it until the gutter is in position, and drive roofing nails (*page 121*) into it (*above*). Apply roofing cement (*page 115*) on each nail head. Use the same procedure to install at least one strap hanger every 24 or 32 inches along the gutter.

INSTALLING A DRIP EDGE

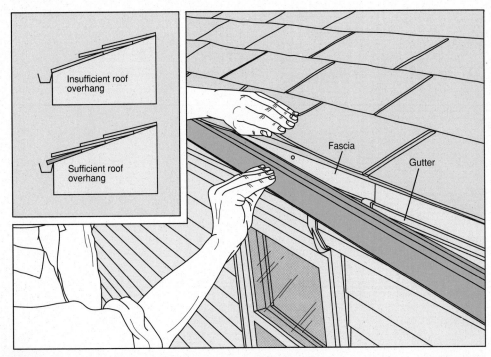

Putting up a drip edge. Prepare to work safely along the roof edge (*page 24*) and install a drip edge if the roofing material does not overhang the roof edge by at least 1 inch (*inset*). Buy drip edge equal to the length of the roof edge at a building supply center. If necessary, cut the drip edge to length using a hacksaw or tin snips (*page 120*) or assemble it in sections following the manufacturer's instructions; the sections of the vinyl drip edge shown are spliced to interlock. Remove burrs from a cut metal edge and smooth rough spots off a cut vinyl edge with a flat file (*page 123*). To install the drip edge, fit one side between the roofing material and the building paper along the roof edge (*left*), pushing until the other side is aligned along the inside gutter edge and overhanging it by at least 1 inch. Following the manufacturer's instructions, install any fasteners (*page 121*) required to secure the drip edge; the drip edge shown is held in place by the roofing material and requires no fasteners.

REPLACING A METAL GUTTER SECTION

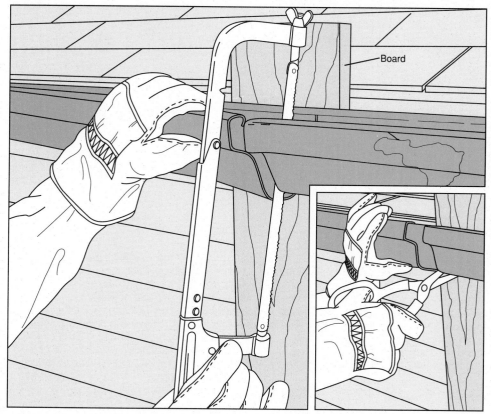

Board

1 Removing the damaged section.
Prepare to work safely along the gutter *(page 24)*, having a helper on hand. Remove any downspout assembly from the damaged section *(page 44)*. Mark a cutting line on the gutter at one end of the damaged section and wedge a board at it between the gutter and the roof edge. Wearing work gloves and safety goggles, use a hacksaw *(page 120)* to cut off the damaged section *(left)*; remove any hangers in the way *(page 39)*. If necessary, use tin snips *(page 120)* to finish the cut *(inset)*. Repeat the procedure at the other end of the damaged section. Take off the damaged section by removing its spikes and ferrules or releasing it from its strap or bracket hangers; if necessary, remove them along with it. Lower the damaged section to the ground. Use a chalkline *(page 117)* to mark the position of a replacement section along the roof edge, ensuring a gutter slope of about 1/16 inch per foot toward the downspout.

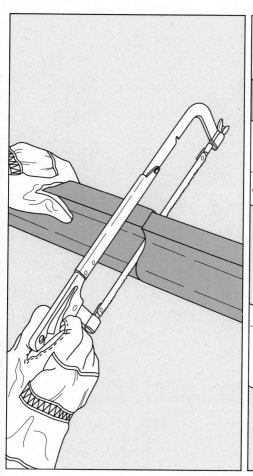
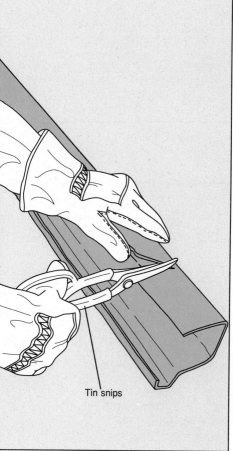

Tin snips

2 Measuring and cutting a replacement section. Calculate the length of gutter needed, adding a few feet for waste, and determine the number of end caps, corner pieces, drop outlets, and hangers required; if there is a fascia, using spikes and ferrules to replace any strap or bracket hangers removed is easiest. For each joint, using a sealant *(page 115)* and a slip joint connector is easiest; or, use a sealant alone or, if you live in a region of heavy rainfall or snow, with rivets *(page 121)*. Buy components for a replacement section at a building supply center.
  Mark off the replacement gutter: equal in length to the damaged section if you are using a slip joint connector at each joint; long enough for about 6 inches of overlap at each joint if you are using a sealant alone; long enough for about 2 inches of overlap at each joint if you are using rivets. Wearing work gloves and safety goggles, cut the gutter to length: use a hacksaw *(page 120)* if it is unpainted *(far left)*, placing a 2-by-4 as a brace inside it; use tin snips *(page 120)* if it is prefinished *(near left)*. Remove burrs from the cut edges with a flat file *(page 123)*. If more than one gutter length is needed, mark off and cut each one the same way; then, assemble the gutter lengths *(step 3)*. If only one gutter length is needed, add any end cap, corner piece and drop outlet required *(step 4)*; otherwise, prepare the replacement section for installation *(step 5)*.

REPLACING A METAL GUTTER SECTION (continued)

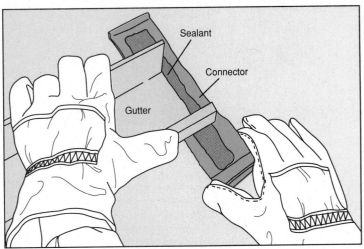

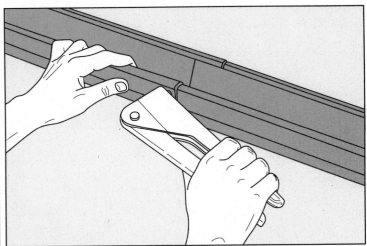

3 **Assembling gutter lengths.** Wearing work gloves, assemble as many gutter lengths as needed for the replacement section, adding any corner piece or drop outlet required *(step 4)*. To join two gutter lengths with a slip joint connector, apply a wide band of sealant along the center on the inside surface of the connector using a caulking gun *(page 116)*. Position the end of the first gutter length on the connector, centering it as shown, and press it into the sealant *(above, left)*. Repeat the procedure with the end of the second gutter length, butting it against the end of the first gutter length. Bend the connector around the sides of the gutter lengths and use pliers to crimp it onto their edges. Smooth any extruded sealant with a small putty knife.

To join two gutter lengths with sealant alone, overlap by 6 inches the one closest to the drop outlet with the one farthest from it. Apply a 6-inch band of sealant along the bottom on the inside of the first gutter length and slide in the second gutter length to overlap it; wearing safety goggles, use tin snips *(page 120)* to cut enough of the lip off the second gutter length to fit it, if necessary. Then, press the two gutter lengths together. To join two gutter lengths with rivets, use the same procedure to overlap them by 2 inches; then, install a rivet in the bottom and each side of the overlap *(above, right)* with a pop riveter *(page 122)* and cover each rivet head with sealant. If no end cap, corner piece or drop outlet is required, prepare the replacement section for installation *(step 5)*.

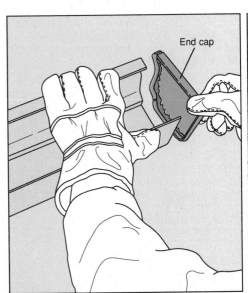

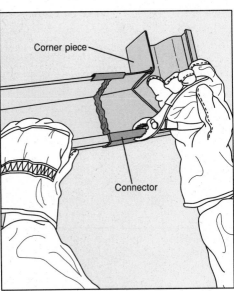

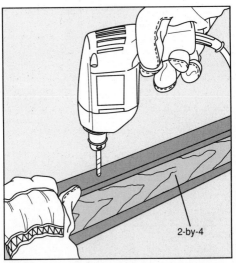

4 **Adding accessory pieces.** Wear work gloves to add any end cap, corner piece and drop outlet required. To install an end cap, apply a band of sealant along the inside edges of it using a caulking gun *(page 116)* and push it onto the end of the gutter length *(above, left)*. Smooth any extruded sealant with a small putty knife. To install a corner piece with a slip joint connector, apply a wide band of sealant along the center on the inside surface of the connector. Position the end of the corner piece and the end of the gutter length on the connector, centering them and butting the ends together, and press them into the sealant. Bend the connector around the sides of the corner piece and the gutter length, and use pliers to crimp it onto their edges *(above, right)*. Install a drop outlet with a slip joint connector the same way. Install a corner piece or a drop outlet using sealant alone or with rivets as you would to join gutter lengths *(step 3)*.

5 **Preparing the replacement section for installation.** If necessary, paint *(page 124)* the replacement section to match the original; first, wipe off any grease using a clean rag soaked in paint thinner and apply an appropriate primer. If there is no fascia, install the replacement section *(step 6)*. If there is a fascia, drill a hole *(page 121)* in the lip of the replacement section for each spike and ferrule required *(above)*, placing a 2-by-4 as a brace inside it; space the holes 24 or 32 inches apart using the damaged section as a guide, positioning each one, if possible, at a rafter—usually located every 12 or 16 inches behind the fascia.

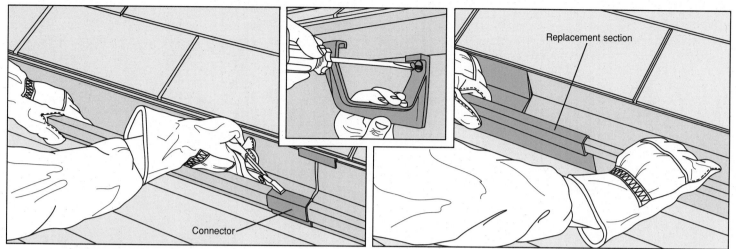

6 **Installing the replacement section.** If you are replacing bracket hangers, screw each one to the fascia at the chalkline and 1 inch away from the old holes *(inset)*; be sure to install one for each joint in the replacement section. To join the replacement section and the undamaged section with a slip joint connector, wear work gloves and apply a wide band of sealant along the center on the inside surface of the connector using a caulking gun *(page 116)*. Position the end of the replacement section on the connector, centering it, and press it into the sealant; then, bend the connector around the sides of it. Repeat the procedure at the other end of the replacement section if you are also joining it and another undamaged section. Working with a helper, raise

the replacement section into position, butting it against the end of the undamaged section. Press the connector around the sides of the two sections and use pliers to crimp it onto their edges *(above, left)*. Smooth any extruded sealant with a small putty knife. Join the other end of the replacement section with another undamaged section the same way. Join the replacement section and the undamaged section using sealant alone *(above, right)* or with rivets as you would to join gutter lengths *(step 3)*, overlapping the section closest to the drop outlet with the section farthest from it. Seat the replacement section securely in its bracket hangers or install spikes and ferrules or strap hangers *(page 40)*. Reinstall any downspout assembly you removed *(page 45)*.

REPLACING A VINYL GUTTER SECTION

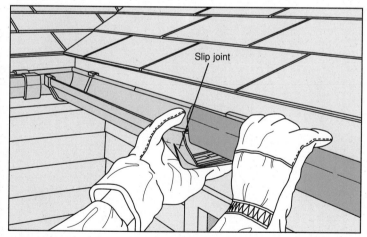

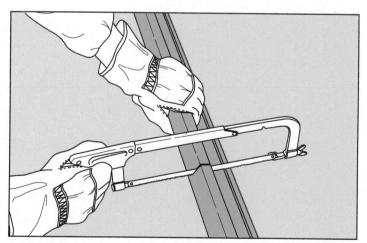

1 **Removing the damaged section.** Prepare to work safely along the gutter *(page 24)*, having a helper on hand. Remove any downspout assembly from the damaged section *(page 45)*. Wearing work gloves, unsnap the damaged section from the slip joint at each end of it *(above)* and from each hanger holding it; if necessary, remove the hangers along with it *(page 39)*. Carefully lower the damaged section to the ground. Use a chalkline *(page 117)* to mark the position of a replacement section along the roof edge, ensuring a gutter slope of about 1/16 inch per foot toward the downspout.

2 **Measuring and cutting a replacement section.** Calculate the length of gutter needed, adding a few feet for waste, and determine the number of corner pieces, end caps, drop outlets, hangers and slip joints required; a corner piece, end cap and drop outlet may have built-in rubber gaskets that serve as a slip joint. Buy components for a replacement section at a building supply center. Mark off the replacement gutter equal in length to the damaged section; wearing work gloves and safety goggles, cut it *(above)* using a hacksaw *(page 120)*. Smooth any rough edges with a flat file *(page 123)*. If more than one gutter length is needed, mark off and cut each one the same way. If only one gutter length is needed, install the replacement section *(step 4)*.

REPLACING A VINYL GUTTER SECTION (continued)

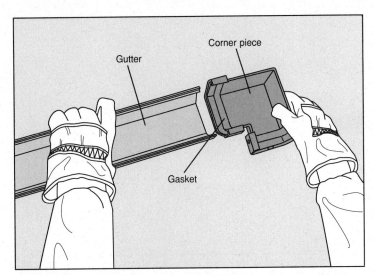

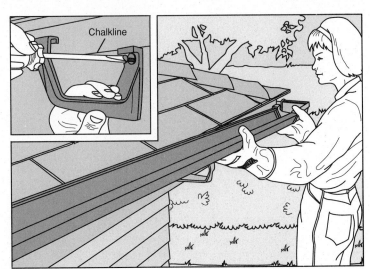

3 **Assembling the replacement section.** Wearing work gloves, assemble the replacement section following the manufacturer's instructions; a 1/4- to 1/2-inch overlap of components is usually required. To install a corner piece equipped with a rubber gasket, position it and the gutter length together *(above)* and snap each clip of the gasket in turn onto the edge of the gutter length. Install an end cap the same way. To join two gutter lengths, use the same procedure to snap on a slip joint between them; if the slip joint is of a screw-on type that also serves as a hanger, join the gutter lengths as you install the replacement section *(step 4)*.

4 **Installing the replacement section.** If you are replacing bracket hangers, screw each one to the fascia at the chalkline and 1 inch away from the old holes *(inset)*; be sure to install one for each joint in the replacement section. Install any replacement strap hangers *(page 40)* following the manufacturer's instructions; install any slip joint that also serves as a hanger at the joint between gutter lengths. Working with a helper, raise the replacement section into position and seat it securely *(above)*, snapping it in place. Repeat the procedure, if necessary, to install other gutter lengths. Then, reinstall any downspout assembly you removed *(page 45)*.

REPLACING A METAL DOWNSPOUT SECTION

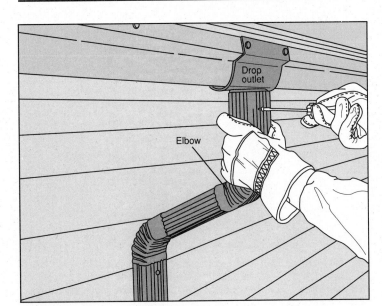

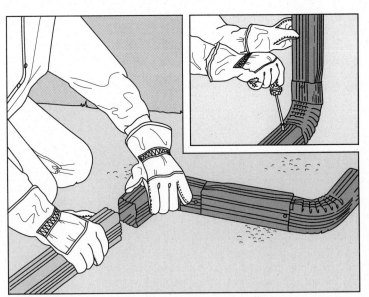

1 **Removing the damaged section.** Prepare to work safely at the downspout *(page 24)*. To remove the entire downspout assembly, have a helper steady the bottom; wearing work gloves, unscrew the elbow from the drop outlet *(above)* and then the brackets from the siding. Pull the elbow off the drop outlet and lower the downspout assembly to the ground. To remove a damaged section, take off it and any downspout assembly below it using the same procedure; then, unscrew the bottom end of it from the downspout assembly removed.

2 **Preparing a replacement section.** Buy a replacement section at a building supply center. Wearing work gloves and safety goggles, cut the replacement section to length using a hacksaw *(page 120)* and remove any burrs from the cut edges with a flat file *(page 123)*, if necessary. Fit the narrow end of the replacement section into the wide end of the downspout assembly removed *(above)*, pushing it in tightly. Drill a hole *(page 121)* through the overlap of the ends and drive in *(inset)* a sheet metal screw *(page 121)*.

REPLACING A METAL DOWNSPOUT SECTION (continued)

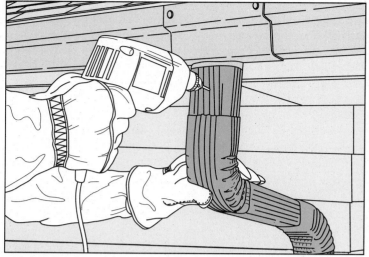

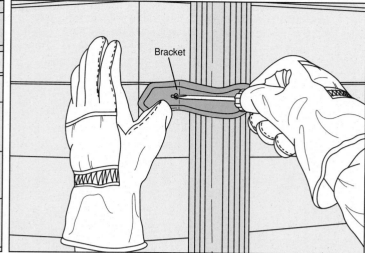

Bracket

3 **Installing the replacement section.** Wearing work gloves, install the downspout assembly removed with its wide end at the top. Having a helper steady the bottom of the downspout assembly removed, fit the top of it onto the bottom of the downspout assembly already in place, pushing the ends together tightly; if the top is a replacement section, drill a hole *(page 121)* through the overlap of the ends *(above, left)* and drive in a sheet metal screw *(page 121)*. Fit each bracket removed back into position around the downspout assembly and screw it onto the siding *(above, right)*, installing one

at the top and bottom of the downspout assembly, and every 10 feet along it or according to the manufacturer's instructions. If you are relocating a bracket on wood, vinyl or aluminum siding, first drill a pilot hole for each screw using a wood bit; if you are relocating a bracket on a masonry wall, first drill a hole for an anchor *(page 121)* using a masonry bit and set the anchor flush with the wall. If necessary, paint *(page 124)* the replacement section to match the original; first, wipe off any grease using a clean rag soaked in paint thinner and apply an appropriate primer, if necessary.

REPLACING A VINYL DOWNSPOUT SECTION

1 **Removing the damaged section.** Prepare to work safely at the downspout *(page 24)*. To remove the entire downspout assembly or a damaged section, work upward from the bottom and one section at a time. Unscrew the bracket for the first section from the siding and pull the first section off the downspout assembly still in place *(above)*; the second section also may come off if it is not held in place by its own bracket. Continue the procedure until the entire downspout assembly or the damaged section is removed. Buy a replacement section at a building supply center; wearing work gloves and safety goggles, cut it to length using a hacksaw *(page 120)* and smooth any rough edges with a flat file *(page 123)*, if necessary.

2 **Installing the replacement section.** Working downward from the bottom of the downspout assembly already in place, install each section one at a time, having a helper steady the bottom, if necessary *(above)*; follow the manufacturer's instructions for any special steps to hold it in place. Position the bracket for the section and screw it onto the siding. If you are relocating a bracket on wood, vinyl or aluminum siding, first drill *(page 121)* a pilot hole for each screw using a wood bit; if you are relocating a bracket on a masonry wall, first drill a hole for an anchor *(page 121)* using a masonry bit and set the anchor flush with the wall. Continue the procedure until the entire downspout assembly is installed.

FASCIAS

Fascias, the trim boards over the rafters along the eaves and rakes, and soffits, the finished underside of the eaves and rakes, are not major roofing and siding troublespots; whether of wood alone or covered with a vinyl or aluminum siding material, they are usually well protected from the elements and need only periodic cleaning and refinishing. A fascia, however, is more exposed than a soffit and can be vulnerable to marking, warping and rot. When a problem develops, consult the Troubleshooting Guide in Your Roofing and Siding *(page 16)* and below for guidance.

Replacing a fascia or a fascia cover is easy, although working at heights can be intimidating. Before undertaking a repair, read the chapter on Working Safely at Heights *(page 24)* to properly set up and use any ladders or scaffolding necessary. Call for a professional evaluation if you find that a soffit or a rafter is damaged. Most repairs require only basic tools such as a pry bar, a hammer, a saw and tin snips; for repairs to a vinyl fascia cover, you may also need a special snaplock punch. Refer to Tools & Techniques *(page 112)* for instructions on using tools and choosing materials.

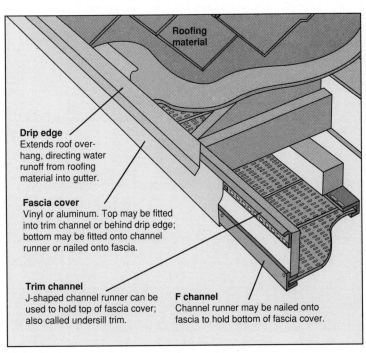

Roofing material

Drip edge
Extends roof overhang, directing water runoff from roofing material into gutter.

Fascia cover
Vinyl or aluminum. Top may be fitted into trim channel or behind drip edge; bottom may be fitted onto channel runner or nailed onto fascia.

Trim channel
J-shaped channel runner can be used to hold top of fascia cover; also called undersill trim.

F channel
Channel runner may be nailed onto fascia to hold bottom of fascia cover.

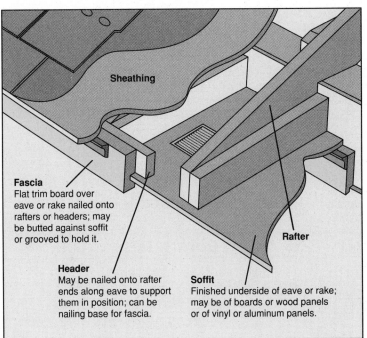

Sheathing

Fascia
Flat trim board over eave or rake nailed onto rafters or headers; may be butted against soffit or grooved to hold it.

Rafter

Header
May be nailed onto rafter ends along eave to support them in position; can be nailing base for fascia.

Soffit
Finished underside of eave or rake; may be of boards or wood panels or of vinyl or aluminum panels.

TROUBLESHOOTING GUIDE

SYMPTOM	POSSIBLE CAUSE	PROCEDURE
Soffit wet or leaking; wood spongy, pitted or crumbling	Water penetrating roofing	Call for professional evaluation
Fascia spongy, pitted or crumbling	Rot or insect damage	Replace fascia *(p. 47)* ▣◕; if insect infestation suspected, call for professional evaluation
Fascia warped	Gutter or downspout damaged or faulty	Troubleshoot and repair roofing and siding system *(p. 16)*
	Water damage	Replace fascia *(p. 47)* ▣◕
	Condensation in soffit; structural damage	Call for professional evaluation
Fascia cover buckled, bent, gouged, dented, cracked or broken	Weather stress; impact damage	Replace vinyl or aluminum fascia cover *(p. 48)* □◕▲
	Fascia warped	Replace fascia *(p. 47)* ▣◕
Fascia nicked, gouged, or cracked; dirty or stained; finish faded or damaged	Weather stress; impact damage	Repair as for Wood Siding *(p. 86)*
Fascia cover nicked or scratched; dirty or stained; finish faded or damaged	Weather stress; impact damage	Repair as for Vinyl and Aluminum Siding *(p. 102)*

DEGREE OF DIFFICULTY: □ Easy ▣ Moderate ■ Complex
ESTIMATED TIME: ○ Less than 1 hour ◕ 1 to 3 hours ● Over 3 hours
(For ladder and scaffolding set-up, see page 24)

▲ Special tool required

REPLACING A FASCIA

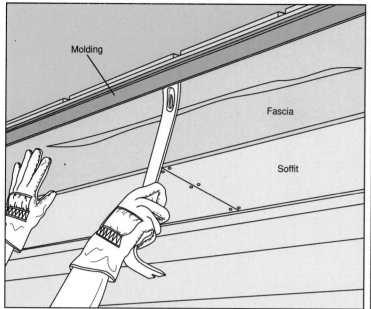

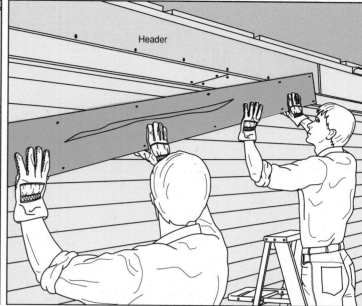

1 **Removing the damaged fascia.** Prepare to work safely along the fascia *(page 24)*, having a helper on hand. Remove any gutter section of metal *(page 41)* or vinyl *(page 43)* from the fascia; if there is a vinyl or an aluminum fascia cover, also remove it *(page 48)*. Test the fascia for rot and patch minor damage *(page 116)*; if the damage is extensive, replace the fascia. To remove the fascia, pull off any molding at the top using a pry bar *(above, left)* and lower it to the ground. Loosen the nails in the fascia by working the pry bar under it and along its bottom edge, if possible; then, having your helper steady it, pull out the nails and lower it to the ground *(above, right)*. If there is a header behind the fascia, test it for rot and patch minor damage; if the damage is extensive, remove the header as you did the fascia, also pulling out any nails driven through the soffit and into it. If the rafter ends are damaged, call for a professional evaluation.

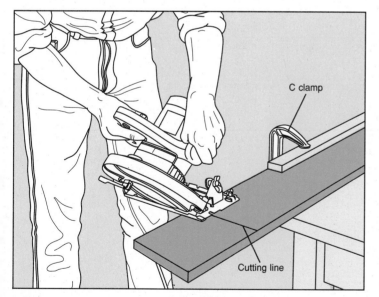

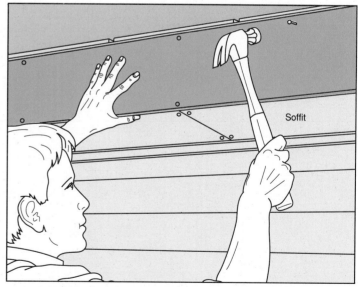

2 **Preparing a new fascia.** Buy replacement lumber of the same dimensions as the fascia, header and molding at a building supply center; if the old fascia is grooved to hold the soffit, have the lumber for the new fascia routed to match it or rout it yourself. Measure the length of the old fascia and mark the new fascia for cutting. Wearing safety goggles, cut the new fascia to length *(page 118)*, using a circular saw to bevel the end at a corner, if necessary *(above)*. Use the same procedure to mark and cut any new header and molding. Apply preservative or finish *(page 124)* on the new fascia, header and molding, ensuring the end grain, in particular, is adequately coated; also preserve or finish any exposed rafter ends to protect them.

3 **Installing the new fascia.** Install any new header first, as you would the new fascia. To install the new fascia, raise it into position with your helper steadying it; if it is grooved to hold the soffit, ensure it fits snugly. Drive nails *(page 121)* into the new fascia *(above)*, using the nailing pattern of the old fascia. Reinstall any vinyl *(page 48)* or aluminum *(page 49)* fascia cover you removed. Install any molding at the top of the new fascia the same way. If necessary, refinish the repaired surfaces *(page 124)*. Apply sealant *(page 115)* along the joint between the new fascia and the soffit. Reinstall any gutter section of metal *(page 43)* or vinyl *(page 44)* you removed. Install a drip edge *(page 40)* to protect the new fascia, if necessary.

REPLACING A VINYL OR ALUMINUM FASCIA COVER

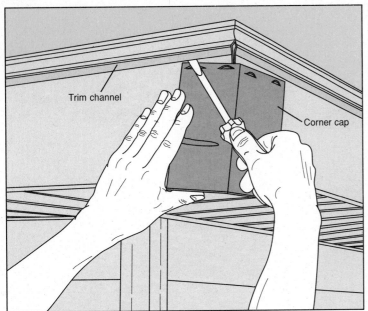

1 **Removing the fascia cover.** Prepare to work safely along the fascia *(page 24)*, having a helper on hand. To take off the fascia cover, remove any gutter section of metal *(page 41)* or vinyl *(page 43)* from it. To remove a vinyl fascia cover, work from one end to the other end, first taking off any corner cap. To remove a corner cap, unsnap the bottom of it from the F channel; if it is nailed, pull out the nails with a pry bar. Then, slide out the top of the corner cap; if it is fitted into a trim channel, use an old, flat-tipped screwdriver to gently pry it out *(above, left)*. Work along the fascia cover with the screwdriver the same way *(above, right)*; if the end is overlapped by another fascia cover, remove as much of it as necessary to free the end. Lower the fascia cover to the ground. To remove an aluminum fascia cover, wear work gloves and use the same procedure; if an end is folded around a corner and overlapped by another fascia cover, remove as much of it as necessary to free the end. After removing a vinyl or an aluminum fascia cover, test the fascia for rot and patch minor damage *(page 116)*; if the damage is extensive, replace the fascia *(page 47)*. Then, install a new vinyl *(step 2)* or aluminum *(step 3)* fascia cover.

2 **Fitting and installing a vinyl fascia cover.** Buy a replacement fascia cover at a building supply center; to fit it into a trim channel, also buy a snaplock punch. Measure the old fascia cover and mark the new fascia cover for cutting. Use tin snips *(page 120)* to cut the new fascia cover to size; notch the bottom at each end, if necessary, following the manufacturer's instructions. To fit the fascia cover into a trim channel, dimple it every 6 inches along the top with the snaplock punch *(inset)*. If the fascia cover does not fit onto an F channel, use an awl to punch holes for nails along the bottom, if necessary, at intervals specified by the manufacturer.

To install the fascia cover, raise it into position with your helper steadying it. Slide the top of the fascia cover into the trim channel *(left)* or behind any drip edge. Snap the bottom of the fascia cover onto the F channel or nail it *(page 121)* onto the fascia, driving each nail until its head just touches the fascia cover. If you removed a corner cap, replace it *(page 49)*. Reinstall any gutter section of metal *(page 43)* or vinyl *(page 44)* you removed. Install a drip edge *(page 40)* to protect the new fascia cover, if necessary.

REPLACING A VINYL OR ALUMINUM FASCIA COVER (continued)

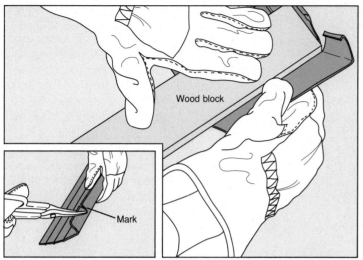

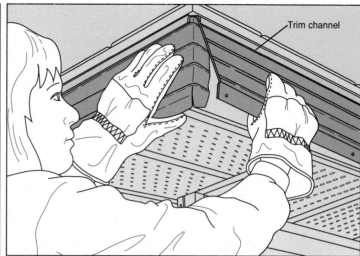

Trim channel

Wood block

Mark

3 **Fitting and installing an aluminum fascia cover.** Buy a replacement fascia cover at a building supply center. Wearing work gloves, measure the old fascia cover and mark the new fascia cover for cutting. To fit the new fascia cover around a corner, mark a line across the back and bottom 1 inch from the end. Notch the bottom, cutting at a 45-degree angle on each side of the line *(inset)* using tin snips *(page 120)*. Fold the back at a 90-degree angle along the line, using a wood block as a guide *(above, left)*. Cut the fascia cover to size with tin snips. Use an awl to punch holes for nails along the bottom of the fascia cover, if necessary, at intervals specified by the manufacturer.

To install the fascia cover, raise it into position with your helper steadying it. Slide the top of the fascia cover into the trim channel or behind any drip edge. To fit the end of the fascia cover around a corner, slide it into place behind the fascia cover on the other side of the corner *(above, right)*. Nail *(page 121)* the bottom of the fascia cover onto the fascia, driving each nail until its head just touches the fascia cover. Reinstall any gutter section of metal *(page 43)* or vinyl *(page 44)* you removed. Install a drip edge *(page 40)* to protect the new fascia cover, if necessary.

REPLACING A VINYL CORNER CAP

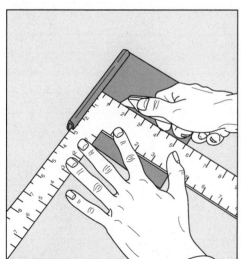

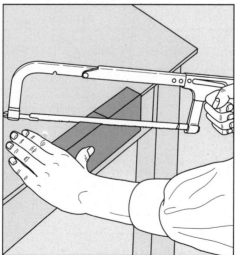

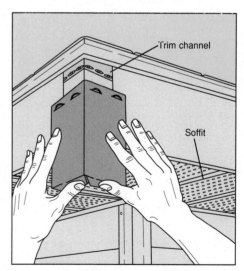

Trim channel

Soffit

1 **Making a corner cap.** If the corner cap you removed is undamaged, reinstall it *(step 2)*. To make a new corner cap, use tin snips *(page 120)* to cut off a section of fascia cover 6 inches long. Score a line across the center on the back and bottom of the fascia cover with a utility knife *(page 120)* and a carpenter's square *(above, left)*. Notch the bottom, cutting at a 45-degree angle on each side of the line using a hacksaw *(above, right)* or the tin snips. Fold the back at a 90-degree angle along the line, using the carpenter's square as a guide. To fit the corner cap into a trim channel, dimple it every 1 1/2 inches along the top with a snaplock punch. If the corner cap does not fit onto an F channel, use an awl to punch holes for nails along the bottom, if necessary, at intervals specified by the manufacturer.

2 **Installing the corner cap.** To install the corner cap, raise it into position over the end of the fascia cover on each side of the corner, sliding the top into the trim channel *(above)* or behind any drip edge. Snap the bottom of the corner cap onto the F channel or nail it *(page 121)* onto the fascia, driving each nail until its head just touches the corner cap. Reinstall any gutter section of metal *(page 43)* or vinyl *(page 44)* you removed. Install a drip edge *(page 40)* to protect the new fascia cover, if necessary.

ASPHALT SHINGLES

The low cost, easy application and few maintenance needs of asphalt shingles make them the roofing choice of most homeowners; compatible with traditional and contemporary housing, they are available in many colors and styles—from the common 3-tab to the newer embossed and laminated types. Usually, an asphalt shingle has three layers: organic felt or fiberglass mat for strength; asphalt for water and weather resistance; and mineral granules to shelter the asphalt, add color and retard fire. A typical roof of asphalt shingles is shown at right. Installed in straight, overlapping rows, or courses, the shingles are laid on building paper and nailed to the wooden sheathing under it. Nails are driven into shingles just below the self-sealing adhesive at intervals specified by the manufacturer—and are hidden by the tabs of the next course, typically sealed onto the self-sealing adhesive.

If a leak develops in the attic or from an upstairs ceiling, consult the Troubleshooting Guide in Your Roofing and Siding *(page 14)* and in this chapter *(below)*. Often, the problem may originate with the gutters and downspouts, the vents or the flashing, and not the roofing. If you find damaged shingles, however, you can easily replace them—one tab or one shingle at a time, or a small section of shingles at once. Before undertaking a repair, read the chapter on Working Safely at Heights *(page 24)* to properly set up and use any ladders or scaffolding necessary; do not work on a roof with a pitch greater than 6 in 12. Refer to Tools & Techniques *(page 112)* for instructions on using tools and choosing materials. Make repairs on a dry, cool, overcast day. If you cannot locate the source of a leak or if the roofing is damaged extensively, call for a professional evaluation.

TROUBLESHOOTING GUIDE

SYMPTOM	POSSIBLE CAUSE	PROCEDURE
Leak into attic or from ceiling	Water penetrating roofing; hole in plumbing	Minimize immediate water damage *(p. 10)* □○
	Flashing, vent, gutter or downspout damaged or faulty	Troubleshoot and repair roofing and siding system *(p. 16)*
	Nail popped	Replace popped nail *(p. 52)* □○
	Tab damaged	Repair *(p. 53)* □○ or replace *(p. 53)* □○ tab
	Shingle or shingles damaged	Replace shingle *(p. 54)* □○ or section of shingles *(p. 55)* ◨●: at open valley *(p. 56)* ◨○; at closed cut valley *(p. 57)* ■●; at ridge or hip *(p. 59)* ◨○; at chimney *(p. 60)* ◨○; at vent *(p. 61)* ◨●; if roofing damaged extensively, call for professional evaluation
Ice buildup at roof edge under shingles	Soffit vent blocked or turbine roof vent faulty	Unblock soffit vent *(p. 22)* □●; service turbine roof vent *(p. 23)* □○
	Attic ventilation inadequate	Call for professional evaluation
Flashing rusted or broken	Weather stress; impact damage	Troubleshoot roofing and siding system and repair flashing *(p. 16)*
Shingle tab lifted or curled	Wind damage	Repair tab *(p. 53)* □○
Shingle tab cracked, torn or perforated	Nail popped	Replace popped nail *(p. 52)* □○
	Weather stress; wear	Repair *(p. 53)* □○ or replace *(p. 53)* □○ tab
Shingle or shingles broken, hanging out of position or missing	Wind damage; impact damage	Replace shingle *(p. 54)* □○ or section of shingles *(p. 55)* ◨●: at open valley *(p. 56)* ◨○; at closed cut valley *(p. 57)* ■●; at ridge or hip *(p. 59)* ◨○; at chimney *(p. 60)* ◨○; at vent *(p. 61)* ◨●; if roofing damaged extensively, call for professional evaluation
Shingle or shingles cracked, curled, or crumbling	Soffit vent blocked or turbine roof vent faulty	Unblock soffit vent *(p. 22)* □●; service turbine roof vent *(p. 23)* □○
	Weather stress; wear	Replace shingle *(p. 54)* □○ or section of shingles *(p. 55)* ◨●: at open valley *(p. 56)* ◨○; at closed cut valley *(p. 57)* ■●; at ridge or hip *(p. 59)* ◨○; at chimney *(p. 60)* ◨○; at vent *(p. 61)* ◨●; if roofing damaged extensively, call for professional evaluation
Shingles dark, damp, bald in spots; frost patches in cool weather; accumulation of mineral granules in gutter	Weather stress; wear	Replace shingle *(p. 54)* □○ or section of shingles *(p. 55)* ◨●: at open valley *(p. 56)* ◨○; at closed cut valley *(p. 57)* ■●; at ridge or hip *(p. 59)* ◨○; at chimney *(p. 60)* ◨○; at vent *(p. 61)* ◨●; if roofing damaged extensively, call for professional evaluation
Shingles dirty, debris-covered; growth of moss	Wear; wind-borne material; pollution	Sweep off roof; trim back overhead and adjacent vegetation
Shingles stained dark brown or black	Flashing or vent rusted; gutter or downspout faulty or rusted	Troubleshoot and repair roofing and siding system *(p. 16)*
	Algae, mold or mildew	Wash with solution of 1 part 5% bleach and 1 part water; rinse well

DEGREE OF DIFFICULTY: □ **Easy** ◨ **Moderate** ■ **Complex**
ESTIMATED TIME: ○ **Less than 1 hour** ◐ **1 to 3 hours** ● **Over 3 hours**
(For ladder and scaffolding set-up, see page 24)

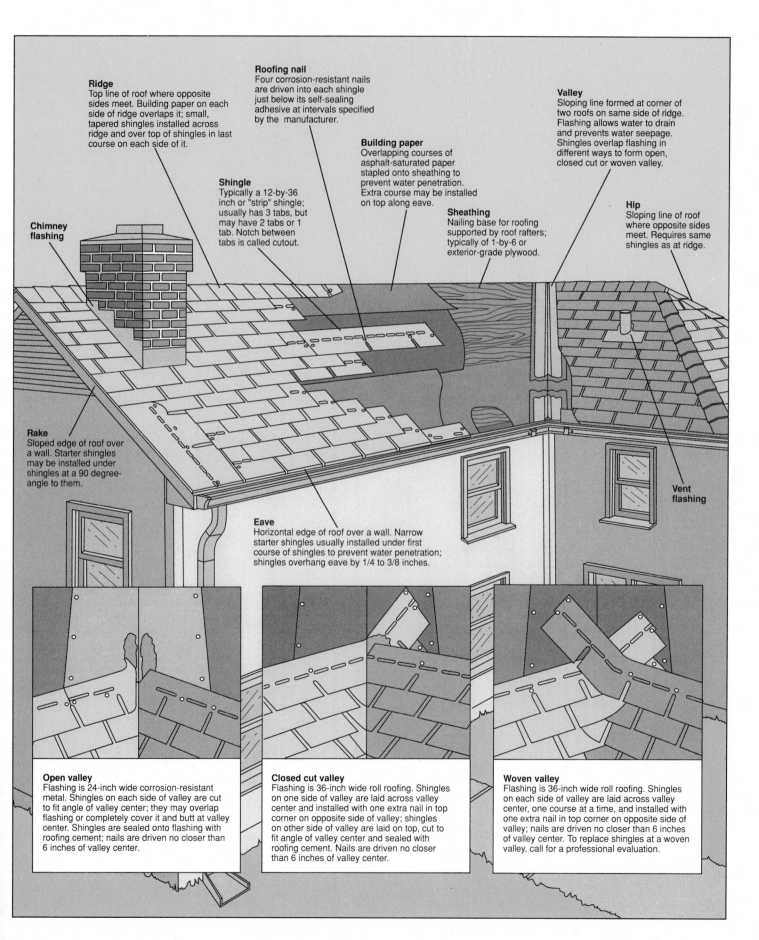

Ridge
Top line of roof where opposite sides meet. Building paper on each side of ridge overlaps it; small, tapered shingles installed across ridge and over top of shingles in last course on each side of it.

Roofing nail
Four corrosion-resistant nails are driven into each shingle just below its self-sealing adhesive at intervals specified by the manufacturer.

Building paper
Overlapping courses of asphalt-saturated paper stapled onto sheathing to prevent water penetration. Extra course may be installed on top along eave.

Valley
Sloping line formed at corner of two roofs on same side of ridge. Flashing allows water to drain and prevents water seepage. Shingles overlap flashing in different ways to form open, closed cut or woven valley.

Shingle
Typically a 12-by-36 inch or "strip" shingle; usually has 3 tabs, but may have 2 tabs or 1 tab. Notch between tabs is called cutout.

Sheathing
Nailing base for roofing supported by roof rafters; typically of 1-by-6 or exterior-grade plywood.

Hip
Sloping line of roof where opposite sides meet. Requires same shingles as at ridge.

Chimney flashing

Rake
Sloped edge of roof over a wall. Starter shingles may be installed under shingles at a 90 degree-angle to them.

Vent flashing

Eave
Horizontal edge of roof over a wall. Narrow starter shingles usually installed under first course of shingles to prevent water penetration; shingles overhang eave by 1/4 to 3/8 inches.

Open valley
Flashing is 24-inch wide corrosion-resistant metal. Shingles on each side of valley are cut to fit angle of valley center; they may overlap flashing or completely cover it and butt at valley center. Shingles are sealed onto flashing with roofing cement; nails are driven no closer than 6 inches of valley center.

Closed cut valley
Flashing is 36-inch wide roll roofing. Shingles on one side of valley are laid across valley center and installed with one extra nail in top corner on opposite side of valley; shingles on other side of valley are laid on top, cut to fit angle of valley center and sealed with roofing cement. Nails are driven no closer than 6 inches of valley center.

Woven valley
Flashing is 36-inch wide roll roofing. Shingles on each side of valley are laid across valley center, one course at a time, and installed with one extra nail in top corner on opposite side of valley; nails are driven no closer than 6 inches of valley center. To replace shingles at a woven valley, call for a professional evaluation.

REPLACING A POPPED NAIL

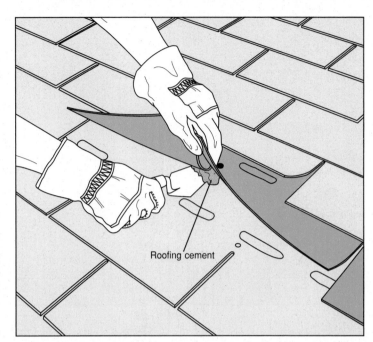

Tab

Roofing cement

1 **Removing the nail.** Prepare to work safely on the roof *(page 24)*. If a tab is bulging, cracked, torn or perforated, replace any popped nail in the shingle one course below it; otherwise, repair or replace the tab *(page 53)*. Lift the damaged tab high enough to expose the nail; if it is sealed down, gently work a trowel or a putty knife under it and along its edges to loosen it. Holding up the tab, use a pry bar to pull the nail out of the shingle *(above)*.

2 **Sealing the nail hole.** Lift as many tabs of the shingle as necessary to reach the nail hole in the bottom of it; if a tab is sealed down, gently work a trowel or a putty knife under it and along its edges to loosen it. Wearing work gloves, use the trowel or putty knife to apply roofing cement *(page 115)* on the bottom of the shingle over the nail hole *(above)* and about 2 inches from the edges at the corners of each lifted tab. Press each tab down firmly to seal it.

3 **Installing a new nail.** To install a new nail in the shingle, lift the damaged tab one course above it, exposing the sealed nail hole. Drive a roofing nail *(page 121)* into the shingle about 1 inch to the side of the sealed hole using a hammer, setting the nail head flush with the surface *(above)*. If the damaged tab is cracked, torn, or perforated, repair or replace it *(page 53)*. Otherwise, seal the damaged tab *(step 4)*.

4 **Sealing the damaged tab.** Wearing work gloves, hold up the damaged tab and use a trowel or a putty knife to apply a small amount of roofing cement *(page 115)* on the bottom of it about 2 inches from the edges at each corner *(above)*. Reposition the tab and press it down firmly to seal it. Lay a brick on top of the tab, if necessary, to help the bonding of the roofing cement and remove it when the roofing cement cures.

REPAIRING A SHINGLE TAB

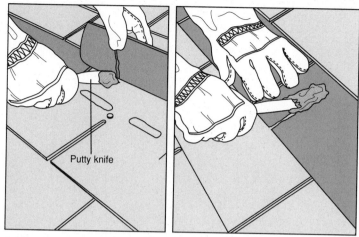

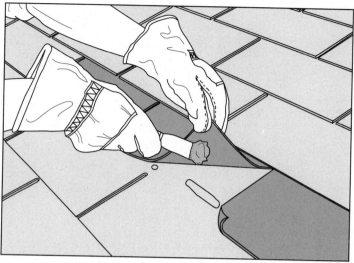

Putty knife

Sealing a crack, tear or perforation. Prepare to work safely on the roof *(page 24)*. Lift the tab high enough to expose the damage on the bottom of it; if it is sealed down, gently work a putty knife or a trowel under it and along its edges to loosen it. If the tab is damaged beyond its exposed portion, replace it *(steps below)*. Otherwise, wear work gloves and use the putty knife or trowel to apply roofing cement *(page 115)* on the bottom of the tab over the damage *(above, left)* and about 2 inches from the edges at each corner. Press the tab down firmly to seal it. Then, apply roofing cement on the top of the tab over the damage *(above, right)*. Scrape off excess roofing cement and smooth the edges.

Sealing a lifted or curled edge. Prepare to work safely on the roof *(page 24)*. To seal a lifted or curled edge, lift the tab high enough to reach under it; if it is partly sealed down, gently work a putty knife or a trowel under it and along its edges to loosen it. Wearing work gloves, hold up the tab and use the putty knife or trowel to apply roofing cement *(page 115)* on the bottom of it about 2 inches from the edges at each corner *(above)*. Press the tab down firmly to seal it. Lay a brick on top of the tab to help the bonding of the roofing cement and remove it when the roofing cement cures.

REPLACING A SHINGLE TAB

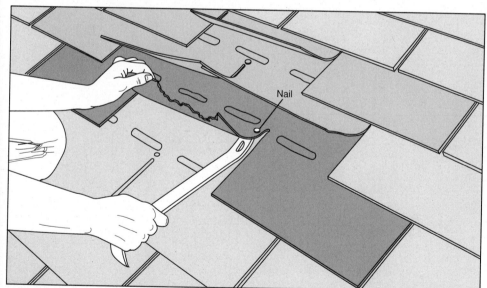

Nail

1 **Removing the nails.** Prepare to work safely on the roof *(page 24)*. If a shingle has one tab or more than one damaged tab, replace the shingle *(page 54)*; otherwise, replace the damaged tab. To locate the nails holding the damaged tab, lift the tab two courses above it and then the two adjacent tabs one course above it; lift the shingles above it if you are at a ridge or hip *(page 59)*. If a tab is sealed down, gently work a putty knife or a trowel under it and along its edges to loosen it. Lift the damaged tab the same way. To remove the nails holding the damaged tab, work from it to the tab two courses above it. To raise each nail head, fit a pry bar under the tab and around the nail shaft *(above)*; to pull out the nail, remove the pry bar and fit it around the raised nail head on top of the tab. Continue the procedure until all the nails holding the damaged tab are removed.

2 **Cutting off the damaged tab.** Cut the damaged tab off the shingle using tin snips *(page 120)*, working from each cutout at the side of the damaged tab *(above)* straight to the top of the shingle; hold up the tab one course above the damaged tab, as shown, to avoid damaging it. After cutting off the damaged tab, carefully pull it out.

REPLACING A SHINGLE TAB (continued)

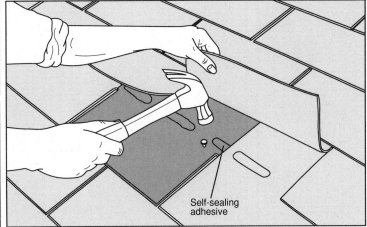

Self-sealing adhesive

3 **Installing the replacement tab.** Buy a shingle that matches the originals at a building supply center. Use tin snips *(page 120)* to cut a replacement tab off the shingle; if necessary, also trim the tab to size. Wearing work gloves, hold up the adjacent tabs one course above the opening for the new tab and use a putty knife or a trowel to apply roofing cement *(page 115)* on the area to be covered by the new tab—including building paper *(inset)* and other tabs. Slide the new tab into position under the adjacent tabs one course above it *(above, left)* and aligned with the tabs on each side of it. Press the new tab down firmly to seal it onto the roofing cement.

Holding up in turn the adjacent tabs one course above the new tab, drive a roofing nail *(page 121)* into the new tab just below the self-sealing adhesive and about 1 inch from each side *(above, right)*; likewise nail a cutoff tab adjacent to it. Apply roofing cement on the bottom of the adjacent tabs one course above the new tab over each nail hole and about 2 inches from the edges at each corner; press each tab down firmly to seal it. Using the same procedure, nail the adjacent tabs one course above the new tab about 1 inch to the side of each sealed hole; then, seal the tab two courses above the new tab with roofing cement. If you are at a ridge or hip, reinstall the shingles above the new tab *(page 60)*.

REPLACING A SHINGLE

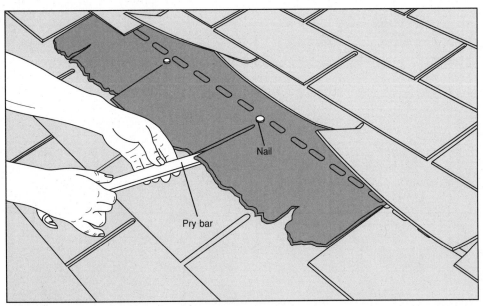

Nail

Pry bar

1 **Removing the damaged shingle.** Prepare to work safely on the roof *(page 24)*. If a shingle has two or three tabs and only one is damaged, replace the tab *(page 24)*; otherwise, replace the damaged shingle. To locate the nails holding the damaged shingle, lift the tabs two courses above it and then the adjacent tabs one course above it; lift the shingles above it if you are at a ridge or hip *(page 59)*. If a tab is sealed down, gently work a putty knife or a trowel under it and along its edges to loosen it. Lift each tab of the damaged shingle the same way. To remove the nails holding the damaged shingle, work from it to the tabs two courses above it. To raise each nail head, fit a pry bar under the tab and around the nail shaft *(above)*; to pull out the nail, remove the pry bar and fit it around the raised nail head on top of the tab. Continue until all the nails holding the damaged shingle are removed. Then, pull out the damaged shingle; replace any damaged starter shingle you find under it at an eave *(page 58)* or a rake *(page 59)*.

2 **Fitting a replacement shingle.** Buy a replacement shingle at a building supply center. Slide the new shingle into position under the adjacent tabs one course above it *(above)* and aligned with the tabs on each side of it; if necessary, trim it using tin snips *(page 120)*. Wearing work gloves, use a putty knife or a trowel to apply roofing cement *(page 115)* on the bottom of the new shingle about 2 inches from the edges at the corners of each tab. Press each tab down firmly to seal it.

REPLACING A SHINGLE (continued)

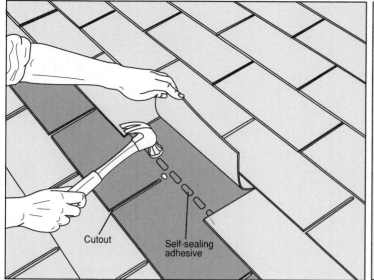

Cutout

Self-sealing adhesive

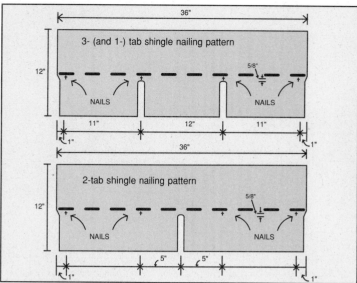

36"

3- (and 1-) tab shingle nailing pattern

12"

5/8"

NAILS   NAILS

11"   12"   11"

1"   1"

36"

2-tab shingle nailing pattern

12"

5/8"

NAILS   NAILS

5"   5"

1"   1"

3 **Installing the replacement shingle.** Holding up in turn the adjacent tabs one course above the new shingle, drive a roofing nail *(page 121)* into the new shingle just below the self-sealing adhesive and about 1 inch from each side. Also nail at intervals specified by the manufacturer: for a 3-tab shingle, at each cutout *(above, left)*; for a 1-tab shingle, 12 inches from each side *(above right, top)*; for a 2-tab shingle, 5 inches from each side of the cutout *(above right, bottom)*. Wearing work gloves, use a putty knife or a trowel to

apply roofing cement *(page 115)* on the bottom of the adjacent tabs one course above the new shingle over each nail hole and about 2 inches from the edges at each corner; press each tab down firmly to seal it onto the roofing cement. Using the same procedure, nail the adjacent tabs one course above the new shingle about 1 inch to the side of each sealed hole; then, seal the tab two courses above each tab of the new shingle with roofing cement. If you are at a ridge or hip, reinstall the shingles above the new shingle *(page 60)*.

REPLACING A SECTION OF SHINGLES

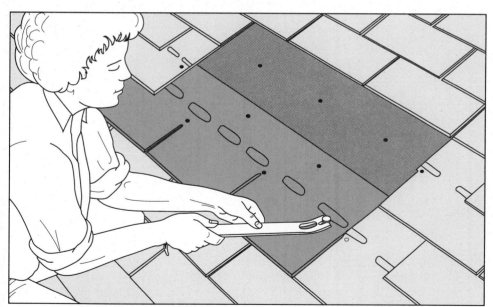

Building paper

1 **Removing the damaged section.** Prepare to work safely on the roof *(page 24)*. To remove a damaged section of shingles, work one course at a time from the top to the bottom and from one end to the other end. Take off each shingle of the first course as you would to remove one shingle *(page 54)*. To take off a shingle of a subsequent course, remove each nail holding it. Raise a nail head by fitting a pry bar under the shingle and around the nail shaft; to pull out the nail, remove the pry bar and fit it around the raised nail head on top of the shingle *(above)*. Continue until all the nails holding the shingle are removed and then pull out the shingle. Repeat the procedure until all the shingles of the damaged section are removed; replace any damaged starter shingle you find under the section at an eave *(page 58)* or a rake *(page 59)*.

2 **Sealing the building paper.** If the sheathing is spongy, soft or crumbly, test for and repair minor rot *(page 116)*; if the damage is extensive, call for a professional evaluation. Patch any damaged building paper *(page 117)*. Wearing work gloves, use a putty knife or a trowel to apply roofing cement *(page 115)* on each nail hole in the building paper *(above)*.

REPLACING A SECTION OF SHINGLES (continued)

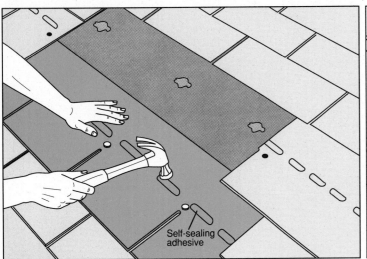

Self-sealing
adhesive

3 **Installing the replacement section.** Buy replacement shingles at a building supply center. To install the replacement section of shingles, work one course at a time from the bottom to the top and from one end to the other end. To install each new shingle, slide it into position under the adjacent tabs of any shingle one course above it and aligned with the tabs of the shingles on each side of it; if necessary, cut it to size using tin snips *(page 120)*. Wearing work gloves, use a putty knife or a trowel to apply roofing cement *(page 115)* on the bottom of the new shingle about 2 inches from the edges at the corners of each tab; press each tab down firmly to seal it.

Holding up any adjacent tabs one course above the new shingle, drive a roofing nail *(page 121)* into the new shingle just below the self-sealing adhesive and about 1 inch from each side. Also nail at intervals specified by the manufacturer *(page 55)*: for a 3-tab shingle, at each cutout *(above, left)*; for a 1-tab shingle, 12 inches from each side; for a 2-tab shingle, 5 inches from each side of the cutout. Install all but the shingles for the last course the same way. Then, as you would to fit *(page 54)* and install *(page 55)* one shingle, install each shingle of the last course *(above, right)*.

REPLACING A SHINGLE AT AN OPEN VALLEY

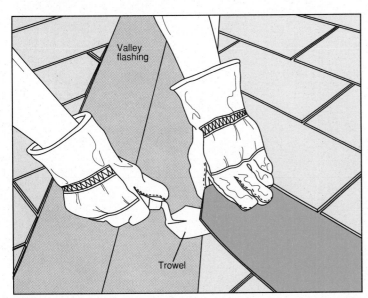

Valley
flashing

Trowel

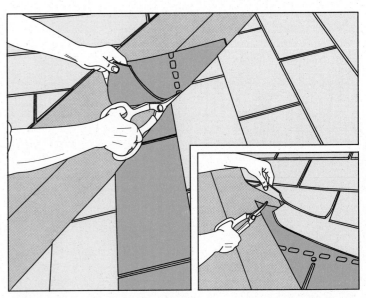

1 **Removing the damaged shingle.** Prepare to work safely on the roof *(page 24)*. To remove a damaged shingle at an open valley, pull out the nails holding it as you would to remove another shingle *(page 54)*. Wearing work gloves, gently work a trowel or a putty knife under and along the edge of the shingle at the valley flashing *(above)*, breaking the seal of the roofing cement; work carefully to avoid damaging the flashing. Then, pull out the shingle. If the valley flashing is damaged, repair it *(page 16)*.

2 **Fitting a replacement shingle.** Buy a replacement shingle at a building supply center. Slide the new shingle into position under the adjacent tabs one course above it and aligned with the tabs of the shingle beside it. With tin snips *(page 120)*, trim off the new shingle along the edge of the valley *(above)*, using the edge of the shingles one course above and below it as a guide. Then, holding up the tab at the valley one course above the new shingle, snip 1 inch off the top corner of the new shingle at a 45-degree angle *(inset)*.

REPLACING A SHINGLE AT AN OPEN VALLEY (continued)

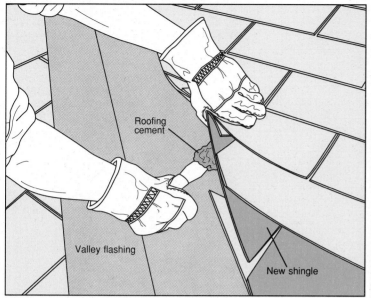

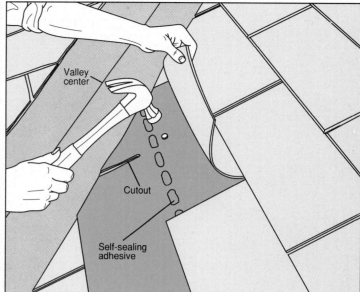

3 **Installing the replacement shingle.** Wearing work gloves, hold up the edge of the new shingle at the valley and use a putty knife or a trowel to apply a band of roofing cement *(page 115)* 3 inches wide on the bottom of it along the edge of the valley *(above, left)*; press it down firmly to seal it onto the flashing and any shingle under it. Then, apply roofing cement on the bottom of the new shingle about 2 inches from the edges at the unsealed corners of each tab; press each tab down firmly to seal it.

Holding up in turn the adjacent tabs one course above the new shingle, drive a roofing nail *(page 121)* into the new shingle just below the self-sealing adhesive and about 1 inch from each side. Also nail at intervals specified by the manufacturer *(page 55)*: for a 3-tab shingle, at each cutout; for a 1-tab shingle, 12 inches from each side; for a 2-tab shingle, 5 inches from each side of the cutout. Reposition a nail to avoid driving it within 6 inches of the valley center *(above, right)*. Seal and nail the tabs above the new shingle as you would to install another shingle *(page 55)*.

REPLACING A SHINGLE AT A CLOSED CUT VALLEY

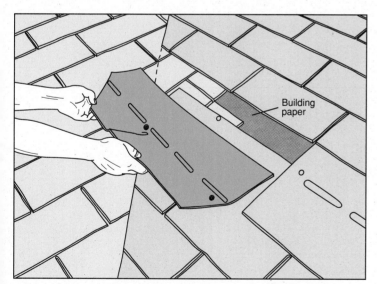

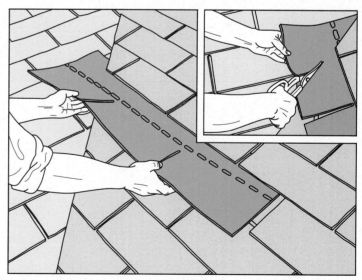

1 **Removing a cut shingle.** Prepare to work safely on the roof *(page 24)*. To replace a damaged cut shingle at a closed cut valley, take it off as you would to remove another shingle *(page 54)* and install a replacement cut shingle *(step 2)*. To replace a damaged uncut shingle at a closed cut valley, take off as many cut shingles on the opposite side of the valley as necessary to reach the end of it; work from the cut shingle adjacent to the uncut shingle toward the ridge, one course at a time *(above)*. Then, remove the damaged uncut shingle and install a replacement *(step 3)*.

2 **Installing a replacement cut shingle.** Buy a replacement shingle at a building supply center. Slide the new shingle into position under the adjacent tabs one course above it *(above)* and aligned with the tabs of the shingle beside it. With tin snips *(page 120)*, trim off the new shingle along the edge of the valley, using the edge of the shingles one course above and below it as a guide *(inset)*. Holding up the tab at the valley one course above the new shingle, snip 1 inch off the top corner of it at a 45-degree angle. Seal and nail the new shingle as you would to install a shingle at an open valley *(step 3, above)*.

REPLACING A SHINGLE AT A CLOSED CUT VALLEY (continued)

3 **Replacing an uncut shingle.** Remove the damaged uncut shingle as you would to remove another shingle *(page 54)*, also pulling out the extra nail in the top corner of it on the cut side of the valley *(left)*. Patch any damaged building paper *(page 117)* and apply roofing cement *(page 115)* on any holes in the flashing at the valley. Buy a replacement shingle at a building supply center. As you would to fit *(page 54)* and install *(page 55)* another shingle, seal and nail the new shingle; reposition a nail slightly, if necessary, to avoid driving it within 6 inches of the valley center. Add an extra nail at the top corner of the new shingle on the cut side of the valley. Then, reinstall each cut shingle removed as you would to install a replacement cut shingle *(step 2)*.

REPLACING A STARTER SHINGLE AT AN EAVE

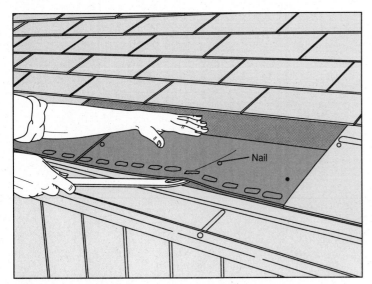

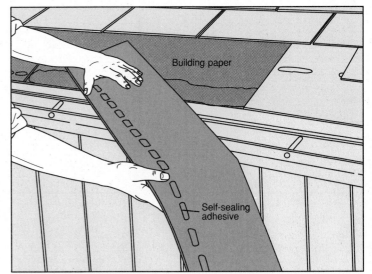

1 **Removing the damaged starter shingle.** Remove as large a section of shingles as necessary to reach the damaged starter shingle *(page 55)* and then lift the edge of it at the eave; if it is sealed down, gently work a putty knife or a trowel under and along it. To raise each nail head, fit a pry bar under the starter shingle and around the nail shaft *(above)*; to pull out the nail, remove the pry bar and fit it around the raised nail head on top of the starter shingle. When all the nails holding the starter shingle are removed, pull it out. If the sheathing is spongy, soft or crumbly, test for and repair minor rot *(page 116)*; if the damage is extensive, call for a professional evaluation. Patch any damaged building paper *(page 117)*; apply roofing cement *(page 115)* on each nail hole in it.

2 **Installing the replacement starter shingle.** Buy a replacement shingle at a building supply center; to make it into a starter shingle, cut off the tabs just below the self-sealing adhesive with tin snips *(page 120)*. Use a putty knife or a trowel to apply a band of roofing cement *(page 115)* 3 inches wide along the building paper at the eave. Position the starter shingle with the cut edge along the eave *(above)* and overhanging it by 1/4 to 3/8 inch. Press the starter shingle down firmly to seal it onto the roofing cement. Drive a roofing nail *(page 121)* into the starter shingle 3 to 4 inches from the eave and about 1 inch and 12 inches from each side. Then, install the replacement section of shingles on top of the starter shingle *(page 56)*.

REPLACING A STARTER SHINGLE AT A RAKE

Building paper

Removing and installing a starter shingle.
Remove as large a section of shingles as necessary to reach the damaged starter shingle *(page 55)*; cut off a damaged section using tin snips *(page 120)*. Pull out the nails holding the starter shingle using a pry bar; then, pull out the starter shingle *(left)*. If the sheathing is spongy, soft or crumbly, test for and repair minor rot *(page 116)*; if the damage is extensive, call for a professional evaluation. Patch any damaged building paper *(page 117)*; apply roofing cement *(page 115)* on each nail hole in it.

Buy a replacement shingle to use as a starter shingle at a building supply center. Slide the new starter shingle into position with the top edge along the rake and overhanging it by 1/4 to 3/8 inch. Drive a roofing nail *(page 121)* into the starter shingle 3 to 4 inches from the rake and about 1 inch from each side. Also nail at intervals specified by the manufacturer *(page 55)*: for a 3-tab shingle, at each cutout; for a 1-tab shingle, 12 inches from each side; for a 2-tab shingle, 5 inches from each side of the cutout. Then, install the replacement section of shingles on top of the starter shingle *(page 56)*.

REPLACING A SHINGLE AT A RIDGE OR HIP

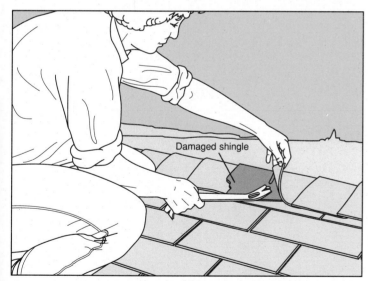

Damaged shingle

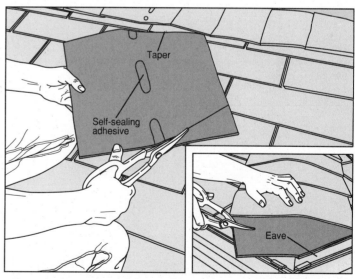

Taper

Self-sealing adhesive

Eave

1 Removing the damaged shingle. Prepare to work safely on the roof *(page 24)*. To locate the nails holding the damaged shingle, lift the shingle two courses above it and then the shingle one course above it; if a shingle is sealed down, gently work a putty knife or a trowel under it and along its edges to loosen it. Lift the damaged shingle the same way. To remove the nails holding the damaged shingle, work from it to the shingle two courses above it. To raise each nail head, fit a pry bar under the shingle and around the nail shaft; to pull out the nail, remove the pry bar and fit it around the raised nail head on top of the shingle *(above)*. Continue until all the nails holding the damaged shingle are removed; then, pull out the damaged shingle.

2 Fitting a replacement shingle. Buy a replacement shingle at a building supply center; to make it into a shingle for the ridge or hip, use tin snips *(page 120)* to cut off a tab 12 inches square and taper it, trimming each side from 3/8 to 5/8 inch below the self-sealing adhesive to about 1 inch from the side at the top *(above)*. Slide the new shingle into position under the shingle one course above it, overlapping the taper. If you are at the end of a ridge over two hips, fit the shingle *(step 3)*. If you are at the end of a hip over the eave, trim the shingle to fit using the edge of the shingles on each side of the corner as a guide *(inset)*. After positioning and fitting the shingle, apply roofing cement *(page 115)* on the bottom of it about 2 inches from the edges at each corner, press it down firmly to seal it and install it *(step 4)*.

REPLACING A SHINGLE AT A RIDGE OR HIP (continued)

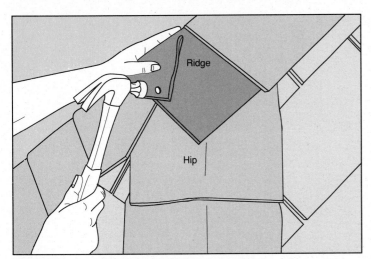

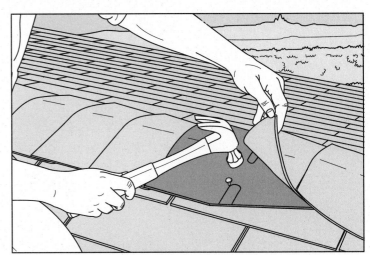

3 **Fitting a replacement shingle at two hips.** To fit the shingle at the end of a ridge over two hips, use tin snips *(page 120)* to cut a straight line about 4 inches long up the center of it. Fold down one cut side of the shingle against the end of the ridge, overlap it with the other cut side of the shingle and drive a roofing nail *(page 121)* into the overlapped sides *(above)*. Wearing work gloves, apply roofing cement *(page 115)* on the nail head with a putty knife or a trowel.

4 **Installing the replacement shingle.** Holding up the shingle one course above the new shingle, drive a roofing nail *(page 121)* into the new shingle just below the self-sealing adhesive and about 1 inch from each side *(above)*. Wearing work gloves, use a putty knife or a trowel to apply roofing cement *(page 115)* on the bottom of the shingle one course above the new shingle over each nail hole and about 2 inches from the edges at each corner; press the shingle down firmly to seal it. Using the same procedure, nail the shingle one course above the new shingle about 1 inch to the side of each sealed hole; then, seal the shingle two courses above the new shingle with roofing cement.

REPLACING A SHINGLE AT A CHIMNEY

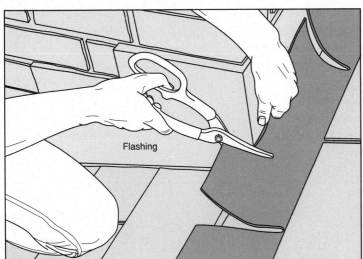

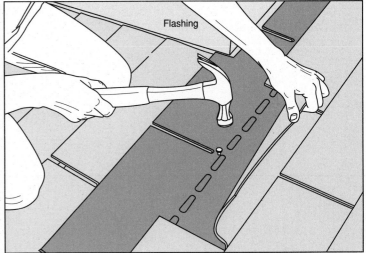

Removing and installing a shingle. Prepare to work safely on the roof *(page 24)*. If a damaged shingle is sealed under base flashing or between layers of step flashing, replace each damaged tab without disturbing the flashing *(page 53)* or call for a professional evaluation; removing the entire shingle may damage the flashing. If a damaged shingle is sealed on top of flashing, take it off as you would to remove another shingle *(page 54)*.

Buy a replacement shingle at a building supply center and slide it into position under the adjacent tabs of the course above it; use tin snips *(page 120)* to trim it to size *(above, left)*. Wearing work gloves, use a putty knife or a trowel to apply a band of roofing cement *(page 115)*

3 inches wide on the bottom of the shingle along the edge of the flashing; press it down firmly to seal it. Then, apply roofing cement on the bottom of the new shingle about 2 inches from the edges at the unsealed corners of each tab; press each tab down firmly to seal it.

Holding up in turn the adjacent tabs one course above the new shingle, drive a roofing nail *(page 121)* into the new shingle just below the self-sealing adhesive and about 1 inch from each side. Also nail at intervals specified by the manufacturer *(page 55)*: for a 3-tab shingle, at each cutout *(above, right)*; for a 1-tab shingle, 12 inches from each side; for a 2-tab shingle, 5 inches from each side of the cutout. Reposition a nail slightly, if necessary, to avoid driving it within 2 inches of the flashing.

REPLACING A SHINGLE AT A VENT

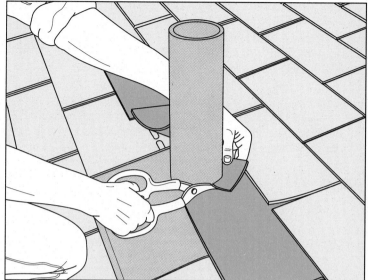

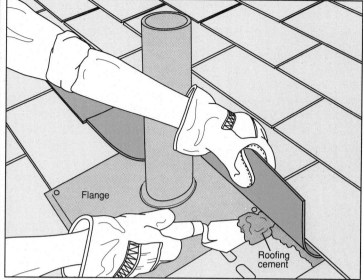

Removing and installing a shingle above the vent. Prepare to work safely on the roof *(page 24)*. Take off a shingle above the vent and sealed on the flashing as you would to remove another shingle *(page 54)*. If the flashing is damaged, repair it *(page 16)*. Replace any damaged shingle below the vent and sealed under the flashing *(step below)*.

Buy a replacement shingle at a building supply center. To fit the new shingle, position it alongside the vent, mark it by eye *(page 118)* and use tin snips *(page 120)* to cut it to shape. Slide the new shingle into position under the adjacent tabs one course above it; trim it to fit snugly around the flashing collar *(above, left)*. Wearing work gloves, use a trowel or a putty knife to apply a band of roofing cement *(page 115)* 3 inches wide

on the bottom of the new shingle along the edge of the flashing flange *(above, right)*; press it down firmly to seal it. Apply roofing cement on the bottom of the new shingle about 2 inches from the edges at the unsealed corners of each tab; press each tab down firmly to seal it.

Holding up in turn the adjacent tabs one course above the new shingle, drive a roofing nail *(page 121)* into the new shingle just below the self-sealing adhesive and about 1 inch from each side. Also nail at intervals specified by the manufacturer *(page 55)*: for a 3-tab shingle, at each cutout; for a 1-tab shingle, 12 inches from each side; for a 2-tab shingle, 5 inches from each side of the cutout. Reposition a nail slightly, if necessary, to avoid driving it within 2 inches of the flashing.

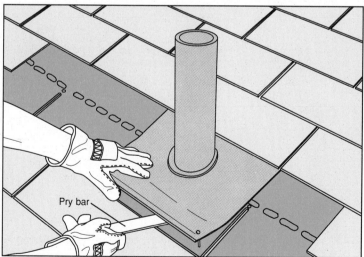

Removing and installing a shingle below the vent. To remove a damaged shingle below the vent and sealed under the flashing, first take off each shingle above the vent and sealed on the flashing *(step above)*. Then, gently work the tip of a pry bar under and along the edge of the flashing flange *(above, left)*, breaking the seal of the roofing cement between it and the damaged shingle, and raising the head of any nail in it; use the pry bar to remove any raised nails. Take off the damaged shingle as you would to remove another shingle *(page 54)*. Patch any damaged building paper *(page 117)*.

Buy a replacement shingle at a building supply center. To fit the new shingle, position it below the vent, mark it by eye *(page 118)* and use tin snips *(page 120)* to cut it to shape. Slide the new shingle into position under the adjacent tabs one course above it *(above, right)*; trim it

to fit snugly around the flashing collar. Wearing work gloves, use a trowel or a putty knife to apply roofing cement *(page 115)* on the bottom of the new shingle about 2 inches from the edges at the corners of each tab; press each tab down firmly to seal it.

Holding up in turn the adjacent tabs one course above the new shingle, drive a roofing nail *(page 121)* into the new shingle just below the self-sealing adhesive and about 1 inch from each side. Also nail at intervals specified by the manufacturer *(page 55)*: for a 3-tab shingle, at each cutout; for a 1-tab shingle, 12 inches from each side; for a 2-tab shingle, 5 inches from each side of the cutout. Apply a band of roofing cement 3 inches wide on the bottom of the flashing flange and press it down firmly to seal it on the new shingle; if necessary, renail it and apply roofing cement on each nail head. Reinstall each shingle removed above the vent *(step above)*.

TILE AND SLATE ROOFING

Clay tile and slate are expensive types of roofing, but their beauty, durability and low maintenance requirements make them a characteristic choice in regions where the material is readily available. Outside these areas, concrete tiles, often made to look like clay tiles and slates, are now popular. Tiles vary in shape, depending on their material; for example, traditional clay types can be a two-piece cap and pan tile or S-shaped, while concrete types can be rounded or flat and are usually interlocking. Slates are rectangular in shape. Common tile and slate roofing types are shown below and on page 63.

Most tile and slate roofs are similar in construction. Tiles and slates usually are laid on waterproof building paper and nailed to the wooden sheathing under it; tiles may be laid on built-up roofing similar to tar and gravel roofing *(page 70)* and hung or nailed onto wooden battens. Tiles and slates are laid in straight, overlapping rows, or courses; while slates of a course are typically positioned side by side, tiles of a course usually also overlap one another. If a problem develops, consult the Troubleshooting Guide in Your Roofing and Siding *(page 14)* and in this chapter *(page 63)*.

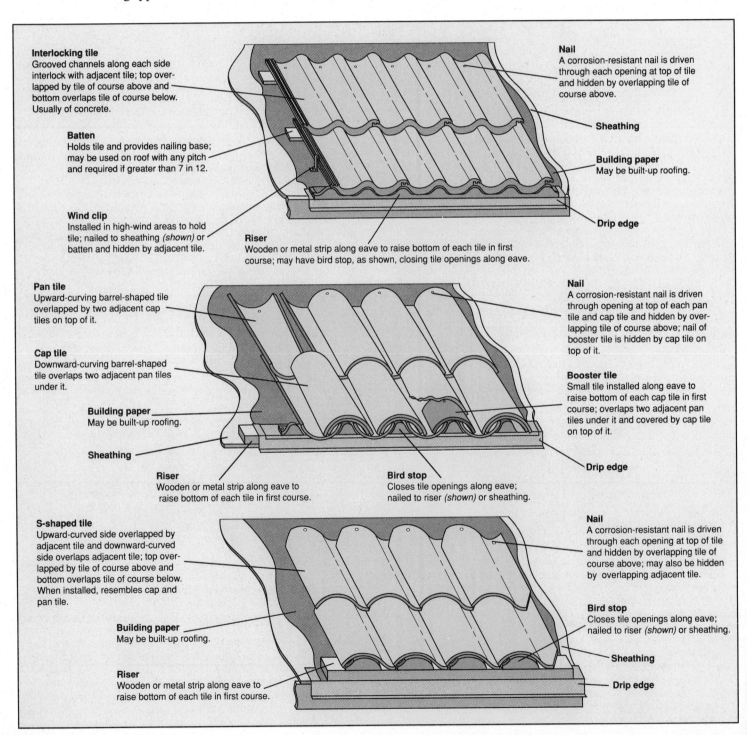

Interlocking tile
Grooved channels along each side interlock with adjacent tile; top overlapped by tile of course above and bottom overlaps tile of course below. Usually of concrete.

Batten
Holds tile and provides nailing base; may be used on roof with any pitch and required if greater than 7 in 12.

Wind clip
Installed in high-wind areas to hold tile; nailed to sheathing *(shown)* or batten and hidden by adjacent tile.

Riser
Wooden or metal strip along eave to raise bottom of each tile in first course; may have bird stop, as shown, closing tile openings along eave.

Nail
A corrosion-resistant nail is driven through each opening at top of tile and hidden by overlapping tile of course above.

Sheathing

Building paper
May be built-up roofing.

Drip edge

Pan tile
Upward-curving barrel-shaped tile overlapped by two adjacent cap tiles on top of it.

Cap tile
Downward-curving barrel-shaped tile overlaps two adjacent pan tiles under it.

Building paper
May be built-up roofing.

Sheathing

Riser
Wooden or metal strip along eave to raise bottom of each tile in first course.

Bird stop
Closes tile openings along eave; nailed to riser *(shown)* or sheathing.

Nail
A corrosion-resistant nail is driven through opening at top of each pan tile and cap tile and hidden by overlapping tile of course above; nail of booster tile is hidden by cap tile on top of it.

Booster tile
Small tile installed along eave to raise bottom of each cap tile in first course; overlaps two adjacent pan tiles under it and covered by cap tile on top of it.

Drip edge

S-shaped tile
Upward-curved side overlapped by adjacent tile and downward-curved side overlaps adjacent tile; top overlapped by tile of course above and bottom overlaps tile of course below. When installed, resembles cap and pan tile.

Building paper
May be built-up roofing.

Riser
Wooden or metal strip along eave to raise bottom of each tile in first course.

Nail
A corrosion-resistant nail is driven through each opening at top of tile and hidden by overlapping tile of course above; may also be hidden by overlapping adjacent tile.

Bird stop
Closes tile openings along eave; nailed to riser *(shown)* or sheathing.

Sheathing

Drip edge

Although tiles and slates usually weather well and require little care, tiles can sometimes crack, break or blow off and slates may chip, break or slip out of position. If you find damaged tiles or slates, you can easily replace them, either one at a time or a small section at once—but only, however, if the damage is along the eave and you can work safely from a ladder or scaffolding. If the damaged roofing is at a valley, hip or rake or is beyond easy reach of the eave, call for a professional evaluation. Walking on the roofing can create further damage to it and is not advised for the homeowner.

Working at heights along the eave can be intimidating. Before undertaking a repair, read the chapter on Working Safely at Heights *(page 24)* to properly set up and use any ladders or scaffolding necessary; when setting up a ladder, be especially careful not to break any tile or slate along the eave. Most repairs require only basic tools such as a pry bar and a hammer; however, if you have a slate roof and are likely to make occasional repairs, you can buy a special slate ripper for removing damaged slates. Refer to Tools & Techniques *(page 112)* for instructions on using tools and choosing materials.

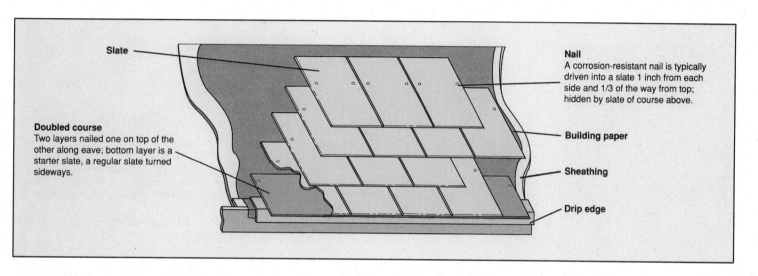

Slate

Nail
A corrosion-resistant nail is typically driven into a slate 1 inch from each side and 1/3 of the way from top; hidden by slate of course above.

Doubled course
Two layers nailed one on top of the other along eave; bottom layer is a starter slate, a regular slate turned sideways.

Building paper

Sheathing

Drip edge

TROUBLESHOOTING GUIDE

SYMPTOM	POSSIBLE CAUSE	PROCEDURE
Leak into attic, from ceiling or through wall	Water penetrating roofing or siding	Minimize immediate water damage *(p. 10)* □○
	Flashing, vent, gutter or downspout damaged or faulty	Troubleshoot and repair roofing and siding system *(p. 16)*; if beyond reach of eave, call for evaluation
	Tiles or slates damaged	Replace interlocking tile *(p. 64)* □○ or section of tiles *(p. 65)* ▱◕; replace S-shaped tile *(p. 65)* □○ or section of tiles *(p. 66)* ▱◕; replace cap and pan tile *(p. 66)* □○ or section of tiles *(p. 67)* ▱◕; replace slate *(p. 68)* □○▲ or section of slates *(p. 69)* ▱◕▲; if at valley, hip or rake or beyond reach of eave, call for evaluation
Ice buildup at roof edge under tiles or slates	Soffit vent blocked	Unblock soffit vent *(p. 22)* □●
	Attic ventilation inadequate	Call for evaluation
Flashing rusted or broken	Weather stress; impact damage	Troubleshoot roofing and siding system and repair flashing *(p. 16)*; if beyond reach of eave, call for evaluation
Interlocking tile cracked, broken or missing	Weather and wear; impact damage	Replace tile *(p. 64)* □○ or section of tiles *(p. 65)* ▱◕; if at valley, hip or rake or beyond reach of eave, call for evaluation
S-shaped tile cracked, broken or missing	Weather and wear; impact damage	Replace tile *(p. 65)* □○ or section of tiles *(p. 66)* ▱◕; if at valley, hip or rake or beyond reach of eave, call for evaluation
Cap or pan tile cracked, broken or missing	Weather and wear; impact damage	Replace tile *(p. 66)* □○ or section of tiles *(p. 67)* ▱◕; if at valley, hip or rake or beyond reach of eave, call for evaluation
Slate loose or hanging out of position	Weather; nail faulty	Reattach slate *(p. 68)* □○; if at valley, hip or rake or beyond reach of eave, call for evaluation
Slate cracked, broken or missing	Weather and wear; impact damage	Replace slate *(p. 68)* □○▲ or section of slates *(p. 69)* ▱◕▲; if at valley, hip or rake or beyond reach of eave, call for evaluation

DEGREE OF DIFFICULTY: □ Easy ▱ Moderate ■ Complex
ESTIMATED TIME: ○ Less than 1 hour ◕ 1 to 3 hours ● Over 3 hours
(For ladder and scaffolding set-up, see page 24)

▲ Special tool required

REPLACING AN INTERLOCKING TILE

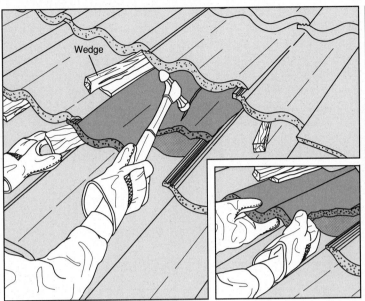

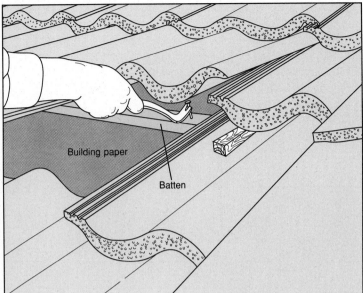

1 **Removing the damaged tile.** Prepare to work safely at the eave *(page 24)*. Wearing work gloves, lift the tile one course above the damaged tile and prop it up with a wooden wedge. Prop up the overlapping tile adjacent to the damaged tile the same way. Grasp the damaged tile firmly and pull it out, working it from side to side to loosen hidden nails *(inset)*. If the tile is stubborn, prop it up with a wedge and break it into pieces with a ball-peen hammer; wearing safety goggles, strike it sharply once or twice at a 45-degree angle to the surface

(above, left). Pull out each piece, lifting it slightly to clear any batten. Use a pry bar to pull out any nail that held the tile in place *(above, right)*; also use the pry bar to remove any wind clip nailed under the overlapping tile adjacent to it. Repair any loose or damaged batten as you would a furring strip *(page 100)*. Repair any damaged building paper *(page 117)*. Seal *(page 71)* or patch *(page 72)* any damaged built-up roofing. If the sheathing is spongy, soft or crumbly, test for and repair minor rot *(page 116)*; if the damage is extensive, call for a professional evaluation.

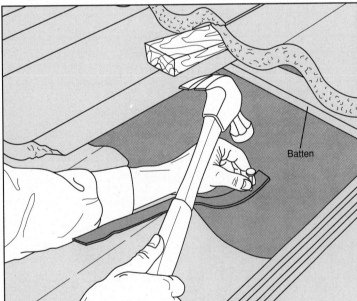

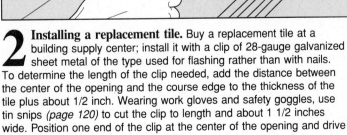

2 **Installing a replacement tile.** Buy a replacement tile at a building supply center; install it with a clip of 28-gauge galvanized sheet metal of the type used for flashing rather than with nails. To determine the length of the clip needed, add the distance between the center of the opening and the course edge to the thickness of the tile plus about 1/2 inch. Wearing work gloves and safety goggles, use tin snips *(page 120)* to cut the clip to length and about 1 1/2 inches wide. Position one end of the clip at the center of the opening and drive

a nail *(page 121)* through it *(above, left)*; cover the nail head with roofing cement *(page 115)*. Then, slide the new tile into position under the tile one course above it and the overlapping tile adjacent to it *(above, right)*, hooking it on any batten and aligning it with its course. Bend the protruding end of the clip up and over the edge of the tile *(inset)*. After securing the new tile, pull out the wedge and reseat the tile one course above it and the overlapping tile adjacent to it; ensure the tiles lie flat and interlocking channels fit properly.

REPLACING A SECTION OF INTERLOCKING TILES

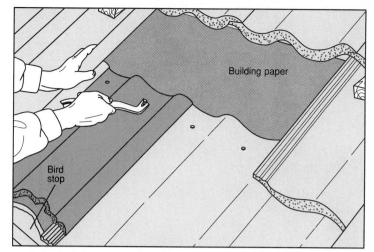

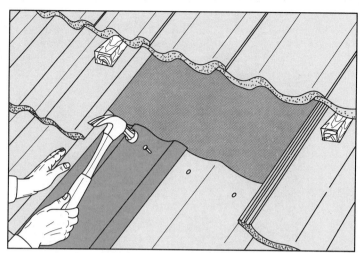

1 **Removing a section of damaged tiles.** Prepare to work safely at the eave *(page 24)* and work from top to bottom one course at a time to remove the damaged section. Take off each tile of the first course as you would to remove one tile *(page 64)*. To take off each tile of the other courses, pull its nails using a pry bar *(above)*. Continue until the section of damaged tiles is removed. Repair or replace any damaged batten as you would a furring strip *(page 100)*. Repair any damaged building paper *(page 117)*. Seal *(page 71)* or patch *(page 72)* any damaged built-up roofing. If the sheathing is spongy, soft or crumbly, test for and repair minor rot *(page 116)*; if the damage is extensive, call for a professional evaluation.

2 **Installing a section of replacement tiles.** Buy replacement tiles at a building supply center and work from bottom to top one course at a time to install the new section; install each tile of the last course with a clip of 28-gauge galvanized sheet metal of the type used for flashing rather than with nails. To install each tile of the other courses, wear work gloves and slide it into position, hooking it on any batten and aligning it with its course; ensure the tile lies flat and interlocking channels fit properly. Then, carefully drive a nail *(page 121)* through each opening in the tile *(above)* until its head just touches the tile. To install each tile of the last course, fit it with a clip as you would to install one tile *(page 64)*.

REPLACING AN S-SHAPED TILE

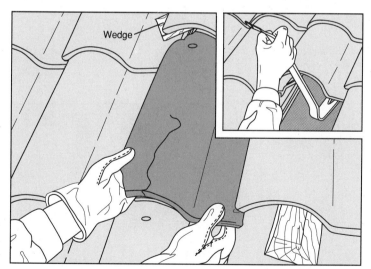

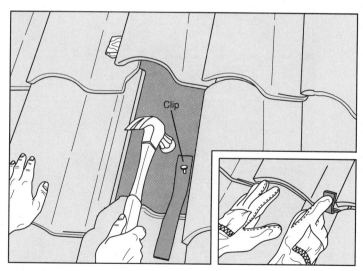

1 **Removing the damaged tile.** Prepare to work safely at the eave *(page 24)*. Wearing work gloves, lift the tile one course above the damaged tile and prop it up with a wooden wedge. Prop up the overlapping tile adjacent to the damaged tile the same way. Grasp the damaged tile firmly and pull it out, working it from side to side to loosen hidden nails *(above)*. If the tile is stubborn, prop it up with a wedge and break it into pieces wearing safety goggles and using a a ball-peen hammer. Use a pry bar to pull out any nail that held the tile in place *(inset)*. Repair any loose or damaged nailer as you would a furring strip *(page 100)*. Repair any damaged building paper *(page 117)*. If the sheathing is spongy, soft or crumbly, test for and repair minor rot *(page 116)*; if the damage is extensive, call for a professional evaluation.

2 **Installing a replacement tile.** Buy a replacement tile at a building supply center; install it with a clip of 28-gauge galvanized sheet metal of the type used for flashing rather than with nails. To determine the length of the clip needed, add the distance between the center of the opening and the course edge to the thickness of the tile plus about 1/2 inch. Wearing work gloves and safety goggles, use tin snips *(page 120)* to cut the clip to length and about 1 1/2 inches wide. Nail *(page 121)* one end of the clip at the center of the opening *(above)* and cover the nail head with roofing cement *(page 115)*. Slide the new tile into position and bend the protruding end of the clip up and over the edge of it *(inset)*. After securing the new tile, pull out the wedge and reseat the tile one course above it and the overlapping tile adjacent to it.

REPLACING A SECTION OF S-SHAPED TILES

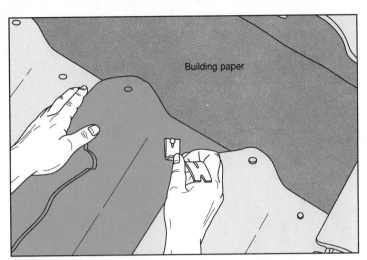

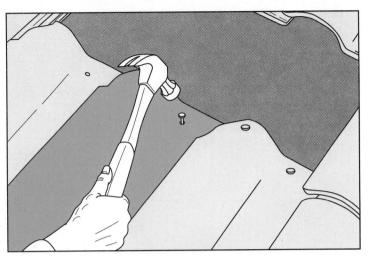

1 **Removing a section of damaged tiles.** Prepare to work safely at the eave *(page 24)* and work from top to bottom one course at a time to remove the damaged section. Take off each tile of the first course as you would to remove one tile *(page 65)*. To take off each tile of the other courses, pull its nails using a pry bar *(above)*. Continue until the section of damaged tiles is removed. Repair or replace any damaged nailer as you would a furring strip *(page 100)*. Repair any damaged building paper *(page 117)*. If the sheathing is spongy, soft or crumbly, test for and repair minor rot *(page 116)*; if the damage is extensive, call for a professional evaluation.

2 **Installing a section of replacement tiles.** Buy replacement tiles at a building supply center and work from bottom to top one course at a time to install the new section; install each tile of the last course with a clip of 28-gauge galvanized sheet metal of the type used for flashing rather than with nails. To install each tile of the other courses, wear work gloves and slide it into position, aligning it with its course and ensuring it lies flat. Then, carefully drive a nail *(page 121)* through each opening in the tile *(above)* until its head just touches the tile. To install each tile of the last course, fit it with a clip as you would to install one tile *(page 65)*.

REPLACING A CAP TILE AND A PAN TILE

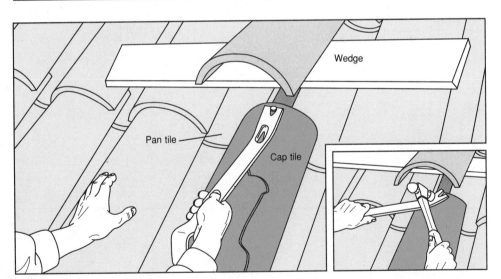

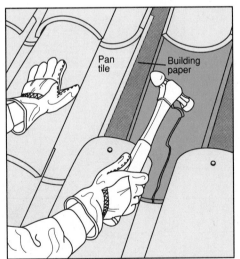

1 **Removing and installing a cap tile.** Prepare to work safely at the eave *(page 24)*. To remove a cap tile, wear work gloves and lift the cap tile one course above it. If the cap tile to be removed is wired in place, call for a professional evaluation; otherwise, prop up the cap tile one course above it with a wooden wedge, pull out its nail using a pry bar *(above)* and lift it off. If there is a damaged booster tile under the cap tile, pull out its nail with the pry bar and lift it off. If a pan tile is damaged, remove the other cap tile and any booster tile on it; then, remove it *(step 2)*. Buy a replacement cap tile and booster tile at a building supply center.
To install a booster tile, wear work gloves and slide it into position, aligning it with its course and ensuring it lies flat. Carefully drive a nail *(page 121)* through the opening in the booster tile until its head just touches the tile. To install a cap tile, use the same procedure, seating it on any booster tile; if the cap tile one course above it is in the way, place the end of a pry bar on the nail head and hammer on the pry bar to drive the nail *(inset)*. After nailing the cap tile, pull out the wedge and reseat the cap tile one course above it.

2 **Removing a damaged pan tile.** To remove a damaged pan tile, break it into pieces using a a ball-peen hammer; wearing work gloves and safety goggles, strike it sharply once or twice at a 45-degree angle to the surface *(above)*. Use a pry bar to pull out the nail that held the pan tile in place under the pan tile one course above it. Repair any damaged building paper *(page 117)*. If the sheathing is spongy, soft or crumbly, test for and repair minor rot *(page 116)*; if the damage is extensive, call for a professional evaluation.

REPLACING A CAP TILE AND A PAN TILE (continued)

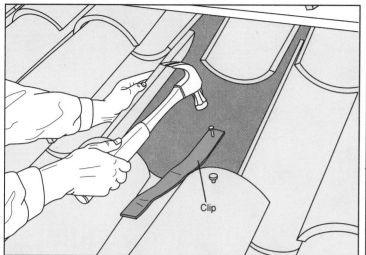

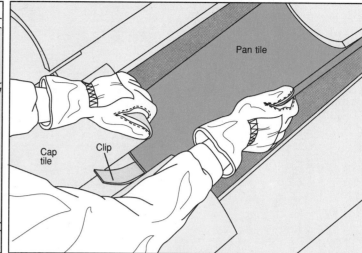

3 **Installing a replacement pan tile.** Buy a replacement pan tile at a building supply center; install it with a clip of 28-gauge galvanized sheet metal of the type used for flashing rather than with a nail. To determine the length of the clip needed, add the distance between the center of the opening and the course edge to the thickness of the pan tile plus about 1/2 inch. Wearing work gloves and safety goggles, use tin snips *(page 120)* to cut the clip to length and about 1 1/2 inches wide. Position one end of the clip at the center of the opening and drive

a nail *(page 121)* through it *(above, left)*; cover the nail head with roofing cement *(page 115)*. Then, slide the new pan tile into position under the pan tile one course above it and between the cap tiles and the pan tile one course below it *(above, right)*; align it with its course and ensure it lies flat. Bend the protruding end of the clip up and over the edge of the pan tile. After securing the new pan tile, reinstall any booster tile and the cap tile on each side of it *(step 1)*.

REPLACING A SECTION OF CAP AND PAN TILES

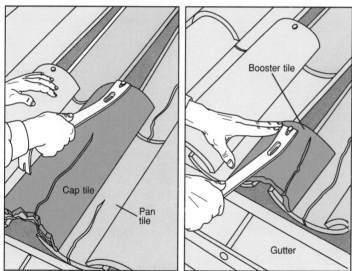

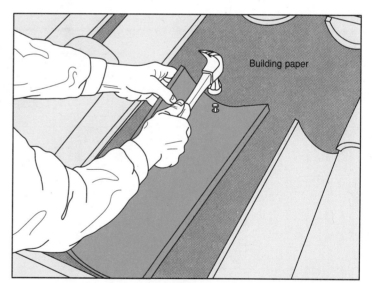

1 **Removing a section of damaged tiles.** Prepare to work safely at the eave *(page 24)*. Work from top to bottom one course at a time to remove the damaged section, taking off first each cap tile and any booster tile, and then each pan tile. Take off each cap tile of the first course as you would to remove one tile *(page 66)*. To take off each cap tile of the other courses, pull its nail using a pry bar *(above, left)*. Continue until the section of damaged cap tiles is removed. To remove any booster tile, pull its nail with the pry bar *(above, right)*. To take off each pan tile, use the same procedure; to reach the nail of each pan tile of the first course, lift the pan tile one course above it. Repair any damaged building paper *(page 117)*. If the sheathing is spongy, soft or crumbly, test for and repair minor rot *(page 116)*; if the damage is extensive, call for a professional evaluation.

2 **Installing a section of replacement tiles.** Buy replacement tiles at a building supply center. Work from bottom to top one course at a time to install the new section, installing first each pan tile and then any booster tile and each cap tile; secure each pan tile of the last course with a clip of 28-gauge galvanized sheet metal of the type used for flashing rather than with a nail. To install each pan tile of the other courses, wear work gloves and slide it into position, aligning it with its course and ensuring it lies flat. Then, carefully drive a nail *(page 121)* through the opening in the pan tile *(above)* until its head just touches the tile. To install each pan tile of the last course, fit it with a clip as you would to install one tile *(step 3, above)*. Install any booster tile and each cap tile as you would to install one cap tile *(page 66)*.

REATTACHING A SLATE

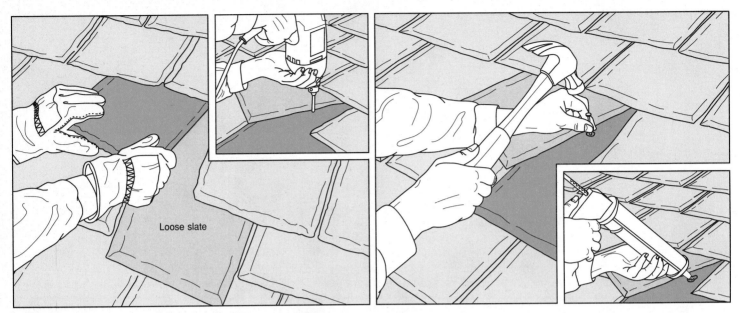

Loose slate

Securing a loose slate. Prepare to work safely at the eave *(page 24)*. If a slate is loose or has slipped out of position, you may be able to reposition and secure it. Wearing work gloves, gently lift an overlapping slate one course above the loose slate off one nail and swing it slightly at an angle *(above, left)*, exposing as much of the loose slate under it as possible. If you cannot move an overlapping slate one course above the loose slate, do not apply force; instead, remove the loose slate *(step 1, below)* and reinstall it *(page 69)*. Otherwise, slide the loose slate back into position under the overlapping slates one course above it, aligning it

with its course and ensuring it lies flat. Wearing safety goggles, use a power drill fitted with a 3/16-inch masonry bit *(page 121)* to drill a hole through the loose slate and into the slate under it *(inset, left)*; drill near the top of the loose slate and as close as possible to the angled slate one course above it, as shown. Apply a small dab of roofing cement *(page 115)* into the hole with a caulking gun *(inset, right)*. Then, drive a nail *(page 121)* through the hole in the slate until its head just touches the slate *(above, right)*. After nailing the loose slate, swing the angled slate one course above it back into position, covering the nail head.

REPLACING A SLATE

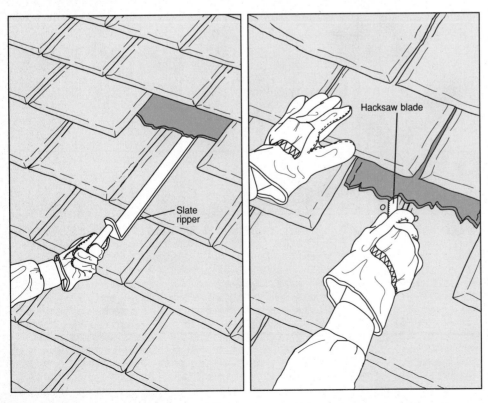

Slate ripper

Hacksaw blade

1 **Removing the damaged slate.** Prepare to work safely at the eave *(page 24)*. To remove a damaged slate, cut off each nail holding it in place—located near the top of it, usually at each corner, and hidden under the overlapping slates one course above it. To cut off each nail, wear work gloves and use a special slate ripper or a hacksaw blade; a slate ripper usually can be rented or purchased at a roofing supply center or slate company. To use the slate ripper, slide its hooked tip under the damaged slate and around a nail; then, pull sharply on the handle to cut the nail *(far left)*. If the nail is stubborn, strike the handle sharply using a mallet. To use the hacksaw blade, slide it under the damaged slate and saw off each nail *(near left)*. After cutting off each nail, pull out the damaged slate. Remove any damaged starter slate using the same procedure. Repair any damaged building paper *(page 117)*. If the sheathing is spongy, soft or crumbly, test for and repair minor rot *(page 116)*; if the damage is extensive, call for a professional evaluation.

REPLACING A SLATE (continued)

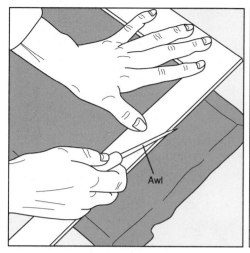

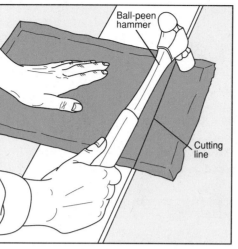

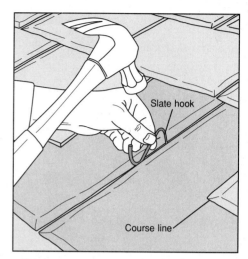

2 **Fitting a new slate.** Buy a replacement slate of the same size, color and texture and, if possible, from the same quarry at a roofing supply center or a slate company; take a piece of the old slate to ensure a match. Also buy a 3-inch copper or stainless steel slate hook to secure the new slate. To determine the length of the new slate needed, measure the side of a slate at a rake; or, measure the exposed length of a slate, multiply by 2 and add 3 inches. To determine the width of the new slate needed, measure the width of the old slate; or, measure the width of the opening and subtract the size of the gap needed on each side of it, using the gap between other slates as a guide. To trim the new slate, score cutting lines on each side of it using a carpenter's square and an awl *(above, left)*. Then, place the slate on a raised surface with the cutting line along its edge and the waste side overhanging it; wearing safety goggles, work from end to end along the cutting line to break the slate, gently striking the waste side with a ball-peen hammer *(above, right)* or at the cutting line with a hatchet.

3 **Installing the new slate.** To install the new slate, drive the pointed end of a slate hook into the opening *(above)*, positioning it in the gap between the slates and aligning its hooked end with the course line, as shown. Wearing work gloves, slide the new slate into position under the slates one course above it, lifting it slightly to clear the hook; then, lower the slate to seat it securely on the hook.

REPLACING A SECTION OF SLATES

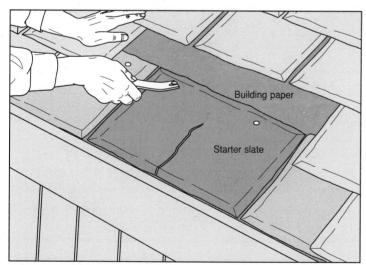

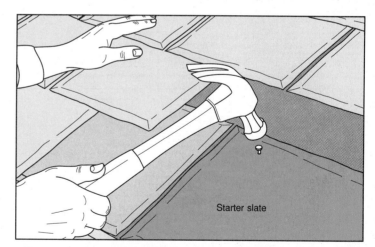

1 **Removing a section of damaged slates.** Prepare to work safely at the eave *(page 24)* and work from top to bottom one course at a time to remove the damaged section. Take off each slate of the first course as you would to remove one slate *(page 68)*. To take off each slate of the other courses, pull any exposed nail using a pry bar and cut off any hidden nail as you would to remove one slate. Take off any damaged starter slate the same way *(above)*. Continue until the section of damaged slates is removed. Repair any damaged building paper *(page 117)*. If the sheathing is spongy, soft or crumbly, test for and repair minor rot *(page 116)*; if the damage is extensive, call for a professional evaluation.

2 **Installing a section of replacement slates.** Buy replacement slates and fit each one *(step 2, above)*, if necessary, working from bottom to top one course at a time to install the new section; secure each slate of the last course with a 3-inch copper or stainless steel slate hook. To install each slate of the other courses, including any starter slate, wear work gloves and slide it into position, aligning it with its course and ensuring it lies flat. Then, carefully drive a nail *(page 121)* through each exposed opening in the slate *(above)* until its head just touches the slate; if there is no opening in the slate, wear safety goggles and use a power drill fitted with a 3/16-inch masonry bit *(page 121)* to drill a hole on each exposed side of it about 1 inch from the edge and 1/3 of the way from the top. Secure each slate of the last course with a slate hook as you would to install one slate *(step 3, above)*.

TAR AND GRAVEL ROOFING

Tar and gravel, or built-up, roofing is found on flat and low-sloped roofs; a typical section of roofing membrane is shown below. Over a sheathing, 3 to 5 layers, or plies, of building paper are built up; between each ply, liquid asphalt or coal tar is applied. A thick flood coat of asphalt or tar is poured on top and gravel is spread over it. Although the roofing can provide years of problem-free shelter, it requires proper care. Consult the Troubleshooting Guide in Your Roofing and Siding (*page 14*) and below; often, the flashing or the gutters and downspouts are the source of problems. If a leak is caused by damaged roofing, call for a professional evaluation.

Keep the roofing free of debris, especially at any drain cage (*page 71*). If wind and rain shift the gravel, seal the roofing membrane, if necessary, and add gravel to protect it (*page 71*). Patch cracks (*page 72*) and repair blisters (*page 73*) as soon as you detect them to prevent potential leaks. Before undertaking a repair on the roof, read the chapter on Working Safely at Heights (*page 24*); follow the safety tips in the Emergency Guide (*page 8*). Most repairs require only basic tools—a spade or shovel, a broom, a utility knife, and a trowel or a putty knife. Refer to Tools & Techniques (*page 112*) for information on tools and roofing materials.

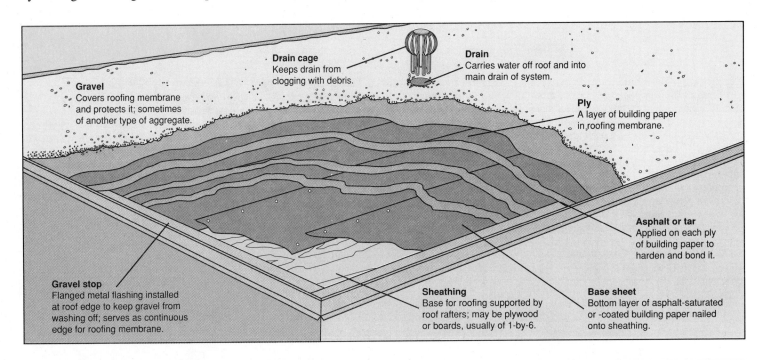

Drain cage
Keeps drain from clogging with debris.

Drain
Carries water off roof and into main drain of system.

Gravel
Covers roofing membrane and protects it; sometimes of another type of aggregate.

Ply
A layer of building paper in roofing membrane.

Asphalt or tar
Applied on each ply of building paper to harden and bond it.

Gravel stop
Flanged metal flashing installed at roof edge to keep gravel from washing off; serves as continuous edge for roofing membrane.

Sheathing
Base for roofing supported by roof rafters; may be plywood or boards, usually of 1-by-6.

Base sheet
Bottom layer of asphalt-saturated or -coated building paper nailed onto sheathing.

TROUBLESHOOTING GUIDE

SYMPTOM	POSSIBLE CAUSE	PROCEDURE
Leak into attic or from ceiling	Water penetrating roofing; hole in plumbing	Minimize immediate water damage (*page 10*) □○
	Flashing, vent, gutter or downspout damaged or faulty	Troubleshoot and repair roofing and siding system (*page 16*)
	Drain cage clogged	Clean off roofing (*page 71*) □○
	Roofing membrane damaged	Call for professional evaluation
Roofing edge cracked, separated from gravel stop	Weather stress; wear	Repair roofing at gravel stop (*page 73*) □○
Roofing blistered	Moisture penetrating roofing membrane	Repair blistered roofing (*page 73*) ▪○
Roofing cracked	Weather stress; impact damage	Patch roofing (*page 72*) ▪○; if roofing damaged extensively, call for professional evaluation
Roofing membrane exposed	Gravel shifted by wind and rain	Protect roofing (*page 71*) □○
Water pooling on roof	Drain cage clogged	Clean off roofing (*page 71*) □○
	Drain faulty; structural damage	Call for professional evaluation
Roofing debris-covered; moss	Wind-borne material; overhead vegetation	Clean off roofing (*page 71*) □○; trim back overhead vegetation

DEGREE OF DIFFICULTY: □ Easy ▪ Moderate ■ Complex
ESTIMATED TIME: ○ Less than 1 hour ◑ 1 to 3 hours ● Over 3 hours
(For ladder and scaffolding set-up, see page 24)

CLEANING OFF THE ROOFING

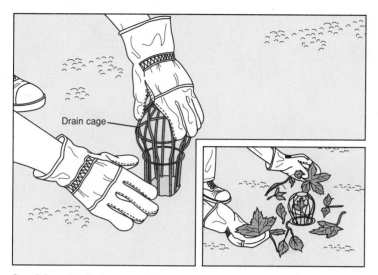

Servicing the drain cage. Prepare to work safely on the roof *(page 24)*. Inspect the drain cage and clean it at least once a year, each fall or spring. Wearing work gloves, remove leaves, mud and other debris at the base of the drain cage and from the area around it *(inset)*; do not let gravel or debris fall into the drain. If the drain cage is corroded, bent, or broken, replace it. To remove the drain cage, grasp it firmly with one hand and pull it out of the drain. Buy a replacement drain cage at a building supply center. To install a new drain cage, squeeze its tines together and push it into the drain *(above)*, seating it securely.

Removing moss and embedded debris. Prepare to work safely on the roof *(page 24)*. As soon as moss or other embedded debris appears, wear work gloves and use a flat-bladed spade to gently scrape away the gravel covered by it *(above)*; collect the gravel in a bucket and lower it to the ground *(page 30)*. Scrub stubborn deposits off the roofing membrane with a soft-bristled brush. Buy replacement gravel at a building supply center, raise it to the roof in the bucket and use a stiff-bristled broom to spread it evenly; ensure all the roofing membrane is covered. To prevent moss and other embedded debris, trim back overhead foliage and keep the drain cage clean *(step left)*.

PROTECTING THE ROOFING

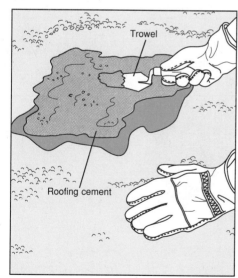

1 Brushing aside the gravel. Prepare to work safely on the roof *(page 24)*. To inspect an area of the roofing membrane, wear work gloves and use a stiff-bristled broom to brush the gravel and any dirt aside into a pile *(above)*; clear an area 3 to 4 inches longer and wider than the roofing membrane to be inspected. If the roofing membrane is dried, grayed or alligatored (a series of hairline cracks), seal the damaged area *(step 2)*. If the roofing membrane has a large or deep crack, patch it *(page 72)*. If the roofing membrane is blistered, repair it *(page 73)*. Otherwise, brush the gravel removed back over the roofing membrane, spreading it evenly; ensure all the roofing membrane is covered. If necessary, buy additional gravel at a building supply center and raise it to the roof in a bucket *(page 30)*.

2 Sealing the roofing membrane. Wearing work gloves, use a trowel or a putty knife to apply an even layer of roofing cement *(page 115)* on the damaged roofing membrane *(above)*. Use a stiff-bristled broom to brush the gravel removed back over the roofing membrane immediately, spreading it evenly; ensure all the roofing membrane is covered. If necessary, buy additional gravel at a building supply center and raise it to the roof in a bucket *(page 30)*.

PATCHING THE ROOFING

1 **Measuring and cutting patches.** Prepare to work safely on the roof *(page 24)*. Wearing work gloves, use a stiff-bristled broom to brush the gravel and any dirt off the damaged roofing membrane, clearing an area at least 16 inches longer and wider than it. Measure the damaged roofing membrane with a tape measure and use scissors to cut off 2 patches of fiberglass screen *(above)* or 15-pound perforated building paper longer and wider than it: the first patch by about 6 inches; the second patch by about 12 inches.

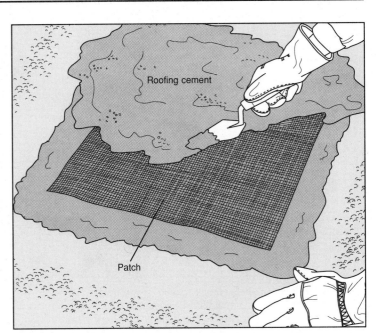

2 **Installing the first patch.** Wearing work gloves, use a trowel or a putty knife to apply an even layer of roofing cement *(page 115)* on the damaged roofing membrane, covering an area 3 to 4 inches longer and wider than the first, small patch. Center the first patch on the damaged roofing membrane and press it down lightly into the roofing cement to bond it. Then, use the trowel or putty knife to apply an even layer of roofing cement on the patch *(above)*, covering an area 3 to 4 inches longer and wider than the second, large patch.

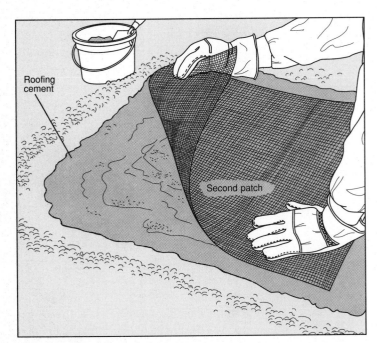

3 **Installing the second patch.** Wearing work gloves, center the second patch on the first patch and press it down lightly into the roofing cement to bond it *(above)*. Then, use a trowel or a putty knife to apply an even layer of roofing cement on the patch, covering an area 3 to 4 inches longer and wider than it; ensure all the patch is covered and its corners are embedded.

4 **Brushing back the gravel.** Wearing work gloves, use a stiff-bristled broom to brush the gravel removed back over the roofing membrane immediately, spreading it evenly *(above)*; work carefully to avoid lifting the edges of the patches. Ensure all the roofing membrane is covered. If necessary, buy additional gravel at a building supply center and raise it to the roof in a bucket *(page 30)*.

REPAIRING BLISTERED ROOFING

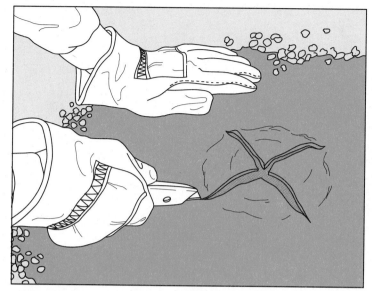

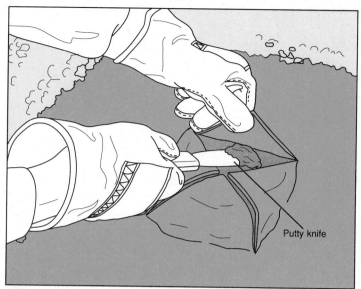

Putty knife

1 **Cutting open a blister.** Prepare to work safely on the roof *(page 24)*. If there are many or large blisters in the roofing membrane, call for a professional evaluation. To repair a few, small blisters, wear work gloves and use a stiff-bristled broom to brush the gravel and any dirt off the damaged roofing membrane, clearing an area at least 16 inches longer and wider than it. Use a utility knife *(page 120)* to lance each blister, scoring an "X" through the roofing membrane and into the air pocket *(above)*. Press down firmly on the roofing membrane to flatten it and expel any air. Gently lift each flap of the blister and use a clean rag to soak up any moisture.

2 **Sealing the blister.** Wearing work gloves, use a putty knife or a trowel to apply a layer of roofing cement *(page 115)* under each flap *(above)*, forcing as much as possible against the uncut edges. Press each flap down firmly into the roofing cement to bond it. Then, patch the roofing *(page 72)*. If there was moisture inside the blister, check for and repair any damaged roofing at the gravel stop *(steps below)*; also repair any damaged flashing *(page 16)*. If blisters recur, call for a professional evaluation.

REPAIRING THE ROOFING AT THE GRAVEL STOP

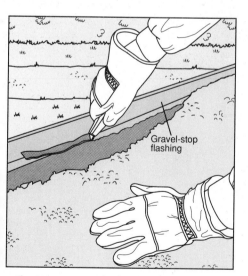

Gravel-stop flashing

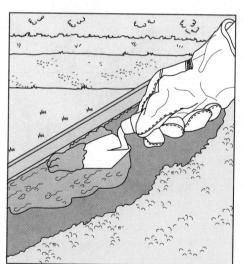

1 **Preparing the area.** Prepare to work safely on the roof *(page 24)*. If the roofing membrane is dried and separated from the gravel stop, repair it. Wearing work gloves, use a stiff-bristled broom to brush the gravel and any dirt off the damaged roofing membrane, clearing within at least 6 inches of the roof edge. Then, use a utility knife *(page 120)* to trim the damaged edge off the roofing membrane *(above)*.

2 **Filling the gap.** Wearing work gloves, clean loose gravel and debris out of the gap between the gravel stop and the roofing membrane. If the gravel stop is loose, add nails *(page 121)*. Use a trowel or a putty knife to fill the gap with roofing cement *(page 115)* until it is level with the roofing membrane *(above)*. Smooth the roofing cement and apply an even layer of it on the 6 inches of roofing membrane brushed off at the roof edge.

3 **Putting back the gravel.** Wearing work gloves, use a stiff-bristled broom to brush the gravel removed back over the roofing membrane immediately; spread it evenly by hand *(above)*. Ensure all the roofing membrane is covered. If necessary, buy additional gravel at a building supply center and raise it to the roof in a bucket *(page 30)*.

WOOD SHINGLES AND SHAKES

Although shingles and shakes can be used for roofing or siding, the uniform size and finished appearance of shingles make them ideal for siding, while the thicker, handsplit texture of shakes makes them a traditional roofing choice. Left to weather or finished, shingles and shakes offer durability and attractiveness as a contemporary roofing and siding material.

A typical home constructed with siding of shingles and roofing of shakes is shown at right. Nailed onto a sheathing, usually of plywood, or spaced 1-by-4s or 1-by-6s, shingles and shakes are positioned in straight, overlapping rows, or courses, with gaps, or keyways, between them to permit wood expansion and contraction; keyways of alternate courses are offset by about 1 1/2 inches. For siding, shingle or shake courses are installed over overlapping courses of building paper which is applied directly on the sheathing. For roofing, shingle courses are likewise installed, although building paper is applied on only the first 3 feet of sheathing above the eaves; shake courses are interlayed with courses of building paper. The nails holding a shingle or shake in place are driven in at the top of it—and are thereby hidden under the bottom, or butt edge, of the shingles or shakes in the course installed above it.

Keep your roofing and siding free of moisture-retaining debris that can produce the growth of wood-destroying fungus and mildew, cause rot and encourage insect damage. Regularly brush off leaves, conifer needles and other matter; if dirt, moss, algae or lichen buildup is extensive, clean using a pressure washer *(page 77)*. Hand-clean or spray-clean stains *(page 78)*. Keep nearby vegetation trimmed back to let in sunlight and increase air circulation. If shingles or shakes are subjected to extreme weather conditions, treat them with a preservative every 3 to 5 years *(page 79)*—even those of naturally decay-resistant wood such as western red cedar.

If a leak develops in the attic, from an upstairs ceiling or through an outside wall of your home, consult the Troubleshooting Guide in Your Roofing and Siding *(page 14)* and in this chapter *(page 76)*. Often, the problem may originate with the gutters and downspouts, vents or flashing and not with the roofing or siding. If, however, you find damaged shingles or shakes, you can easily replace them—one at a time or a small section at once. If you cannot locate the source of a leak or if the roofing or siding is damaged extensively, call for a professional evaluation.

Although shingle and shake repairs are not difficult, working at heights on the roof or siding can be intimidating. Read the chapter on Working Safely at Heights *(page 24)* to properly set up and use any ladders or scaffolding necessary; do not work on a roof with a pitch greater than 6 in 12. Most repairs require only basic carpentry tools such as a hammer, a nailset, a pry bar, a wood chisel and a mallet. Refer to Tools & Techniques *(page 112)* for instructions on using equipment such as a pressure washer *(page 115)* and a commercial airless sprayer *(page 125)*. Follow the manufacturer's instructions when working with sealants, finishes and preservatives, and read the safety tips in the Emergency Guide on page 8. Always wear the proper safety equipment for the job.

Shake
Typically available in lengths of 18 and 24 inches. Tapered end at top overlapped by course above; butt edge at bottom overlaps course below. Keyway or space between shakes is 1/2 inch. Butt edges of a course form butt line.

Ridge
Top line of roof where opposite sides meet. Special bevel-sided shingles or shakes are butted together lengthwise and installed along ridge in similar way to standard shingles and shakes; building paper on each side of ridge overlaps it.

Hip
Sloping line of roof where opposite sides meet; requires same bevel-sided shingles or shakes as a ridge.

Woven corner
Shingles or shakes butted together at corner; butt joint formed on opposite side of corner each alternate course. If trim installed at corner, shingles or shakes fit flush against it.

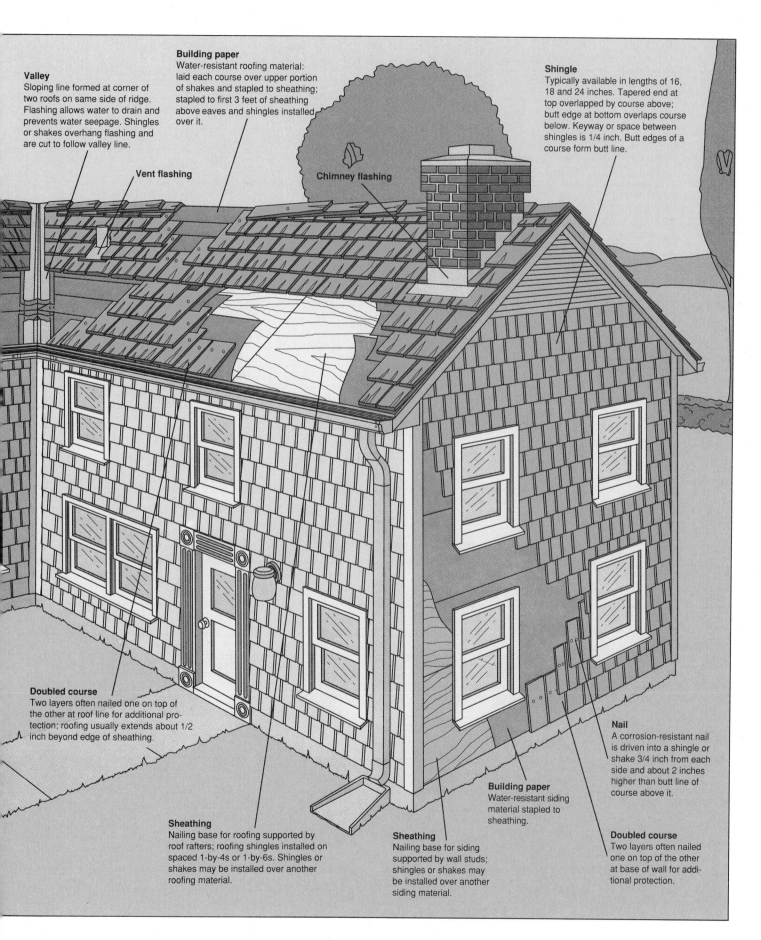

Valley
Sloping line formed at corner of two roofs on same side of ridge. Flashing allows water to drain and prevents water seepage. Shingles or shakes overhang flashing and are cut to follow valley line.

Vent flashing

Building paper
Water-resistant roofing material: laid each course over upper portion of shakes and stapled to sheathing; stapled to first 3 feet of sheathing above eaves and shingles installed over it.

Chimney flashing

Shingle
Typically available in lengths of 16, 18 and 24 inches. Tapered end at top overlapped by course above; butt edge at bottom overlaps course below. Keyway or space between shingles is 1/4 inch. Butt edges of a course form butt line.

Doubled course
Two layers often nailed one on top of the other at roof line for additional protection; roofing usually extends about 1/2 inch beyond edge of sheathing.

Sheathing
Nailing base for roofing supported by roof rafters; roofing shingles installed on spaced 1-by-4s or 1-by-6s. Shingles or shakes may be installed over another roofing material.

Sheathing
Nailing base for siding supported by wall studs; shingles or shakes may be installed over another siding material.

Building paper
Water-resistant siding material stapled to sheathing.

Nail
A corrosion-resistant nail is driven into a shingle or shake 3/4 inch from each side and about 2 inches higher than butt line of course above it.

Doubled course
Two layers often nailed one on top of the other at base of wall for additional protection.

TROUBLESHOOTING GUIDE

SYMPTOM	POSSIBLE CAUSE	PROCEDURE
Leak into attic, from ceiling or through wall	Water penetrating roofing or siding, or hole in plumbing pipe	Minimize immediate water damage (p. 10) □○
	Flashing, vent, gutter or downspout damaged or faulty	Troubleshoot and repair roofing and siding system (p. 16)
	Shingles or shakes damaged	Replace shingle (p. 80) □○ or shake (p. 81) □○; replace section of shingles (p. 82) ◨● or shakes (p. 83) ◨●; replace shingles or shakes at ridge or hip (p. 85) □◒; if roofing or siding damaged extensively, call for professional evaluation
Ice buildup at roof edge under shingles or shakes	Soffit vent blocked or turbine roof vent faulty	Unblock soffit vent (p. 22) □●; service turbine roof vent (p. 23) □○
	Attic ventilation inadequate	Call for professional evaluation
Flashing rusted or broken	Weather stress; impact damage	Troubleshoot roofing and siding system and repair flashing (p. 16)
Shingles or shakes spongy, pitted or crumbling	Flashing, vent, gutter or downspout damaged or faulty	Troubleshoot and repair roofing and siding system (p. 16)
	Air circulation or sunlight exposure inadequate	Trim back overhead and adjacent vegetation
	Rot or insect damage	Replace shingle (p. 80) □○ or shake (p. 81) □○; replace section of shingles (p. 82) ◨● or shakes (p. 83) ◨●; replace shingles or shakes at ridge or hip (p. 85) □◒; if insect infestation suspected or if roofing or siding damaged extensively, call for professional evaluation
Shingles or shakes buckling, broken, hanging out of position or missing	Weather stress; impact damage	Replace shingle (p. 80) □○ or shake (p. 81) □○; replace section of shingles (p. 82) ◨● or shakes (p. 83) ◨●; replace shingles or shakes at ridge or hip (p. 85) □◒; if roofing or siding damaged extensively, call for professional evaluation
	Structural damage	Call for professional evaluation
Shingles or shakes warped or cracked	Flashing, vent, gutter or downspout damaged or faulty	Troubleshoot and repair roofing and siding system (p. 16)
	Air circulation or sunlight exposure inadequate	Trim back overhead and adjacent vegetation
	Weather stress	Replace shingle (p. 80) □○ or shake (p. 81) □○; replace section of shingles (p. 82) ◨● or shakes (p. 83) ◨●; replace shingles or shakes at ridge or hip (p. 85) □◒; if roofing or siding damaged extensively, call for professional evaluation
	Structural damage	Call for professional evaluation
Shingles or shakes dry, bleached or checked; starting to split, cup or curl	Weather stress	Preserve or finish shingles and shakes (p. 79) ◨●; if roofing or siding damaged extensively, call for professional evaluation
Finish on shingles or shakes faded, patchy or chipped	Weather stress; wear	Finish shingles and shakes (p. 79) ◨●
Finish on shingles or shakes blistered or peeling	Weather stress	Finish shingles and shakes (p. 79) ◨●
	Condensation behind roofing or siding	Call for professional evaluation
Shingles or shakes stained: dark blue-black rundown	Flashing or vent rusted; gutter or downspout faulty or rusted	Troubleshoot and repair roofing and siding system (p. 16); remove stains (p. 78) □◒; if necessary, preserve or finish shingles and shakes (p. 79) ◨●
Shingles or shakes stained: gray-black specks or streaks	Mildew, especially on shaded or protected exposures; sunlight discoloration, especially on southern or western exposures	Remove stains (p. 78) □◒; if necessary, preserve or finish shingles and shakes (p. 79) ◨●; trim back overhead and adjacent vegetation from shaded or protected exposures
	Condensation behind roofing or siding	If stains extensive or recur, call for professional evaluation
Shingles or shakes stained: reddish-brown streaks, especially below butt edges	Extractive stains due to bleeding of wood pigments	Remove stains (p. 78) □◒; if necessary, preserve or finish shingles and shakes (p. 79) ◨●
	Condensation behind roofing or siding	If stains extensive or recur, call for professional evaluation
Shingles or shakes dirty, debris-covered; growth of moss, algae or lichen	Wear; wind-borne material; pollution	Remove debris (p. 77) □○ or pressure-wash (p. 77) ◨●; trim back overhead and adjacent vegetation

DEGREE OF DIFFICULTY: □ Easy   ◨ Moderate   ■ Complex
ESTIMATED TIME: ○ Less than 1 hour   ◒ 1 to 3 hours   ● Over 3 hours
(For ladder and scaffolding set-up, see page 24)

REMOVING DEBRIS FROM SHINGLES OR SHAKES

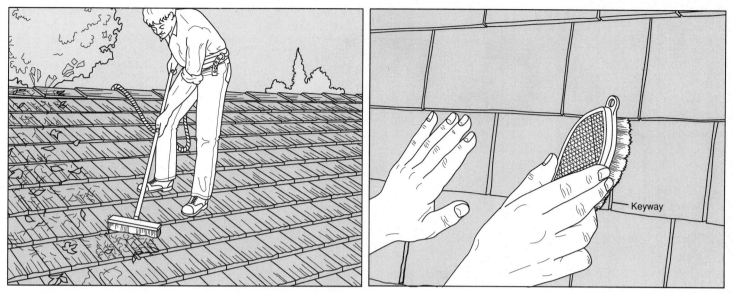

Brushing off debris. Brush debris off shingles and shakes to maintain them, and before applying a cleaner, a preservative or a finish. If dirt, moss, lichen or algae buildup is extensive, pressure-wash the roofing *(step below)* or siding *(page 78)*. Prepare to work safely on the roof or siding *(page 24)*. On the roof, work from ridge to eave, first cleaning raised surfaces such as dormer roofing. Use a stiff-bristled broom to sweep off the surface *(above, left)*; use a stiff-bristled brush to clean out keyways. Then, clean the gutters and downspouts *(page 36)*. On the siding, work from soffit to foundation, using a stiff-bristled brush to scrub the surface and clean out keyways *(above, right)*. Remove stains *(page 78)*; if necessary, apply a preservative or a finish *(page 79)*.

PRESSURE-WASHING SHINGLES OR SHAKES

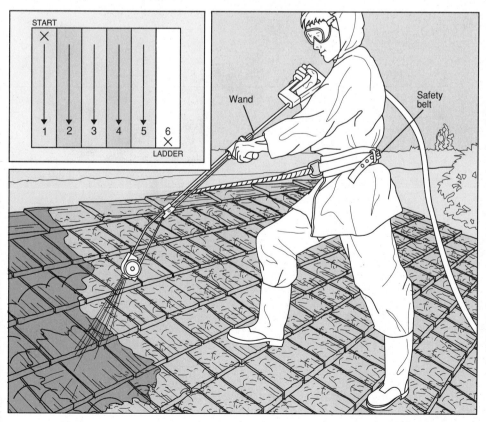

Pressure-washing the roofing. If dirt, moss, lichen or algae buildup is extensive, rent a pressure washer and set it up on the ground *(page 115)*. Prepare to work safely on the roof *(page 24)*, placing a ladder at one end of it. Wearing a safety belt, rain gear, rubber boots, rubber gloves and safety goggles, start at the end of the roof farthest from the ladder; clean raised surfaces such as dormer roofing first. Clean from ridge to eave in successive 5-foot wide sections *(inset)*. Always stand on dry roofing and do not point the spray wand into chimney flues or vents. Gripping the wand firmly with both hands and bracing it against your shoulder to steady it, hold it perpendicular to the roofing with the nozzle 12 to 18 inches from the surface and squeeze the trigger *(left)*. To stop the flow of water, release the trigger. Work back to the ladder, cleaning all but the last 5-foot wide section of roofing. Use the same procedure to clean all but the last 5-foot wide section of roofing on the other side of the ridge. When the roofing is dry, relocate the ladder and repeat the procedure on the remaining two sections. Clean debris out of the gutters and downspouts *(page 36)*. Remove any stains from the roofing *(page 78)* and, if necessary, apply a preservative or a finish *(page 79)* .

PRESSURE-WASHING SHINGLES OR SHAKES (continued)

Pressure-washing the siding. If dirt, moss, lichen or algae buildup is extensive, rent a pressure washer and set it up *(page 115)*. Prepare to work safely on the siding *(page 24)*, starting at one end of a wall. Wearing rubber boots, rubber gloves and safety goggles, clean from soffit to foundation in successive 5-foot wide sections; do not point the spray wand at doors or windows. Gripping the wand firmly with both hands and bracing it against you to steady it, hold it perpendicular to the siding with the nozzle 12 to 18 inches from the surface and squeeze the trigger *(left)*. To stop the flow of water, release the trigger. Work to the other end of the wall. Clean the siding on other walls the same way. Remove any stains from the siding *(page 78)* and, if necessary, apply a preservative or a finish *(page 79)*.

REMOVING STAINS FROM SHINGLES OR SHAKES

Hand-cleaning a stain. If the roofing or siding is stained extensively, spray-clean it *(page 79)*. If a stain is localized, prepare to work safely on the roof or siding *(page 24)*. Brush off debris *(page 77)* and remove any peeling or lifting finish *(page 123)*. Cover vegetation near the stained surface with plastic sheeting. Wearing rubber gloves, safety goggles and long sleeves, mix as many gallons of cleaner as needed in a plastic bucket. For embedded dirt and rundown stains from gutters and flashing, mix 1 cup of household detergent per 4 quarts of water and scrub using a stiff-bristled brush *(above, left)*. Let the cleaner soak in for 15 to 20 minutes, then rinse the surface thoroughly with fresh water *(above, right)* and allow it to dry. For stubborn rundown stains, mildew or weather

discoloration, use the same procedure, mixing 1 cup of trisodium phosphate (TSP) per 1 quart of 5% household bleach and 3 quarts of warm water. For an extractive stain (caused by the bleeding of wood pigments) or a rust stain, buy oxalic acid concentrate at a building supply center and mix it with water according to the manufacturer's instructions. **Caution:** Oxalic acid is highly caustic; prevent contact with eyes, skin and vegetation. Apply the cleaner with a paintbrush, rinse it off after 30 minutes and allow the surface to dry for 2 to 3 days; if the stain does not disappear, repeat the procedure. When the stain disappears, rinse the surface thoroughly with fresh water and allow it to dry. If necessary, apply a preservative or a finish *(page 79)*.

REMOVING STAINS FROM SHINGLES OR SHAKES (continued)

Spray-cleaning roofing or siding. If a stain is localized, hand-clean the surface *(page 78)*. If the roofing or siding is stained extensively, prepare to work safely on it *(page 24)*; on the roof, place a ladder at one end of it. Brush off debris *(page 77)* and remove any peeling or lifting finish *(page 123)*. Cover nearby vegetation with plastic sheeting. Rent a pump-up sprayer and set it up *(page 114)*. Wearing rubber gloves, safety goggles and long sleeves, mix enough cleaner to fill the cannister *(page 78)*. **Caution:** Do not spray-clean with oxalic acid. To use the sprayer, hold the spray wand at a 60-degree angle to the surface with the nozzle about 12 inches from it and squeeze the trigger; release it to stop the flow of cleaner. Pressurize the sprayer and refill the cannister as needed. On the roof, also wear a safety belt and rubber boots. Start at the end of the roof farthest from the ladder and work from ridge to eave in successive 5-foot wide sections *(above, left)*; clean raised surfaces such as dormer roofing first. Always stand on dry roofing and do not point the wand into chimney flues or vents. Work back to the ladder, cleaning all but the last 5-foot wide section. Use the same procedure on the other side of the ridge. When the roofing is dry, relocate the ladder and clean the remaining two sections. On the siding, use the same procedure, starting at one end of a wall and working from soffit to foundation *(above, right)*; do not point the wand at doors or windows. Rinse the surface thoroughly; if necessary, apply a preservative or a finish *(step below)*.

PRESERVING OR FINISHING SHINGLES OR SHAKES

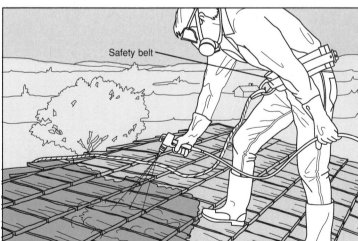

Applying a preservative or a finish. Prepare to work safely on the roof or siding *(page 24)*; on the roof, place a ladder at one end of it. Brush off debris *(page 77)* and remove any peeling or lifting finish *(page 123)*. Choose a preservative or a finish *(page 124)* and follow the manufacturer's instructions for applying it. Use plastic sheeting and duct tape to protect nearby vegetation and surfaces not to be coated. Work on a calm, dry and cloudy day; wear rubber gloves and safety goggles. For a small job, use a paintbrush, a roller *(page 124)* or a sprayer *(page 125)*. For an entire roof or wall, rent a commercial airless sprayer and set it up *(page 125)*; to use it, also wear a respirator and long sleeves. Hold the spray wand at a 60-degree angle to the surface with the nozzle about 12 inches from it and squeeze the trigger; release it to stop the spray. On the roof, also wear a safety belt and rubber boots. Start at the end of the roof farthest from the ladder and work from ridge to eave in successive 5-foot wide sections *(above, left)*; spray raised surfaces such as dormer roofing first. Always stand on dry roofing and do not point the wand into chimney flues or vents. Be sure that end grain and sides of the shingles or shakes are adequately coated; remove excess using a dry paintbrush or a roller. Work back to the ladder, spraying all but the last 5-foot wide section. Use the same procedure on the other side of the ridge. When the roofing is dry, relocate the ladder and spray the remaining two sections. On the siding, use the same procedure, starting at one end of a wall and working from soffit to foundation *(above, right)*; do not point the wand at doors or windows. If necessary, repeat the procedure.

REPLACING A SHINGLE

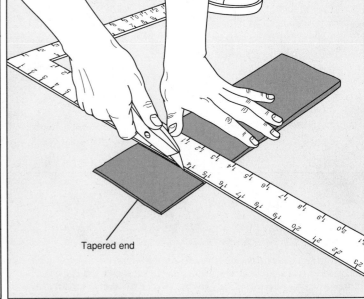

1 Removing the damaged shingle. Prepare to work safely on the roof or siding *(page 24)*. Wearing safety goggles, use a mallet to drive a wood chisel into the butt edge of the shingle *(above, left)* at several places, splitting it into narrow pieces. Wearing work gloves, lift the end of each piece and pull it out, working it from side to side to break it off hidden nails. For a stubborn piece, grip the end of it with old locking pliers and tap the jaws of the pliers using a ball-peen hammer *(inset)*. Using a hacksaw blade, cut off the hidden nails that held the shingle in place; usually the nails are located about 2 inches higher than the butt line of the course above the shingle. Wearing work gloves, fit the hacksaw blade behind the course and saw off each nail flush with the surface *(above, right)*.

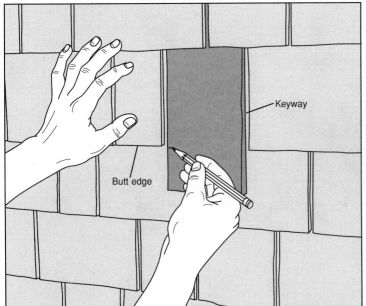

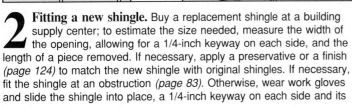

2 Fitting a new shingle. Buy a replacement shingle at a building supply center; to estimate the size needed, measure the width of the opening, allowing for a 1/4-inch keyway on each side, and the length of a piece removed. If necessary, apply a preservative or a finish *(page 124)* to match the new shingle with original shingles. If necessary, fit the shingle at an obstruction *(page 83)*. Otherwise, wear work gloves and slide the shingle into place, a 1/4-inch keyway on each side and its butt edge even with the butt line of its course. If the shingle is too wide, mark it to width and use a utility knife *(page 120)* or a block plane *(page 123)* to trim it. If the shingle is too long, mark it to length, using the butt edge of the shingle on each side of it as a guide *(above, left)*. Measure the excess length, transfer the measurement to the tapered end, and use a carpenter's square and a utility knife to cut the excess off the tapered end *(above, right)*.

REPLACING A SHINGLE (continued)

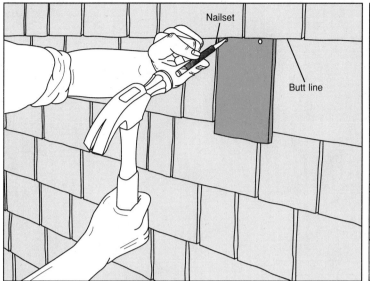

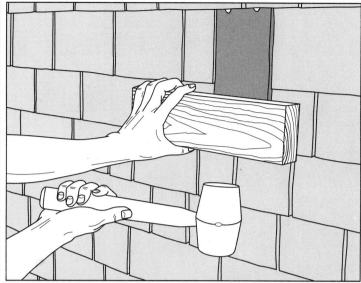

3 **Installing the new shingle.** Wearing work gloves, slide the shingle into place, a 1/4-inch keyway on each side, but leave its butt edge about 1 inch below the butt line of its course. Mark two holes for nails in the shingle, each one at the butt line of the course above it and 3/4 inch from opposite sides. Bore *(page 121)* a 45-degree angle pilot hole at each mark, sloping it toward the butt line of the course above the shingle. Drive a nail *(page 121)* into each hole with a hammer; set its head using a nailset and the hammer *(above, left)*. Holding a wood block under the butt edge of the shingle, tap it using a mallet *(above, right)* until the shingle is in position, its butt edge even with the butt line of its course. If necessary, apply a preservative or a finish on the roofing or siding *(page 79)*.

REPLACING A SHAKE

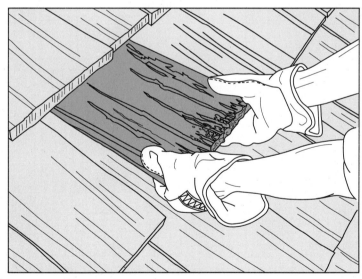

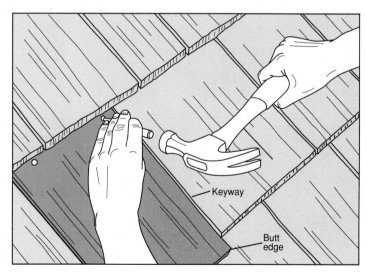

1 **Removing the damaged shake.** Prepare to work safely on the roof or siding *(page 24)*. Wearing work gloves, lift the butt edge of the shake and pull it out *(above)*, working it from side to side to break it off hidden nails; avoid damaging any building paper. If the shake is difficult to remove, split it and pull out the pieces as you would to remove a shingle *(page 80)*. Fit a hacksaw blade behind the course above the shake removed and cut off hidden nails that held it—usually located about 2 inches higher than the butt line. Buy a replacement shake at a building supply center; if necessary, apply a preservative or a finish *(page 124)* to match it with original shakes.

2 **Fitting and installing a new shake.** If necessary, fit the shake at an obstruction *(page 83)*. Otherwise, wear work gloves and slide the shake into place, a 1/2-inch keyway on each side; if it is too wide, trim it with a saber saw *(page 120)*. Position the shake with its butt edge about 1 inch below the butt line of its course and bore *(page 121)* two pilot holes: each one at the butt line of the course above the shake and at a 45-degree angle toward it, and 3/4 inch from opposite sides. Drive a nail *(page 121)* into each hole; set its head with a nailset and the hammer *(above)*. Hold a wood block under the butt edge of the shake and tap it using a mallet until the butt edge is even with the butt line of its course. If necessary, apply a preservative or a finish on the roofing or siding *(page 79)*.

REPLACING A SECTION OF SHINGLES

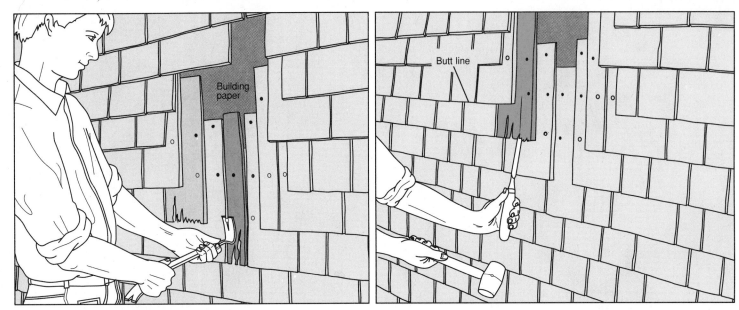

1 **Removing a section of damaged shingles.** Prepare to work safely on the roof or siding *(page 24)*. To remove a section of damaged shingles, work from top to bottom, one course at a time and from one end to the other end. Take out each shingle of the first course as you would to remove one shingle *(page 80)*. To take out each shingle of the other courses, lift its butt edge slightly with a pry bar to raise the nails, push it back into position and pull out the exposed nails *(above, left)*. Wearing work gloves, pull out the shingle, working it from side to side to break it away from hidden nails, if necessary. If the

shingle is difficult to remove, wear safety goggles and use a mallet to drive a wood chisel into the butt edge *(above, right)* at several places, splitting the shingle into narrow pieces; then, pull out the pieces. Using a hacksaw blade, cut off hidden nails that held the shingle in place; usually the nails are located about 2 inches higher than the butt line of the course above the shingle. Fit the hacksaw blade behind the course above the shingle removed and saw off each nail flush with the surface. Continue the procedure until the entire section of damaged shingles is removed. Then, patch any damaged building paper *(page 117)*.

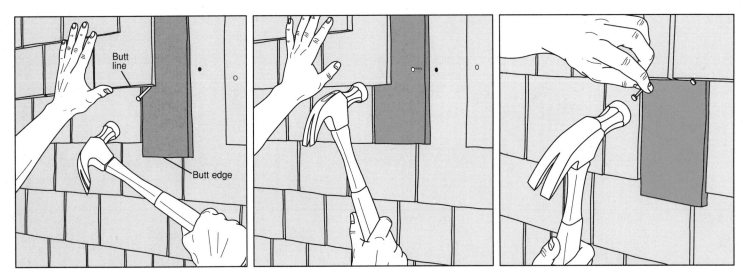

2 **Installing a section of new shingles.** Buy replacement shingles at a building supply center; if necessary, apply a preservative or a finish *(page 124)* to match them with original shingles. To install the shingles, work from bottom to top, one course at a time and from one end to the other end; offset the keyways of alternate courses by about 1 1/2 inches. If necessary, fit a shingle at an obstruction *(page 83)*. Otherwise, wear work gloves and slide each shingle into place, a 1/4-inch keyway on each side and its butt edge even with the butt line of its course; if it is too wide or too long, fit it *(page 80)*. Drive two nails *(page 121)* into the shingle, each one about 2 inches higher than the butt line of the course above it and 3/4 inch from opposite sides. If one side of the shingle is overlapped by the course above it, leave its butt

edge about 1 inch below the butt line of its course and mark a hole for a nail at the butt line of the course above it and 3/4 inch from the overlapped side. Bore *(page 121)* a 45-degree angle pilot hole at the mark, sloping it toward the butt line of the course above the shingle. Drive a nail into the hole *(above, left)*; set its head with a nailset. Holding a wood block under the butt edge of the shingle, use a mallet to tap it until the butt edge is even with the butt line of its course. Drive in a nail 3/4 inch from the other side of the shingle and 2 inches higher than the butt line of the course above it *(above, center)*. Continue the procedure until the last course; then, as you would to install one shingle *(page 81)*, install each shingle of the course *(above, right)*. If necessary, apply a preservative or a finish on the roofing or siding *(page 79)*.

REPLACING A SECTION OF SHAKES

1 **Removing a section of damaged shakes.** Prepare to work safely on the roof or siding *(page 24)*. Work from top to bottom, one course at a time, one end to the other end. Take out each shake of the first course as you would to remove one shake *(page 81)*. To take out each shake of the other courses, lift its butt edge to raise the nails, push it back and pull out the exposed nails. Wearing work gloves, pull out the shake, working it from side to side to break it off hidden nails *(above)*. Fit a hacksaw blade behind the course above the shake removed and cut off the hidden nails—usually located about 2 inches higher than the butt line. Continue until the section is removed. Patch any damaged building paper *(page 117)*. Buy replacement shakes at a building supply center; if necessary, apply a preservative or a finish *(page 124)* to match them with original shakes.

2 **Installing a section of new shakes.** Work from bottom to top, one course at a time, one end to the other end; offset the keyways of alternate courses by about 1 1/2 inches. If necessary, fit a shake at an obstruction *(page 83)*. Otherwise, wear work gloves and slide each shake into place, under the building paper of the course above it on the roof *(above)*, a 1/2-inch keyway on each side and its butt edge even with the butt line of its course; if it is too wide, trim it with a saber saw *(page 120)*. Drive two nails *(page 121)* into the shake, each one about 2 inches higher than the butt line of the course above it and 3/4 inch from opposite sides; avoid nailing into any building paper on it. If one side of the shake is overlapped by the course above it, nail the side as you would to install one shake *(page 81)* and then nail the other side. Continue until the last course; then, as you would to install one shake, install each shake of the last course. If necessary, apply a preservative or a finish on the roofing or siding *(page 79)*.

FITTING SHINGLES OR SHAKES AT OBSTRUCTIONS

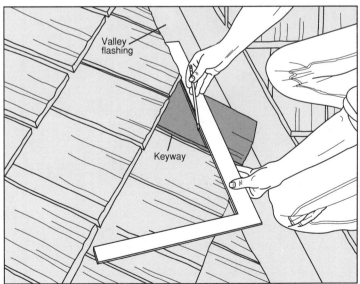

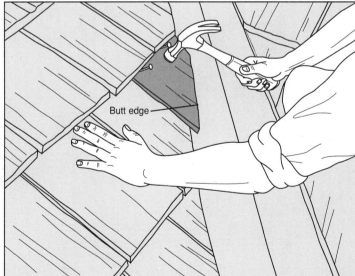

Fitting a shingle or shake at a valley. Inspect the valley flashing *(page 16)* and, if necessary, repair it. To install a shake at the valley, wear work gloves and slide it into place, a 1/2-inch keyway on each side; if it is too wide, trim it with a saber saw *(page 120)*. With a carpenter's square and a pencil, mark the edge of the valley on the shake, using the butt edge of the shake on each side of it as a guide *(above, left)*. Trim the shake to size using the saber saw. Position the shake with its butt edge about 1 inch below the butt line at the valley and bore *(page 121)*

two pilot holes: each one at the butt line of the course above the shake and at a 45-degree angle toward it, and 3/4 inch from opposite sides; avoid drilling into the flashing. Drive a nail *(page 121)* into each hole with a hammer *(above, right)*; set its head with a nailset and the hammer. Hold a wood block under the butt edge of the shake and tap it using a mallet until the butt edge is even with the butt line at the valley. To install a shingle at the valley, use the same procedure, leaving a 1/4-inch keyway on each side.

FITTING SHINGLES OR SHAKES AT OBSTRUCTIONS (continued)

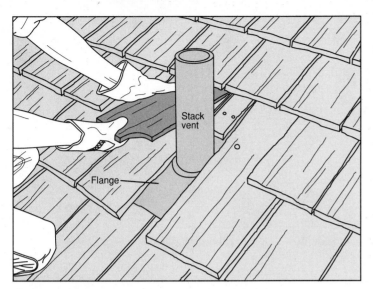

Fitting a shingle or shake at a vent. Inspect the flashing at the stack or roof vent *(page 16)* and, if necessary, repair it. To install a shake above or beside the vent, position it beside the vent and mark it to fit by eye *(page 118)*, allowing for a 1/2-inch keyway on each side. Cut the shake to shape using a saber saw *(page 120)*. Wearing work gloves, slide the shake into place *(above)* and nail it as you would to install another shake *(page 81)*; avoid nailing into the flashing. To install a shake below the vent, fit it under the flashing flange and nail it as you would to install another shake. To install a shingle at the vent, use the same procedure, leaving a 1/4-inch keyway on each side.

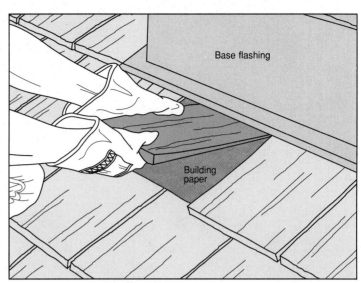

Fitting a shingle or shake at a chimney. Inspect the flashing *(page 16)* and, if necessary, repair it. To fit a shake below the chimney, wear work gloves and slide it into place under the base flashing *(above)*, allowing for a 1/2-inch keyway on each side; beside the chimney, under any step flashing of the course above the shake. If the shake is too wide or too long, trim it with a saber saw *(page 120)*; cut excess length off the tapered end. Position and nail the shake as you would to install another shake *(page 81)*; avoid nailing into the flashing. To install a shingle at the chimney, use the same procedure, leaving a 1/4-inch keyway on each side.

Fitting a shingle or shake at a window or door. To install a shingle at the edge of the window or door, hold it in position and mark it to fit by eye *(page 118)*, allowing for a 1/4-inch keyway on each side. Cut the shingle to size using a saber saw *(page 120)*; trim excess length off the tapered end. Wearing work gloves, slide the shingle into place *(above)* and nail it as you would to install another shingle *(page 81)*. To install a shake at the edge of the window or door, use the same procedure, leaving a 1/2-inch keyway on each side. If necessary, apply a sealant at the edge of the window or door *(page 115)*.

Fitting a shingle or shake at a woven corner. To install a shingle at the woven corner, hold it in position and mark it to fit, allowing for a 1/4-inch keyway on the side not at the corner and for a butt joint on the side at the corner. Mark the shingle to width by tracing the contour of the other shingle at the corner; compensate by an amount equal to the thickness of a shingle to form the butt joint. Trim the shingle to width using a utility knife *(page 120)*. Fit the shingle to length *(page 80)*, use a wood block and a mallet to tap it into place *(above)* and nail it as you would to install another shingle *(page 81)*. To install a shake at the woven corner, use the same procedure, leaving a 1/2-inch keyway.

REPLACING SHINGLES OR SHAKES AT A RIDGE OR A HIP

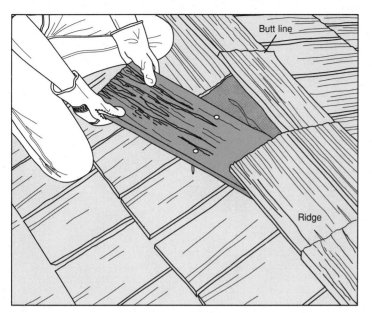

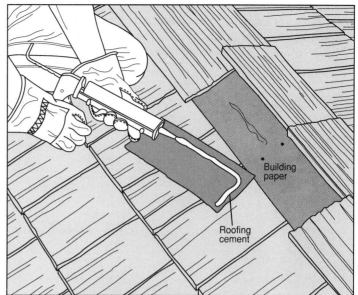

1 **Removing a damaged shingle or shake.** Prepare to work safely on the roof or siding *(page 24)*. To remove a shake at the ridge or hip, wear work gloves to lift its butt edge and pull it out, working it from side to side to break it off hidden nails *(above)*; avoid damaging any building paper. If the shake is difficult to remove, split it and pull out the pieces as you would to remove a shingle *(page 80)*. Fit a hacksaw blade behind the course above the shake removed and cut off hidden nails that held it—usually located about 2 inches higher than the butt line. Remove a shingle at the ridge or hip the same way.

2 **Patching the building paper.** If the building paper is not damaged, install a new shake or shingle *(step 3)*. If the building paper is damaged, remove as many shakes or shingles at the ridge or hip *(step 1)* as necessary to cover the entire damaged area with a patch. Using a utility knife, cut a sheet of building paper for the patch at least 1 inch longer and wider than the damaged area. Wearing work gloves, apply roofing cement *(page 115)* on the bottom of the patch with a caulking gun *(above)*. Turn over the patch, position it and press it into place.

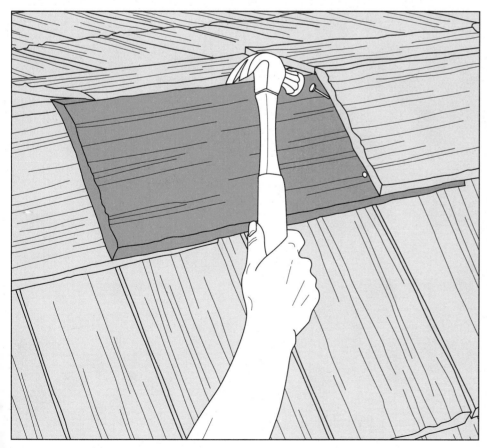

3 **Installing a new shingle or shake.** Buy a replacement shake or shingle for the ridge or hip at a building supply center; if necessary, apply a preservative or a finish *(page 124)* to match it with original shakes or shingles. To install a new shake at the ridge or hip, wear work gloves and slide it into place, but leave its butt edge about 1 inch below the butt line of its course. Bore *(page 121)* two pilot holes: each one at the butt line of the course above the shake and at a 45-degree angle toward it, and 3/4 inch from opposite sides. Drive a nail *(page 121)* into each hole using a hammer *(left)*; set its head with a nailset and the hammer. Hold a wood block under the butt edge of the shake and tap it using a mallet until the butt edge is even with the butt line of its course. To install a new shingle at the ridge or hip, use the same procedure. If necessary, apply a preservative or a finish on the roofing or siding *(page 79)*.

WOOD SIDING

Wood has been a popular siding choice for generations due to its availability, natural beauty and array of styles. Whether of solid wood, plywood or hardboard, of boards or panels, wood siding is suitable for traditional and contemporary homes; typical installations are shown below. All wood siding is nailed onto wall studs or onto furring strips installed on them; for common nailing patterns, see page 88. Sheathing or building paper between the siding and the studs adds water and wind protection. Sealant is applied along any open joints, such as around a window or door.

Undertake repairs to your wood siding as soon as problems are detected to maintain the appearance of your home and prevent interior damage. Clean off dirt and debris, and remove any stains *(page 89)*; patch any nicks, holes or minor rot *(page 91)*. Prevent recurrences of rot and mildew by trimming back overhead and adjacent vegetation, providing the siding with more air circulation and sunlight exposure. If the siding is finished with a stain or treated with a preservative, refinish it every 2 to 5 years; if it is painted, refinish it when the paint deteriorates or fades *(page 90)*.

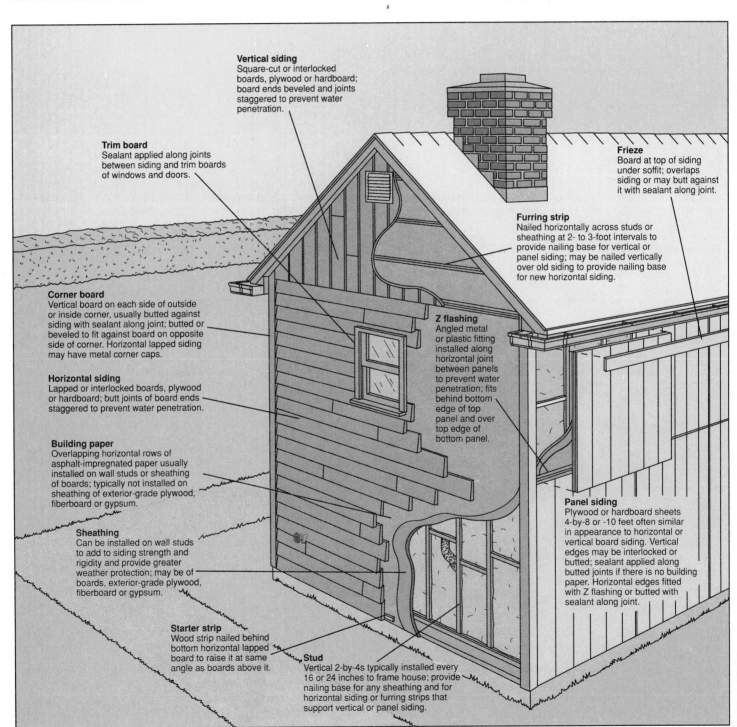

Vertical siding
Square-cut or interlocked boards, plywood or hardboard; board ends beveled and joints staggered to prevent water penetration.

Trim board
Sealant applied along joints between siding and trim boards of windows and doors.

Frieze
Board at top of siding under soffit; overlaps siding or may butt against it with sealant along joint.

Furring strip
Nailed horizontally across studs or sheathing at 2- to 3-foot intervals to provide nailing base for vertical or panel siding; may be nailed vertically over old siding to provide nailing base for new horizontal siding.

Corner board
Vertical board on each side of outside or inside corner, usually butted against siding with sealant along joint; butted or beveled to fit against board on opposite side of corner. Horizontal lapped siding may have metal corner caps.

Z flashing
Angled metal or plastic fitting installed along horizontal joint between panels to prevent water penetration; fits behind bottom edge of top panel and over top edge of bottom panel.

Horizontal siding
Lapped or interlocked boards, plywood or hardboard; butt joints of board ends staggered to prevent water penetration.

Building paper
Overlapping horizontal rows of asphalt-impregnated paper usually installed on wall studs or sheathing of boards; typically not installed on sheathing of exterior-grade plywood, fiberboard or gypsum.

Panel siding
Plywood or hardboard sheets 4-by-8 or -10 feet often similar in appearance to horizontal or vertical board siding. Vertical edges may be interlocked or butted; sealant applied along butted joints if there is no building paper. Horizontal edges fitted with Z flashing or butted with sealant along joint.

Sheathing
Can be installed on wall studs to add to siding strength and rigidity and provide greater weather protection; may be of boards, exterior-grade plywood, fiberboard or gypsum.

Starter strip
Wood strip nailed behind bottom horizontal lapped board to raise it at same angle as boards above it.

Stud
Vertical 2-by-4s typically installed every 16 or 24 inches to frame house; provide nailing base for any sheathing and for horizontal siding or furring strips that support vertical or panel siding.

If interior condensation or a leak occurs, consult the Troubleshooting Guide in Your Roofing and Siding *(page 14)* and in this chapter *(below)*. Often, the problem may originate with the gutters and downspouts or the caulking around windows, doors and fixtures—and not with the siding. If, however, you find damaged siding, repairs are easily made; a split board can be glued, minor rot can be patched, and a warped or badly cracked board or panel can be replaced. If you cannot locate the source of a leak or if the siding is damaged extensively, call for a professional evaluation.

Although wood siding repairs are not difficult, working overhead can be intimidating. Read the chapter on Working Safely at Heights *(page 24)* to properly set up and use any ladders or scaffolding necessary, and work with a helper when handling large boards or panels. Most repairs require only basic carpentry tools such as a hammer, a nailset, a pry bar, a wood chisel, a saw, and a few measuring and marking instruments. Refer to Tools & Techniques *(page 112)* for directions on using tools and choosing materials and equipment required for a job.

TROUBLESHOOTING GUIDE

SYMPTOM	POSSIBLE CAUSE	PROCEDURE
Leak through wall or into basement	Roofing, flashing, vent, gutter or downspout damaged or faulty	Troubleshoot and repair roofing and siding system *(p. 16)*
	Siding damaged	Repair *(p. 93)* ◧◕ or replace *(p. 94)* ◧◕ horizontal lapped board; replace vertical board or batten *(p. 96)* ◧◕; repair or replace horizontal *(p. 97)* ◧◕ or replace vertical *(p. 98)* ◧◕ tongue-and-groove or shiplap board; replace panel *(p. 99)* ◧●
Siding spongy, pitted or crumbling	Gutter or downspout damaged or faulty	Troubleshoot and repair roofing and siding system *(p. 16)*
	Air circulation or sun exposure inadequate	Trim back overhead and adjacent vegetation
	Rot or insect damage	Patch rotted wood *(p. 91)* □○; repair *(p. 93)* ◧◕ or replace *(p. 94)* ◧◕ horizontal lapped board; replace vertical board or batten *(p. 96)* ◧◕; repair or replace horizontal *(p. 97)* ◧◕ or replace vertical *(p. 98)* ◧◕ tongue-and-groove or shiplap board; replace panel *(p. 99)* ◧●; if insect infestation suspected or if siding damaged extensively, call for professional evaluation
Siding board loose or hanging out of position	Fasteners popped or missing	Repair loose board *(p. 92)* □○
Siding board nicked or gouged; small crack or split	Wood shrinkage; weather stress; impact damage	Fill holes and cracks *(p. 91)* □○; repair split board *(p. 92)* □○
Siding board warped; cracked or split extensively	Weather stress; impact damage	Repair *(p. 93)* ◧◕ or replace *(p. 94)* ◧◕ horizontal lapped board; replace vertical board or batten *(p. 96)* ◧◕; repair or replace horizontal *(p. 97)* ◧◕ or replace vertical *(p. 98)* ◧◕ tongue-and-groove or shiplap board
Corner cap rusted or dented	Weather stress; impact damage	Replace corner cap *(p. 95)* □○
Plywood panel blistered	Water penetrating panel	Repair blistered plywood panel *(p. 98)* □○
Plywood or hardboard panel nicked, gouged, warped, cracked or split	Weather stress; impact damage	Replace panel *(p. 99)* ◧●
Trim or corner board spongy, pitted or crumbling	Rot or insect damage	Patch rotted wood *(p. 91)* □○; replace trim or corner board *(p. 100)* □◕; if insect infestation suspected, call for professional evaluation
Trim or corner board warped, cracked or split	Weather stress; impact damage	Replace trim or corner board *(p. 100)* □◕
Siding dry, bleached, checked; finish faded, patchy, chipped	Weather stress; wear	Refinish siding *(p. 90)* □●
Siding finish blistered or peeling	Weather stress	Refinish siding *(p. 90)* □●
	Condensation behind siding	Call for professional evaluation
Siding stained: dark blue-black rundown	Flashing rusted; gutter or downspout faulty or rusted	Troubleshoot and repair roofing and siding system *(p. 16)*; remove stains *(p. 89)* □◕; if necessary, refinish siding *(p. 90)* □●
Siding stained: gray-black specks or streaks	Mildew, especially on shaded or protected exposures; sunlight discoloration, especially on southern or western exposures	Remove stains *(p. 89)* □◕; if necessary, refinish siding *(p. 90)* □●; trim back overhead and adjacent vegetation from shaded or protected exposures
Siding stained: reddish-brown streaks	Extractive stains due to bleeding of wood pigments	Remove stains *(p. 89)* □◕; if necessary, refinish siding *(p. 90)* □●
Siding dirty	Wear; wind-borne material; pollution	Clean siding *(p. 89)* □○

DEGREE OF DIFFICULTY: □ Easy ◧ Moderate ■ Complex
ESTIMATED TIME: ○ Less than 1 hour ◕ 1 to 3 hours ● Over 3 hours
(For ladder and scaffolding set-up, see page 24)

NAILING PATTERNS

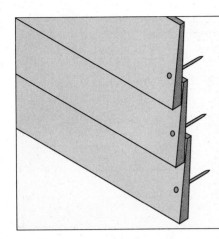

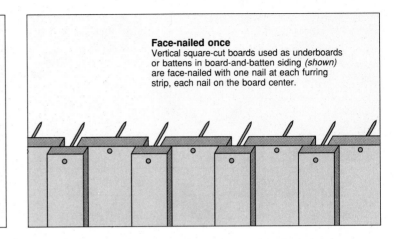

Face-nailed once
Horizontal lapped boards *(shown)* and interlocking boards 6 inches wide or less, except tongue-and-groove, are face-nailed with one nail at each stud or furring strip. Usually, each nail is driven about 1 inch from the bottom edge of the board, clearing the top edge of any board behind it; each nail may be driven through both boards.

Face-nailed once
Vertical square-cut boards used as underboards or battens in board-and-batten siding *(shown)* are face-nailed with one nail at each furring strip, each nail on the board center.

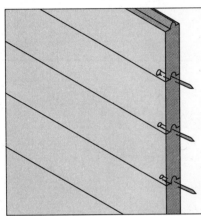

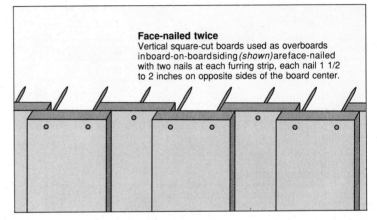

Blind-nailed once
Horizontal and vertical tongue-and-groove boards 6 inches wide or less, *(shown)*, are blind-nailed with one nail at each stud or furring strip. Each nail is driven through the base of the tongue at a 45-degree angle and counter-sunk with a nailset. Tongue-and-groove boards wider than 6 inches are face-nailed twice like other interlocking boards.

Face-nailed twice
Vertical square-cut boards used as overboards in board-on-board siding *(shown)* are face-nailed with two nails at each furring strip, each nail 1 1/2 to 2 inches on opposite sides of the board center.

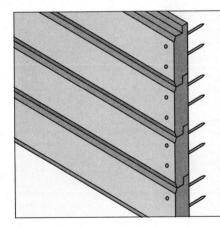

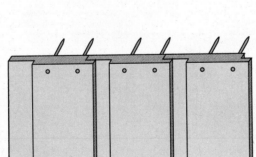

Face-nailed twice
Horizontal and vertical interlocking boards wider than 6 inches, such as the drop shiplap *(left)* and the channel shiplap *(right)*, are face-nailed with two nails at each stud or furring strip, each nail 1 inch from opposite board edges.

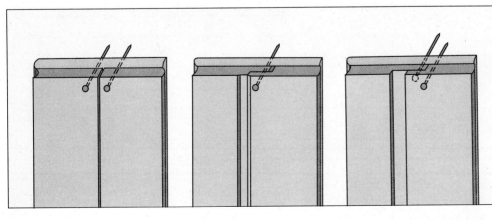

Panel joints
Plywood and hardboard panels are usually nailed every 6 to 8 inches along the edges. Butted panels are face-nailed 3/8 inch from the edge *(far left)*. Interlocking panels may be face-nailed 3/8 inch from the edge of the overlapping panel through both panels *(center left)* or blind-nailed 3/8 inch from the hidden edge of a panel and about 1/2 inch from the edge of the overlapping panel, clearing the hidden edge of the panel behind it *(near left)*.

CLEANING OFF DIRT AND DEBRIS

Washing the siding. Prepare to work safely along the siding *(page 24)*. Remove any loose or lifting finish *(page 90)*. To clean off dirt and debris, use a garden hose fitted with an automobile brush; on stubborn spots, wear rubber gloves and use a solution of mild detergent and warm water. Starting at one end of a wall, work from soffit to foundation, scrubbing the surface with the brush *(above, left)*. If dirt, moss, lichen or algae buildup is extensive, rent and set up a pressure washer *(page 115)*. Wearing rubber boots, rubber gloves and safety goggles, start at one end of a wall and work from soffit to foundation in successive 5-foot wide sections; do not point the spray wand at doors or windows. Gripping the wand firmly with both hands and bracing it against you to steady it, hold it perpendicular to the siding with the nozzle 12 to 18 inches from the surface and squeeze the trigger *(above, right)*. To stop the flow of water, release the trigger. Clean the siding on other walls the same way. Then, remove any stains *(step below)* and, if necessary, apply a preservative or finish *(page 90)*.

REMOVING STAINS

Hand-cleaning a stain. If the siding is stained extensively, spray-clean it *(page 90)*. If a stain is localized, prepare to work safely on the siding *(page 24)* and wash it *(step above)*. Cover nearby vegetation with plastic sheeting. Wearing rubber gloves, safety goggles and long sleeves, mix as many gallons of cleaner as needed in a plastic bucket. For embedded dirt and rundown stains, mix 1 cup of household detergent per 4 quarts of water and scrub using a stiff-bristled brush *(left)*. Let the cleaner soak in for 15 to 20 minutes, then rinse the surface with fresh water and allow it to dry. For stubborn rundown stains, mildew or weather discoloration, use the same procedure, mixing 1 cup of trisodium phosphate (TSP) per 1 quart of 5% household bleach and 3 quarts of warm water. For an extractive stain (caused by the bleeding of wood pigments) or a rust stain, buy oxalic acid concentrate at a building supply center and mix it with water according to the manufacturer's instructions. **Caution:** Oxalic acid is highly caustic; prevent contact with eyes, skin and vegetation. Apply the cleaner with a paintbrush, rinse it off after 30 minutes and allow the surface to dry for 2 to 3 days; if the stain does not disappear, repeat the procedure. When the stain disappears, rinse the surface and allow it to dry. If necessary, apply a preservative or finish *(page 90)*.

REMOVING STAINS (continued)

Spray-cleaning the siding. If a stain is localized, hand-clean the surface *(page 89)*. If the siding is stained extensively, prepare to work safely on it *(page 24)*. Wash the siding *(page 89)* and cover vegetation near the stained surface with plastic sheeting. Rent and set up a pump-up sprayer *(page 114)*. Wearing rubber gloves, safety goggles and long sleeves, mix enough cleaner to fill the cannister *(page 89)*. **Caution:** Do not spray-clean with oxalic acid. Starting at one end of a wall, work from soffit to foundation in successive 5-foot wide sections; do not point the spray wand at doors or windows. Holding the wand at a 60-degree angle to the surface with the nozzle about 12 inches from it, squeeze the trigger *(left)*; release it to stop the flow of cleaner. Pressurize the sprayer and refill the cannister as needed. Rinse the surface thoroughly with fresh water and allow it to dry. Spray-clean the siding on other walls the same way. If necessary, apply a preservative or finish *(steps below)*.

REFINISHING THE SIDING

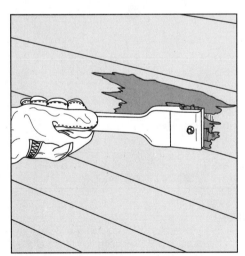

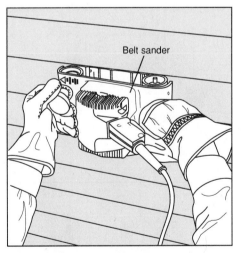

1 **Removing the old finish.** Prepare to work safely along the siding *(page 24)*. If there is no finish or the finish is well adhered, sand the surface *(step 2)*. Wearing work gloves and safety goggles, use a paint scraper to remove loose or lifting finish and hardened wood resins *(above)*; apply even, moderate pressure along the grain. To loosen thick layers of paint or reach tight corners, rub gently with a wire brush. Brush off debris with a whisk and use a putty knife to clean debris out of cracks.

2 **Sanding the surface.** Remove stains *(page 89)*, fill small holes and cracks, patch minor rot *(page 91)*, replace popped nails and repair split boards *(page 92)*. Wearing work gloves and a dust mask, sand along the grain to smooth the surface *(page 123)*, using a power sander on a large, flat area *(above)*. Start with coarse sandpaper if the surface is rough or heavily coated; start with medium sandpaper if it is scratched or moderately coated. Use fine sandpaper for final smoothing or if the surface is unfinished. Brush off dust with a whisk.

3 **Applying a preservative or finish.** Choose a preservative or finish *(page 124)* and follow the manufacturer's instructions for applying it; a primer may be required. Use plastic sheeting to protect nearby vegetation and surfaces not to be coated. Wearing rubber gloves, work from soffit to foundation along the grain on a small area at a time. Coat surfaces hardest to reach first using a paintbrush. On a large, flat area, use a roller *(above)*; fit it with an extension pole, if necessary. Backbrush edges of a penetrating finish with a dry paintbrush or roller.

FILLING SMALL HOLES AND CRACKS

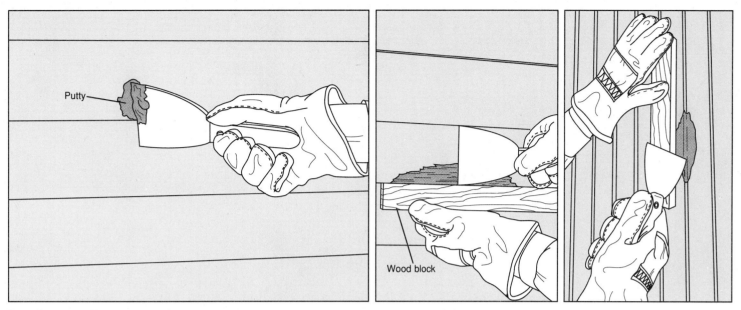

Patching a small hole or crack. Prepare to work safely on the siding *(page 24)*. To fill a small hole or crack in the siding, buy an exterior-grade wood putty at a building supply center and prepare it following the manufacturer's instructions. Wearing work gloves, use a putty knife to pack putty into the hole or crack, overfilling it slightly *(above, left)*. Then, scrape off the excess putty, leveling it with the surrounding surface; position a wood block along the edge of a board as a guide, if necessary *(above, center)*. To replicate any pattern in the siding, rake the patch with the tip of the putty knife blade *(above, right)* or using a wire brush. Allow the wood putty to cure. Then, refinish the damaged siding *(page 90)*.

PATCHING ROTTED WOOD

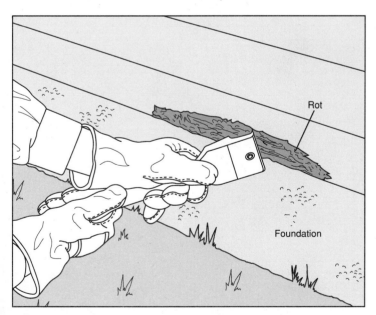

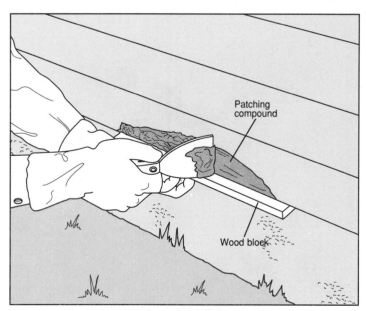

1 **Scraping away the damaged wood.** Prepare to work safely on the siding *(page 24)*. Use an awl, poking it into the wood as deeply as possible, to test for rot—especially at areas where there is chipped, peeling or lifting finish, spongy, pitted or crumbling wood fibers, and gray or dark discoloration; if the damage is extensive, call for a professional evaluation. To patch minor rot, wear work gloves and safety goggles to remove all the soft, rotted wood down to firm, healthy wood using a paint scraper *(above)*, a putty knife or a wire brush.

2 **Applying epoxy patching compound.** Buy epoxy patching compound at a building supply center and prepare it following the manufacturer's instructions. Wearing rubber gloves, use a putty knife to pack patching compound into the damaged area, overfilling it slightly. Then, scrape off the excess patching compound, leveling it with the surrounding surface; position a wood block along the edge of a board as a guide, if necessary *(above)*. To replicate any pattern in the siding, rake the patch with the tip of the putty knife blade or using a wire brush. Allow the patching compound to cure. Then, refinish the damaged siding *(page 90)*.

REPAIRING A LOOSE BOARD

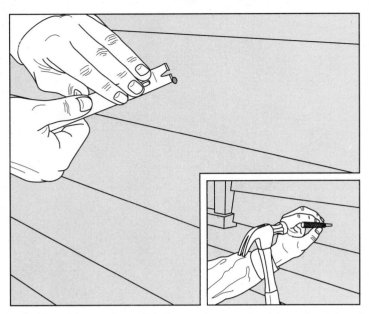

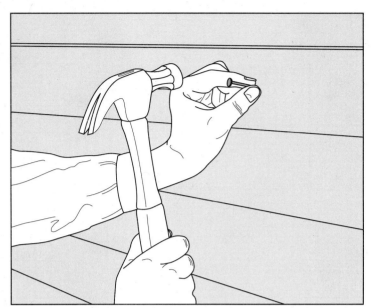

1 **Repairing a popped nail.** Prepare to work safely on the siding *(page 24)*. To reseat a popped nail, drive it below the surface slightly using a nailset and a hammer *(inset)*. To pull out a nail, use a pry bar *(above)*; position a wood block under it to protect the siding, if necessary. If a nail cannot be removed, drive it through the siding with the nailset and the hammer. Fill nail holes and cover nail heads with wood putty *(page 115)*.

2 **Renailing the board.** Buy new nails *(page 121)* at a building supply center. To avoid splitting the board, drive a new nail into each old hole at a 30-degree angle *(above)*; or, bore a pilot hole *(page 121)* about 1/2 inch to one side of each old nail and drive a new nail into it. Seat each nail head below the surface slightly using a nailset and the hammer. Cover the nail heads with wood putty *(page 115)* and refinish the damaged siding *(page 90)*.

REPAIRING A SPLIT BOARD

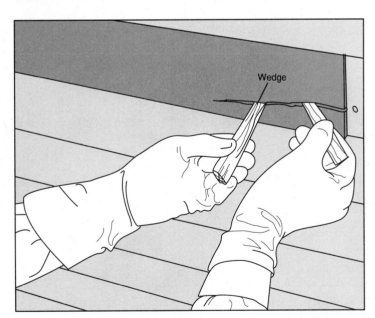

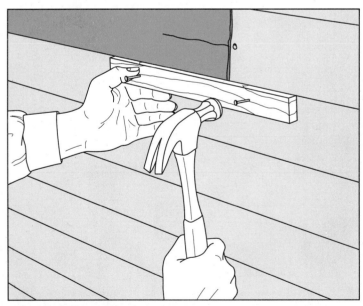

1 **Applying glue.** Prepare to work safely on the siding *(page 24)*. To repair a split board, open the split slightly using a pry bar and fit a small wooden wedge into it to keep the edges apart. Wearing rubber gloves, apply exterior-grade glue *(page 115)* along each edge of the split with a small stick *(above)*. Allow the glue to set according to the manufacturer's instructions and pull out the wedge.

2 **Closing the split.** Hold the split closed until the glue cures. For horizontal lapped siding, keep the edges together by temporarily nailing *(page 121)* a wood block against the bottom of the damaged board *(above)*. For other siding, use the same procedure or bore a pilot hole *(page 121)* and drive in a nail 1/2 inch to each side of the split at a 30-degree angle to it. Wipe off excess glue with a clean, damp cloth. After the glue cures, refinish the damaged siding *(page 90)*.

REPAIRING A HORIZONTAL LAPPED BOARD

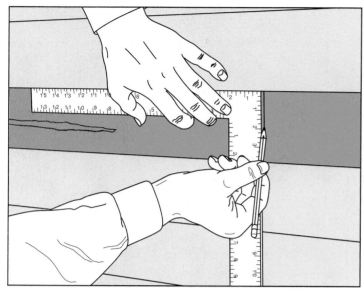

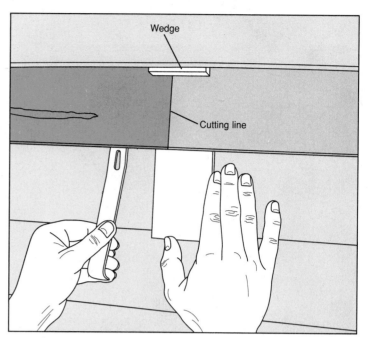

1 **Marking off the damaged section.** Prepare to work safely along the siding *(page 24)*. To repair the board, remove any trim board *(page 100)* and corner cap *(page 95)* or board *(page 101)* necessary to replace the damaged section. Using a carpenter's square and a pencil, mark off each end of the damaged section at the midpoint of the nearest stud or furring strip *(above)*; to locate studs or furring strips, use the nailing or board-end pattern as a guide. If there is no nailing and board-end pattern, the board is nailed onto sheathing and can be marked for cutting at any point along its length.

2 **Wedging the damaged section.** Pull any nails out of the damaged section using a pry bar. To support each end of the damaged section and protect the undamaged boards while cutting, use wooden wedges about 1/4 inch thick. Lift the board one course above the damaged board with the pry bar and fit a wooden wedge under it at the cutting line. Lift the damaged board and fit a wooden wedge under it the same way *(above)*. Temporarily nail *(page 121)* or tape each wedge to keep it in place, if necessary.

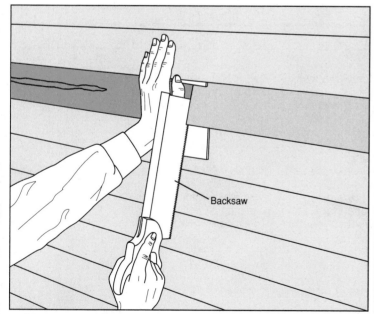

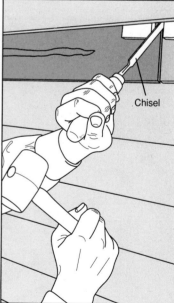

3 **Cutting off the damaged section.** Using a backsaw *(page 118)*, saw off each end of the damaged section along the cutting line as far as possible *(above, left)*; work carefully to avoid damaging the board one course above and below it. Then, shift the top wedge to one side of the cutting line, pull out the bottom wedge and fit it beside the top wedge on the other side of the cutting line. Having a helper support the damaged section, if necessary, use a keyhole saw *(page 119)* to complete the sawcut at each end *(above, center)* or use a chisel and a mallet *(page 120)* to cut off each end *(above, right)*. Remove the wedges and pull out the damaged section; if it is stubborn, use a pry bar to pull any nails holding it out of the board one course above it. Repair any damaged starter strip *(page 95)*, furring strip *(page 100)* and building paper *(page 117)*.

REPAIRING A HORIZONTAL LAPPED BOARD (continued)

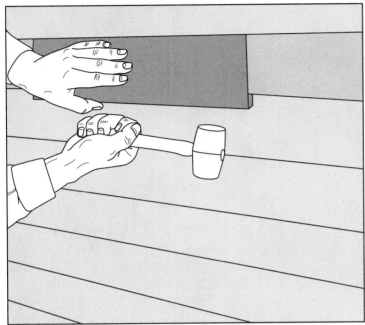

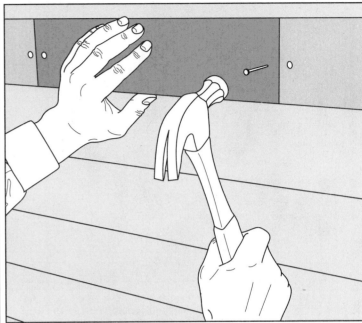

4 **Fitting and installing a replacement section.** Buy a replacement board at a building supply center and cut it *(page 118)* to the length of the opening; if necessary, fit it at an obstruction *(page 101)*. Apply a preservative or finish *(page 124)*, ensuring end grain and cut edges, in particular, are adequately coated. Slide the new board into the opening under the board one course above it; use a mallet to tap it into place *(above, left)*, if necessary. Using the nailing

pattern recommended for the siding *(page 88)* or of the undamaged siding, drive nails *(page 121)* into the new board *(above, right)* and into any unnailed end of a board adjacent to it, as shown. Also replace any nails pulled out of the board one course above the new board. Reinstall any corner cap *(page 95)* or board *(page 101)* and trim board *(page 100)* you removed. Cover the nail heads with wood putty *(page 115)* and refinish the damaged siding *(page 90)*.

REPLACING A HORIZONTAL LAPPED BOARD

Building paper

Starter strip

Removing and installing a horizontal lapped board. Prepare to work safely along the siding *(page 24)*. To replace the damaged board, remove any trim board *(page 100)* and corner cap *(page 95)* or board *(page 101)* necessary to reach its ends. Having a helper support the damaged board, use a pry bar to pull the nails out of it. Then, pull out the damaged board; if it is stubborn, use the pry bar to pull any nails holding it out of the board one course above it. Repair any damaged starter strip *(page 95)*, furring strip *(page 100)* and building paper *(page 117)*.

Buy a replacement board at a building supply center and cut it *(page 118)* to the length of the opening; if necessary, fit it at an obstruction *(page 101)*. Apply a preservative or finish *(page 124)*, ensuring end grain and cut edges, in particular, are adequately coated. Working with a helper, slide the new board into the opening under the board one course above it *(left)*; use a mallet to tap it into place, if necessary. Using the nailing pattern recommended for the siding *(page 88)* or of the undamaged siding, drive nails *(page 121)* into the new board. Also replace any nails pulled out of the board one course above the new board. Reinstall any corner cap *(page 95)* or board *(page 101)* and trim board *(page 100)* you removed. Cover the nail heads with wood putty *(page 115)* and refinish the damaged siding *(page 90)*.

REPLACING A CORNER CAP

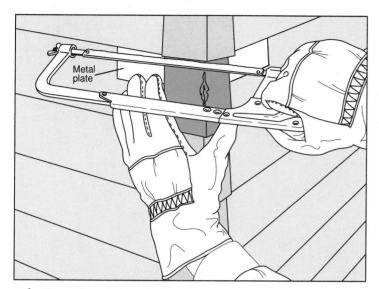

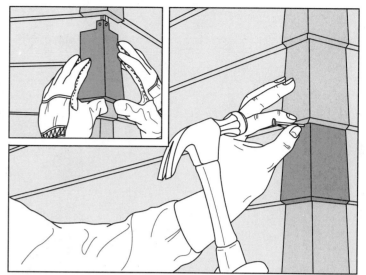

1 **Removing the damaged corner cap.** Prepare to work safely on the siding *(page 24)*. To remove the damaged corner cap, slide a thin metal plate behind the top of it on each side of the corner to protect the siding. Wearing work gloves, use a hacksaw *(page 120)* with a fine-toothed blade to cut off the top of the damaged corner cap just below the corner cap one course above it *(above)*; work carefully to avoid damaging the siding. Then, pull out the damaged corner cap, lifting it off the corner cap one course below it.

2 **Installing a replacement corner cap.** Buy a replacement corner cap 1 inch longer than the opening at a building supply center. Wearing work gloves, slide the new corner cap into the opening under the corner cap one course above it *(inset)*, fitting it onto the board on each side of the corner; trim it to size, if necessary, with tin snips *(page 120)*. Nail *(page 121)* the top of the new corner cap on each side of the corner just below the corner cap one course above it *(above)*, driving each nail until the head just touches it.

REPLACING A STARTER STRIP

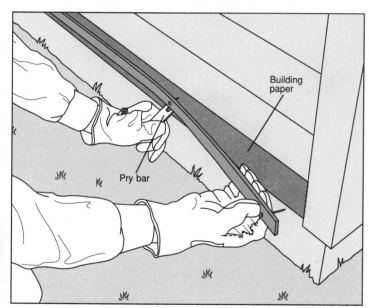

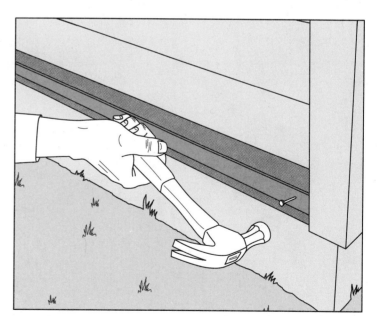

1 **Removing the damaged section.** Remove as many lapped boards as necessary to reach each end of the damaged starter strip *(page 94)*. Wearing work gloves, work from one end to the other end of the damaged starter strip, pulling it off using a pry bar *(above)*. To remove a damaged section, cut off *(page 118)* each end at the midpoint of the nearest stud or furring strip; if the starter strip is nailed onto sheathing, it can be cut at any point along its length. Repair any damaged furring strip *(page 100)* and building paper *(page 117)*.

2 **Installing a replacement section.** Buy a replacement starter strip at a building supply center and cut it *(page 118)* to the length of the opening. Apply a preservative or finish *(page 124)*. Position the new starter strip along the bottom of the opening, aligning it with any starter strip adjacent to it. Drive a nail *(page 121)* into the new starter strip at each stud *(above)* or furring strip, or every 24 inches along the sheathing. Also nail any unnailed end of a starter strip adjacent to it. Reinstall each lapped board you removed *(page 94)*.

REPLACING A VERTICAL BOARD OR BATTEN

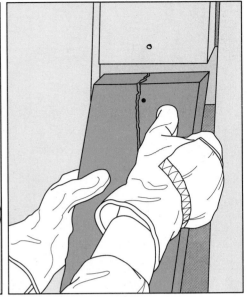

Batten

1 **Removing the damaged board or batten.** Prepare to work safely on the siding *(page 24)*, having a helper on hand. To replace the board or batten on siding of board-and-batten, remove any trim board *(page 100)* necessary to reach each end of it. To remove a batten, wear work gloves and use a pry bar to lift it off *(above, left)*, working from the bottom to the top of it; protect any undamaged board adjacent to it with a wood block, as shown. To remove a board, lift off the batten on each side of it and then lift it off the same way *(above, center)*; pull out the bottom and down on the top of it to clear the beveled edge of any board above it *(above, right)*, if necessary. Use the same procedure on siding of reverse-board-and-batten or board-on-board. Repair any damaged furring strip *(page 100)* and building paper *(page 117)*.

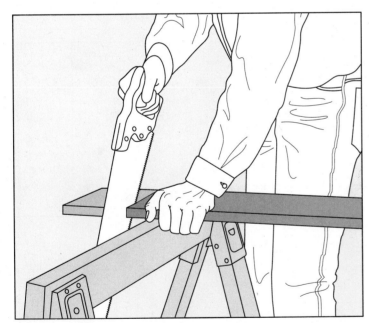

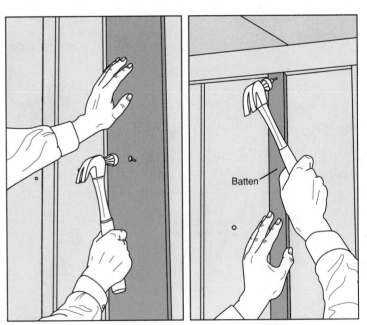

Batten

2 **Marking and cutting a replacement board or batten.** Buy a replacement board and batten at a building supply center. Measure the old board to mark a new board to length. Cut a new board *(page 118)* to length using a crosscut saw *(above)*; bevel the end of it to fit a board above or below it, if necessary, using a circular saw *(page 119)*. Use the same procedure to mark and cut a new batten. Apply a preservative or finish *(page 124)* on a new board and batten, ensuring end grain, in particular, is adequately coated.

3 **Installing the new board or batten.** To install a new board on siding of board-and-batten, center it in the opening, fitting it snugly against any board above and below it. Using the nailing pattern recommended for the siding *(page 88)* or of the undamaged siding, drive nails *(page 121)* into the new board *(above, left)*, working from the top to the bottom of it. Position a batten on each side of the board and nail it the same way *(above, right)*. Use the same procedure on siding of reverse-board-and-batten or board-on-board. Reinstall any trim board *(page 119)*. If necessary, fit the board at an obstruction *(page 101)*. Use the same procedure to mark and cut a new batten. Apply a preservative or finish *(page 124)* on a new board and batten, ensuring end grain, in particular, is adequately coated.

REPAIRING OR REPLACING A HORIZONTAL TONGUE-AND-GROOVE OR SHIPLAP BOARD

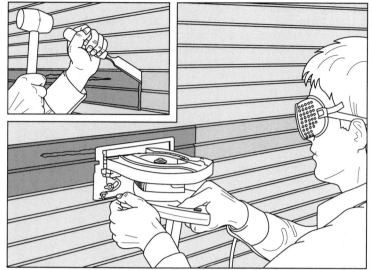

1 **Removing the damaged section or board.** Prepare to work safely along the siding *(page 24)*. To repair a board, replace the damaged section. To replace a damaged section or the entire board, remove any trim board *(page 100)* and corner cap *(page 95)* or board *(page 101)* necessary to reach each end of it. Mark off each end of a damaged section at the midpoint of the nearest stud or furring strip; to locate studs or furring strips, use the nailing or board-end pattern as a guide. If there is no nailing and board-end pattern, the board is nailed onto sheathing and can be marked for cutting at any point along its length. Wearing safety goggles, make a plunge cut along the cutting line at each end of the damaged section using a circular saw *(page 119)*

set to the board thickness—usually 1/2 to 3/4 inch; bore *(page 121)* and chisel *(page 120)* an opening to verify the thickness. Complete the ends of each sawcut with a chisel and a mallet *(inset)*. Then, make a plunge cut at the center of the damaged section and saw along the length of it with the circular saw *(above, left)*; complete the ends of the sawcut with the chisel and mallet. Wearing work gloves, use a pry bar to pull out the top *(above, right)* and then the bottom of the damaged section; use the pry bar also to pull out any nails. Cut along the center of an entire board and pull it out the same way. Repair any damaged furring strip *(page 100)* and building paper *(page 117)*.

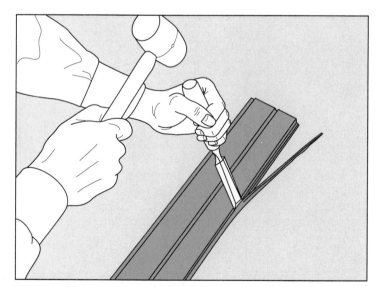

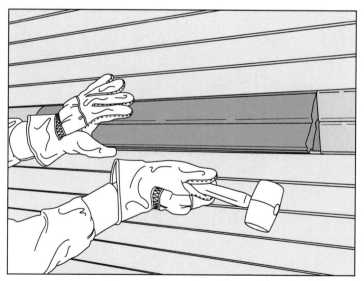

2 **Marking and cutting a replacement board.** Buy a replacement board at a building supply center and cut it *(page 118)* to the length of the opening; if necessary, fit it at an obstruction *(page 101)*. To fit a new tongue-and-groove board, score along the back lip of the groove using a utility knife *(page 120)* and a straight edge; then, wearing safety goggles, cut off the back lip *(above)* with a chisel and a mallet *(page 118)*. Apply a preservative or finish *(page 124)*, ensuring end grain and cut edges, in particular, are adequately coated.

3 **Installing the new board.** Position the new board in the opening; for a tongue-and-groove board, slide its tongue into the groove of the board above it and use a mallet to tap its bottom into place *(above)*. Using the nailing pattern recommended for the siding *(page 88)* or of the undamaged siding *(page 121)* into the new board and any unnailed end of a board adjacent to it; on blind-nailed tongue-and-groove siding, as shown, nail at an angle along the top and bottom, and set each nail head below the surface *(page 122)*. Reinstall any corner cap *(page 95)* or board *(page 101)* and trim board *(page 120)*. Apply a preservative or finish *(page 124)*, ensuring end grain and cut edges, in particular, are adequately coated.

REPLACING A VERTICAL TONGUE-AND-GROOVE OR SHIPLAP BOARD

Removing and installing a board. Prepare to work safely on the siding *(page 24)*, having a helper on hand. To replace the board, remove any trim board *(page 100)* necessary to reach each end of it. Wearing safety goggles, make a plunge cut at the center of the board and saw along the length of it using a circular saw *(page 119)* set to the board thickness—usually 1/2 to 3/4 inch; bore *(page 121)* and chisel *(page 120)* an opening to verify the thickness. Complete the ends of the sawcut with a chisel and a mallet. Wearing work gloves, use a pry bar to pull out each side of the damaged board and any nails. Repair any damaged furring strip *(page 100)* and building paper *(page 117)*.

Buy a replacement board at a building supply center and cut it to the length of the opening; if necessary, fit it at an obstruction *(page 101)*. To fit a new tongue-and-groove board, score along the back lip of the groove using a utility knife *(page 120)* and a straight edge; then, wearing safety goggles, cut off the back lip with the chisel and mallet. Apply a preservative or finish *(page 124)*, ensuring end grain and cut edges, in particular, are adequately coated.

Position the new board in the opening; for a tongue-and-groove board, slide its tongue into the groove of the board beside it and use a mallet to tap its other side into place *(left)*. Using the nailing pattern recommended for the siding *(page 88)* or of the undamaged siding, drive nails *(page 121)* into the new board; on blind-nailed tongue-and-groove siding, as shown, nail at an angle along each side, and set each nail head below the surface *(page 122)*. Reinstall any trim board *(page 100)* you removed. Cover the nail heads with wood putty *(page 115)* and refinish the damaged siding *(page 90)*.

REPAIRING A BLISTERED PLYWOOD PANEL

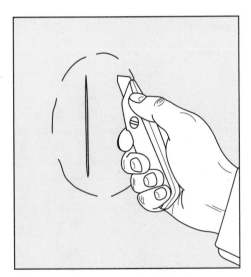

1 Slicing open the blister. Prepare to work safely on the siding *(page 24)*. If the blister is larger than 4 inches square or there is more than one blister, replace the panel *(page 99)*. Otherwise, use a utility knife *(page 120)* to slice through the blister from the top to the bottom of it every 1 to 1 1/2 inches across it *(above)*.

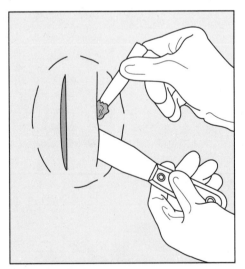

2 Applying glue. If the wood is damp, allow it to dry out for several days. Wearing rubber gloves, gently hold up the top of the blister with a putty knife and apply exterior-grade glue *(page 115)* on the bottom of it and the top of the wood below it with a small stick *(above)*. Allow the glue to set according to the manufacturer's instructions.

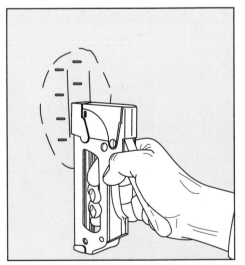

3 Stapling the surface. Wearing rubber gloves, press down on the blister and use a clean, damp cloth to wipe off excess glue. Drive staples about 1 inch apart into the blister with a staple gun *(above)*; wipe off any extruded glue. After the glue cures for about one week, pull out the staples with a staple remover or a pry bar. Fill the holes with wood putty *(page 115)* and refinish the damaged siding *(page 90)*.

REPLACING A PANEL

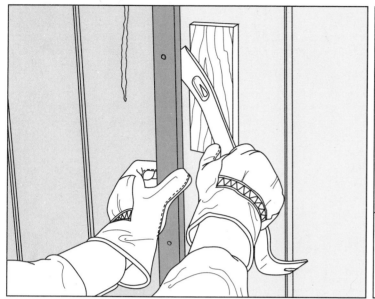

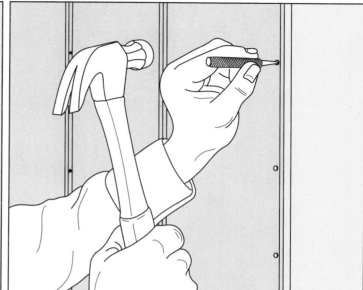

1 **Removing the damaged panel.** Prepare to work safely along the siding *(page 24)*, having a helper on hand. To replace the panel, remove any trim board *(page 100)* and corner board *(page 101)* necessary to reach its edges. To remove a batten, wear work gloves and use a pry bar to lift it off *(above, left)*, working from the bottom to the top of it; protect any undamaged panel adjacent to it with a wood block, as shown. Working from the bottom to the top of the panel, use the pry bar to pull the nails out of it. To reach the nails along any edge of the panel hidden behind an adjacent panel *(page 88)*, pull out the

nails along the edge of it. Drive any stubborn nail through the panel using a nailset and a hammer *(above, right)*. Having your helper steady the panel, carefully pry it out and lower it to the ground. Use self-locking pliers to pull out any broken nails and wood bits around the edges of the opening; if necessary, wedge a wood block under the edge of an adjacent panel to raise it. For nailing a replacement panel, mark the location of each stud or furring strip on any panel above and below the opening and adjacent to it, if necessary. Repair any damaged furring strip *(page 100)* and building paper *(page 117)*.

Z flashing

2 **Fitting and installing a replacement panel.** Buy a replacement panel at a building supply center and cut it *(page 118)* to fit the opening; if necessary, fit it at an obstruction *(page 101)*. Apply a preservative or finish *(page 124)*, ensuring end grain and cut edges, in particular, are adequately coated. If the old panel was installed with sealant, apply sealant *(page 115)* around the edges of the opening. Working with a helper, wear work gloves and position the panel *(above, left)*; if necessary, slide it under the edge of a panel adjacent to it and under the edge of any Z flashing along the bottom of a panel above it *(above, center)*. Using the nailing pattern recommended for the siding *(page 88)* or of the undamaged siding, nail the panel *(page 121)* along each stud or furring strip or onto the sheathing; intervals of 6 to 8 inches and

10 to 12 inches are often specified by the manufacturer. Work from the top to the bottom of the panel, starting along any edge overlapping an adjacent panel and about 1/2 inch from it. To nail along any edge of the panel hidden behind an adjacent panel, raise the edge of it; drive each nail about 3/8 inch from the edge of the panel using a nailset and a hammer, then nail along the edge of the adjacent panel. Finally, nail along the top *(above, right)* and bottom of the panel. If the panel is installed with sealant, ensure the edges are covered. Nail back on any batten and reinstall any corner board *(page 101)* and trim board *(page 100)* you removed. Cover the nail heads with wood putty *(page 115)* and refinish the damaged siding *(page 90)*.

REPAIRING OR REPLACING A FURRING STRIP

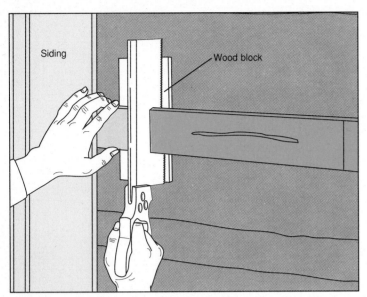

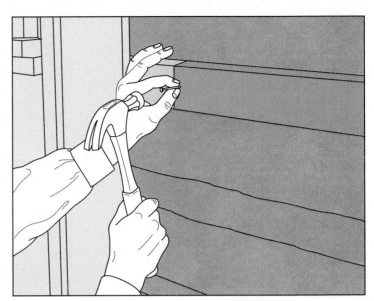

1 **Removing the damaged furring strip.** If the strip is loose, drive extra nails *(page 121)* at each stud or into the sheathing. To repair the strip, mark off each end of the damaged section at the midpoint of the nearest stud. Locate studs using the nailing or board-end pattern as a guide; if there is no pattern, the strip is nailed onto sheathing and can be nailed or cut at any point along its length. Pull any nails out of the damaged section with a pry bar. Using a backsaw *(page 118)*, saw off each end of the damaged section *(above)*; support it using a wood block. Repair any damaged building paper *(page 117)*.

2 **Fitting and installing a replacement furring strip.** Buy a replacement strip of spruce or fir at a building supply center and cut it *(page 118)* to the length of the opening. Apply a preservative or finish *(page 124)*, ensuring end grain, in particular, is adequately coated. Position the new strip in the opening and drive a nail *(page 121)* at each stud *(above)* or every 8 to 10 inches into the sheathing; also nail any unnailed end of a strip adjacent to it.

REPLACING A TRIM BOARD

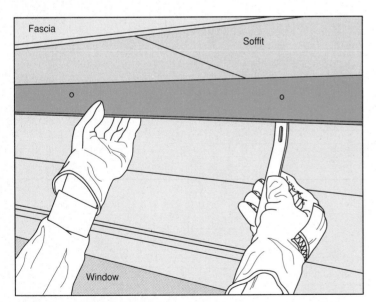

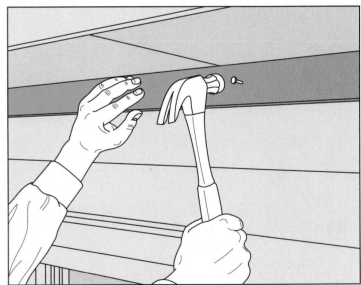

1 **Removing the damaged board.** Prepare to work safely along the siding *(page 24)*. To remove a frieze, wear work gloves and work from one end to the other end along the bottom of it, fitting a pry bar under it at each nail and lifting it off *(above)*; protect any undamaged siding below it with a wood block, if necessary. If the frieze is not damaged, use the pry bar also to pull the nails out of it. For nailing a replacement frieze, mark the location of each stud or furring strip on the siding below the opening, if necessary. Use the same procedure to remove any other trim board.

2 **Fitting and installing a replacement board.** Buy a replacement board at a building supply center and cut it *(page 118)* to fit the opening. Apply a preservative or a finish *(page 124)*, ensuring end grain, in particular, is adequately coated. To install a frieze, position it and drive a nail *(page 121)* at each stud *(above)* or furring strip or every 8 to 10 inches into the sheathing. Use the same procedure to fit and install any other trim board. Cover the nail heads with wood putty *(page 115)* and refinish the damaged siding *(page 90)*. If a board butts the siding without overlapping it, apply sealant *(page 115)* along the joint.

REPLACING A CORNER BOARD

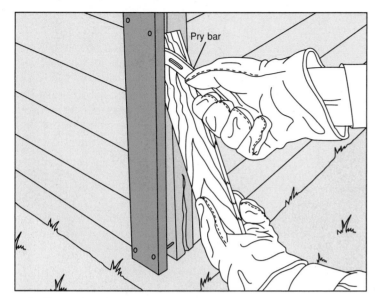

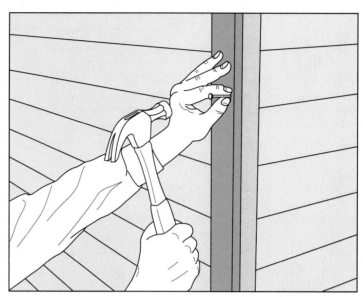

1 **Removing the damaged corner board.** Prepare to work safely on the siding *(page 24)*. If the board is butted against the back of the board on the other side of the corner, as shown, remove the board on the other side of the corner first. To remove a board, wear work gloves and work from the bottom to the top on each side of it, fitting a pry bar under it at each nail and lifting it off *(above)*; protect any undamaged board or siding adjacent to it with a wood block. If the board is not damaged, use the pry bar also to pull the nails out of it.

2 **Fitting and installing a replacement corner board.** Buy a replacement board at a building supply center and cut it *(page 118)* to fit the opening. Apply a preservative or finish *(page 124)*. If the board is to be butted against the side of the board on the other side of the corner, install the board on the other side of the corner first. To install a board, position it and drive nails *(page 121)* every 8 to 10 inches along it *(above)*. Cover the nail heads with wood putty *(page 115)* and refinish the damaged siding *(page 90)*. If a board butts the siding without overlapping it, apply sealant *(page 115)* along the joint.

FITTING SIDING AT AN OBSTRUCTION

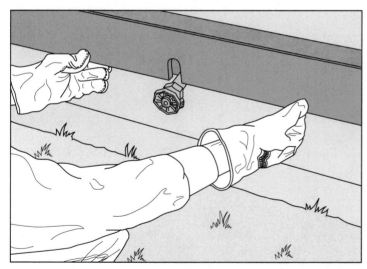

Fitting new siding at a fixture. To fit the siding at a fixture such as a faucet, outlet or vent, use the old siding as a template, if possible; otherwise, measure and mark it *(page 117)* using a compass or by eye for a curve, for example. Cut the siding *(page 118)*, using a keyhole saw or a coping saw on tight or awkward angles and shapes. First, cut the siding slightly larger than the cutting lines, test fit it and, if necessary, adjust the cutting lines; then, cut it to size. Apply a preservative or finish *(page 124)*. Wearing work gloves, slide the siding into position *(above)* and nail it *(page 121)* using the nailing pattern recommended for the siding *(page 88)* or of the undamaged siding. Apply sealant *(page 115)* along the joint around the fixture.

Fitting new siding at a window or door. To fit the siding at a window or door, use the old siding as a template, if possible; otherwise, measure and mark it *(page 117)*, using a carpenter's square or a try square for a 90-degree angle, for example. Cut the siding *(page 118)* slightly larger than the cutting lines, test fit it and, if necessary, adjust the cutting lines; then, cut it to size. Apply a preservative or finish *(page 124)*. Wearing work gloves, slide the siding into position *(above)* and nail it *(page 121)* using the nailing pattern recommended for the siding *(page 88)* or of the undamaged siding. Apply sealant *(page 115)* along the joint around the window or door.

VINYL AND ALUMINUM SIDING

Low cost, good warranties, easy installation and little maintenance make vinyl and aluminum siding tremendously popular for both new-home construction and old-home remodeling. Available in a range of sizes, textures and colors, vinyl or aluminum siding is suitable for most architectural styles of housing. Panels of vinyl or aluminum are installed in horizontal or vertical rows on top of sheathing or old siding and nailed to studs or furring strips. The panels hang on the nails and lock together to form a continuous watertight surface. Accessory pieces are installed at wall, window and door edges to hold the panels. A panel is notched at each end to allow for overlapping and to permit it to expand and contract independently. A typical installation is shown below.

Routine, simple maintenance will keep your vinyl or aluminum siding attractive and sound. Clean off dirt and debris *(page 104)* at least once a year; touch up the finish on aluminum siding *(page 104)* as soon as you notice surface damage. If interior condensation or a leak occurs, consult the Troubleshooting Guide in Your Roofing and Siding *(page 14)* and on page 103. Often, the problem may originate with

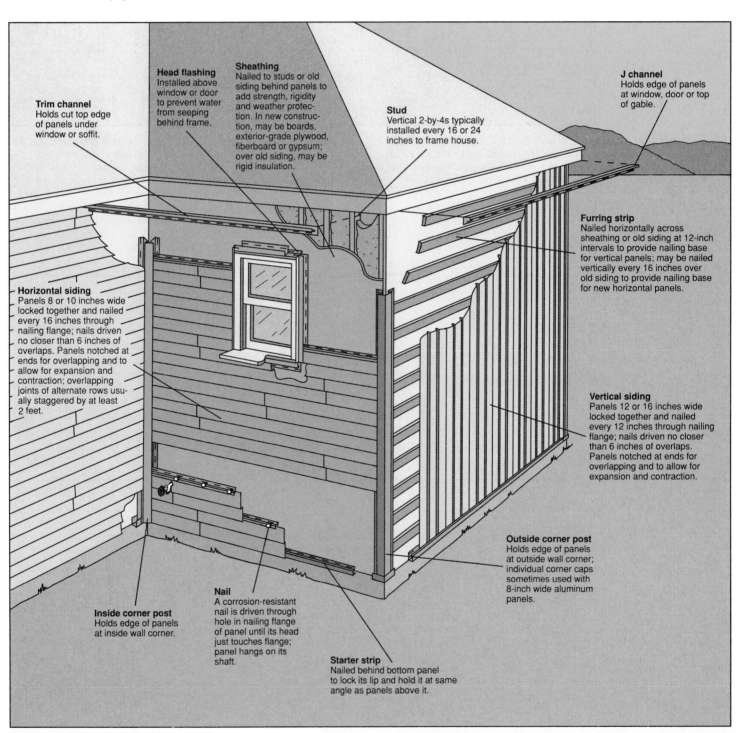

Trim channel
Holds cut top edge of panels under window or soffit.

Head flashing
Installed above window or door to prevent water from seeping behind frame.

Sheathing
Nailed to studs or old siding behind panels to add strength, rigidity and weather protection. In new construction, may be boards, exterior-grade plywood, fiberboard or gypsum; over old siding, may be rigid insulation.

Stud
Vertical 2-by-4s typically installed every 16 or 24 inches to frame house.

J channel
Holds edge of panels at window, door or top of gable.

Horizontal siding
Panels 8 or 10 inches wide locked together and nailed every 16 inches through nailing flange; nails driven no closer than 6 inches of overlaps. Panels notched at ends for overlapping and to allow for expansion and contraction; overlapping joints of alternate rows usually staggered by at least 2 feet.

Furring strip
Nailed horizontally across sheathing or old siding at 12-inch intervals to provide nailing base for vertical panels; may be nailed vertically every 16 inches over old siding to provide nailing base for new horizontal panels.

Vertical siding
Panels 12 or 16 inches wide locked together and nailed every 12 inches through nailing flange; nails driven no closer than 6 inches of overlaps. Panels notched at ends for overlapping and to allow for expansion and contraction.

Inside corner post
Holds edge of panels at inside wall corner.

Nail
A corrosion-resistant nail is driven through hole in nailing flange of panel until its head just touches flange; panel hangs on its shaft.

Starter strip
Nailed behind bottom panel to lock its lip and hold it at same angle as panels above it.

Outside corner post
Holds edge of panels at outside wall corner; individual corner caps sometimes used with 8-inch wide aluminum panels.

gutters and downspouts or the roofing. If you find the siding is damaged and not under warranty, panels are easily replaced. If you cannot locate the source of a leak or if the siding is damaged extensively, call for a professional evaluation.

Working at heights along the siding can be intimidating. Read the chapter on Working Safely at Heights *(page 24)* to properly set up and use any ladders or scaffolding necessary; work with a helper when handling a large panel. Repairs require only basic tools such as a pry bar, a hammer and tin snips; however, to replace a vinyl panel you will need a special unlocking tool for removing it and a snaplock punch for dimpling a replacement that fits into a trim channel. Before removing a damaged panel, buy a replacement; although panels and any accessories needed usually are available at a building supply center, they may have to be ordered from the manufacturer. Bring a small sample or color picture of your siding with you to match its color. Vinyl siding is especially vulnerable to damage in cold weather; undertake repairs to it only on a warm day. Refer to Tools & Techniques *(page 112)* for instructions on using tools and choosing materials.

TROUBLESHOOTING GUIDE

SYMPTOM	POSSIBLE CAUSE	PROCEDURE
Leak through wall or into basement	Roofing, flashing, vent, gutter or downspout damaged or faulty	Troubleshoot and repair roofing and siding system *(p. 16)*
	Siding panel damaged	Replace vinyl siding panel *(p. 105)* ▣◗▲; repair *(p. 107)* ☐○ or replace *(p. 108)* ▣◗ aluminum siding panel
Siding panel buckled, wavy or rippled	Panel faulty or installed incorrectly	Replace vinyl siding panel *(p. 105)* ▣◗▲; repair *(p. 107)* ☐○ or replace *(p. 108)* ▣◗ aluminum siding panel
	Structural damage	Call for professional evaluation
Siding panel dented, gouged, cracked or torn	Weather stress; impact damage	Replace vinyl siding panel *(p. 105)* ▣◗▲; repair *(p. 107)* ☐○ or replace *(p. 108)* ▣◗ aluminum siding panel
Siding panel loose or out of position	High wind; impact damage	Reinstall vinyl siding panel *(p. 106)* ☐○▲ at a trim channel *(p. 107)* ☐○▲ or replace vinyl siding panel *(p. 105)* ▣◗▲; replace aluminum siding panel *(p. 108)* ▣◗
Siding panel punctured	Impact damage	Apply sealant *(p. 115)* ☐○; types color-matched to siding available
Corner post dented, gouged, cracked or torn	Weather stress; impact damage	Repair corner post *(p. 110)* ☐◗
Corner cap dented, gouged or cracked (aluminum)	Weather stress; impact damage	Replace corner cap *(p. 110)* ☐○
Sealant at joint along siding loose or missing	Weather stress; wear	Apply sealant *(p. 115)* ☐○; types color-matched to siding available
Finish dull or faded	Wear; aging	Clean off siding *(p. 104)* ☐○; if siding does not respond to cleaning and over 15 years old, call for professional evaluation
Finish thinning; metal or primer shows (aluminum)	Wear and pollution; aging	Call for professional evaluation
Finish scratched or pitted; dark blistered spots (aluminum)	Impact damage; corrosion due to pollution, salt air	Touch up aluminum siding finish *(p. 104)* ☐○; if damage extensive, call for professional evaluation
Finish blistered or peeling (aluminum)	Panel faulty	Repair *(p. 107)* ☐◗ or replace *(p. 108)* ▣◗ aluminum siding panel; if damage extensive, call for professional evaluation
Siding stained	Flashing or vent rusted; gutter or downspout faulty or rusted	Troubleshoot and repair roofing and siding system *(p. 16)*; clean off siding *(p. 104)* ☐○
	Mildew, especially on shaded or protected exposures	Clean off siding *(p. 104)* ☐○; trim back overhead and adjacent vegetation from shaded or protected exposures
	Condensation behind siding	If stains extensive or recur, call for professional evaluation
Siding dirty	Wear; wind-borne material; pollution	Clean off siding *(p. 104)* ☐○
Chalking; white powdery residue (aluminum)	Natural cleaning action of finish or paint	If not washed off by rain, clean off siding *(p. 104)* ☐○

DEGREE OF DIFFICULTY: ☐ Easy ▣ Moderate ■ Complex
ESTIMATED TIME: ○ Less than 1 hour ◗ 1 to 3 hours ● Over 3 hours
(For ladder and scaffolding set-up, see page 24) ▲ Special tool required

CLEANING OFF DIRT AND DEBRIS

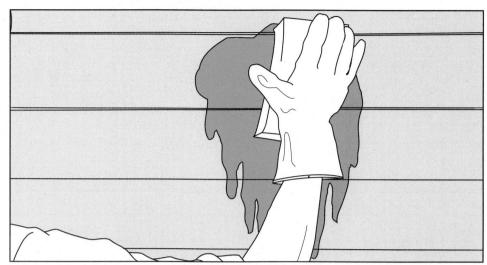

1 **Washing the siding.** Prepare to work safely along the siding *(page 24)*. To clean off dirt and debris, use a garden hose fitted with an automobile brush. Starting at one end of a wall, work from foundation to soffit in successive 5-foot wide sections, scrubbing the surface with the brush *(above)*; apply only moderate pressure and avoid spraying water under panel edges. After washing the siding, remove any stubborn dirt and stains *(step 2)*.

2 **Removing stubborn dirt and stains.** Cover nearby vegetation with plastic sheeting. Wearing rubber gloves, safety goggles and long sleeves, mix as many gallons of cleaner as needed in a plastic bucket. For stubborn dirt, mix 1/3 cup of household detergent per 4 quarts of water and scrub gently with a soft cloth or sponge *(above)*; to avoid streaks, work from bottom to top and rinse thoroughly immediately after scrubbing. For mildew, use the same procedure, mixing 1/3 cup of household detergent and 1/3 cup of trisodium phosphate (TSP) per 1 quart of 5% household bleach and 3 quarts of water. For a rust stain, try the cleaners listed above. For a stubborn stain, contact the siding manufacturer for recommendations on using other cleaners that will not harm the siding finish.

TOUCHING UP ALUMINUM SIDING FINISH

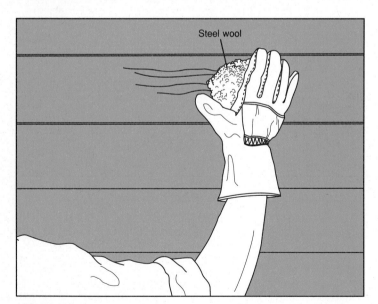

Steel wool

1 **Preparing the surface.** Prepare to work safely along the siding *(page 24)*; work only on a dry, warm day and out of direct sunlight to touch up surface damage such as scratches and corrosion blister spots. Wearing work gloves and safety goggles, remove rough spots and smooth the surface using very fine, grade 2/0 steel wool *(above)*. Then, clean dirt and debris off the surface *(steps above)* and allow it to dry completely.

2 **Applying paint.** Choose a paint *(page 124)* that matches the siding as closely as possible in color and follow the manufacturer's instructions for applying it; a primer may be required. Use plastic sheeting to protect nearby vegetation and surfaces not to be coated. Wearing rubber gloves, use a paintbrush *(page 124)* or paint sprayer *(page 125)* to apply the primer and paint. Apply the primer on any bare metal, allow it to dry and then apply the paint *(above)*; if necessary, apply a second coat of paint after the first coat dries.

REPLACING A VINYL SIDING PANEL

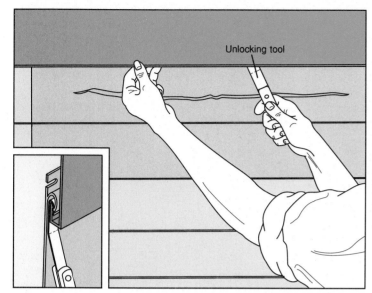

1 **Unlocking a panel.** Prepare to work safely along the siding *(page 24)*, having a helper on hand. Using a special unlocking tool available at a building supply center, unlock the panel overlapping the damaged panel; unlock the damaged panel if there is no panel overlapping it. Starting at one end of the panel, slip the tip of the unlocking tool behind it, hooking onto its lip *(inset)*, and pull firmly. Slowly work along the panel the same way, lifting out its lip *(above)*. Remove the damaged panel by pulling out its nails *(step 2)* or by freeing it from the trim channel *(page 106)*.

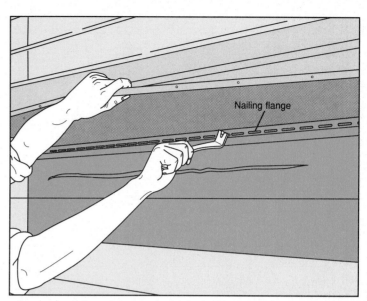

2 **Removing the damaged panel.** Working from one end to the other end of the damaged panel, lift out the lip of the panel overlapping it and use a pry bar to pull out its nails *(above)*. With you and your helper at opposite ends of the damaged panel, push on its nailing flange to unlock it from the panel or starter strip it overlaps; if necessary, unlock it using the unlocking tool *(step 1)*. Slide out the damaged panel, prying it free of the overlapping adjacent panel, J channel or corner post. Replace any damaged furring strip *(page 100)* and starter strip *(page 109)*. Repair any damaged building paper *(page 117)*.

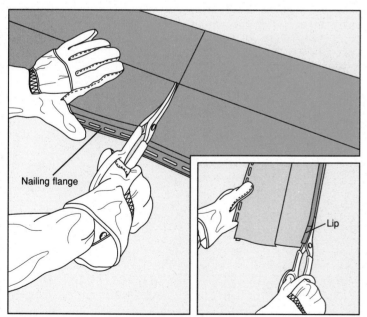

3 **Fitting a replacement panel.** Buy a replacement panel at a building supply center. Using the old panel as a template, measure and mark the new panel to size *(page 117)*; mark cutting lines along the edge to be overlapped by an adjacent panel, J channel or corner post. Wearing work gloves, use tin snips *(page 120)* to cut the new panel to size *(above)* and use a utility knife *(page 120)* to smooth the cut edges. Measure any notches in the nailing flange and lip of the old panel and use the tin snips to cut identical notches in the new panel *(inset)*. If necessary, fit the new panel at an obstruction *(page 111)*.

4 **Positioning the replacement panel.** Working with your helper, slide the new panel into place. First, fit into place the edge of the new panel overlapped by an adjacent panel *(above)*, J channel or corner post. Then, position the nailing flange of the new panel, lifting out the lip of the panel overlapping it. Finally, with you and your helper at opposite ends of the new panel, push on its lip to lock it onto the panel or starter strip it overlaps, setting its nailing flange in place under the panel overlapping it.

REPLACING A VINYL SIDING PANEL (continued)

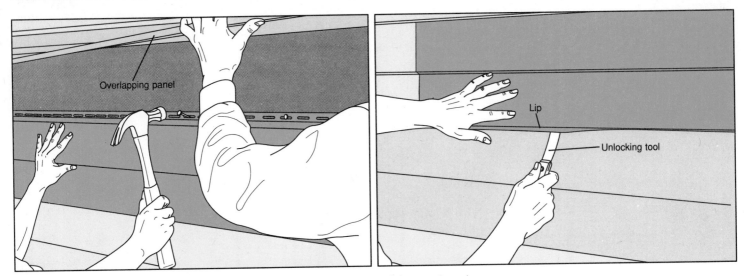

Overlapping panel

Lip

Unlocking tool

5 **Installing the replacement panel.** With your helper lifting out the lip of the panel overlapping the new panel, drive nails *(page 121)* into the nailing flange of the new panel *(above, left)*; drive each nail through the center of a hole until its head just touches the flange. On a horizontal panel, start 6 inches from the overlapped end of the panel and nail every 16 inches along it; on a vertical panel, start at the top and nail every 12 inches along it. Do not nail within 6 inches of an overlapping adjacent panel, J channel or corner post. To lock the panel overlapping the new panel, use the unlocking tool. Starting at one end of the panel overlapping the new panel, slip the tip of the unlocking tool behind it, hooking onto its lip, and pull firmly, snapping it onto the new panel. Slowly work along the panel overlapping the new panel the same way *(above, right)*, locking it in place.

REPLACING A VINYL SIDING PANEL AT A TRIM CHANNEL

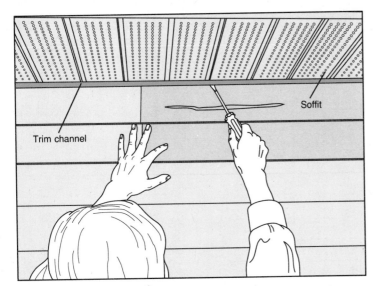

Soffit

Trim channel

Trim channel

1 **Removing the damaged panel.** Prepare to work safely along the siding *(page 24)*, having a helper on hand. Unlock the damaged panel from the panel it overlaps *(page 105)*; also unlock any panel overlapping a section of the damaged panel and pull out its nails. To remove the damaged panel from the trim channel, work from one end to the other end of it, using an old flat-tipped screwdriver to pry it out *(above)*; have your helper support one end, if necessary. Replace any damaged furring strip *(page 100)* and repair any damaged building paper *(page 117)*. If the trim channel is damaged, replace it *(step 2)*. Otherwise, install a new panel *(step 3)*.

2 **Replacing the trim channel.** To remove the trim channel, use a pry bar to pull out its nails; if necessary, cut off a damaged section of trim channel wearing work gloves and using tin snips or a utility knife *(page 120)*. Buy a replacement trim channel at a building supply center and cut it to length, if necessary, allowing for a gap of 1/4 to 1/2 inch between it and any trim channel adjacent to it. Position the new trim channel *(above)* and drive a nail *(page 121)* through its nailing flange every 8 to 10 inches along it, having your helper support it in place, if necessary. Drive each nail until its head just touches the flange.

REPLACING A VINYL SIDING PANEL AT A TRIM CHANNEL (continued)

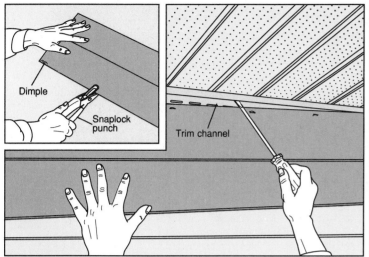

3 **Fitting and installing a replacement panel.** Buy a replacement panel at a building supply center; to fit it into the trim channel, also buy a snaplock punch. Using the old panel as a template, measure and mark the new panel to size *(page 117)*; mark cutting lines along the edge to be overlapped by an adjacent panel, J channel or corner post. Wearing work gloves, use tin snips *(page 120)* to cut the new panel to size and use a utility knife *(page 120)* to smooth the cut edges. Measure any notches in the nailing flange and lip of the old panel and use the tin snips to cut identical notches in the new panel. If necessary, fit the new panel at an obstruction *(page 111)*. Using the snaplock punch, dimple the new panel every 16 inches along the edge to be fitted into the trim channel *(inset)*; ensure the raised surface of

each dimple is on the front of the panel. Working with your helper, slide the new panel into place. First, fit into place the edge of the new panel overlapped by an adjacent panel, J channel or corner post and snap the dimpled edge into the trim channel; if necessary, pry out the trim channel using an old flat-tipped screwdriver *(above, left)*. To lock the new panel onto the panel it overlaps, use the unlocking tool. Starting at one end of the new panel, slip the tip of the unlocking tool behind it, hooking onto its lip, and pull firmly, snapping it onto the panel it overlaps. Slowly work along the new panel the same way *(above, right)*, locking it in place. Nail any section of the new panel overlapped by a panel and lock the panel overlapping it as you would to install another panel *(page 106)*.

REPAIRING AN ALUMINUM SIDING PANEL

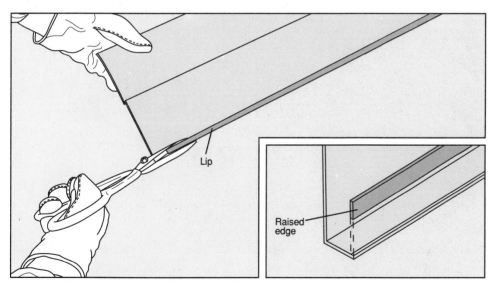

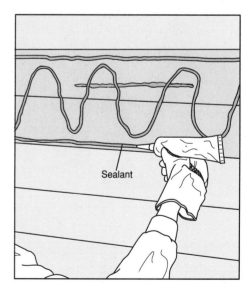

1 **Preparing a patch.** Prepare to work safely along the siding *(page 24)*. If the panel is damaged extensively, replace it *(page 108)*; otherwise, patch it. Buy a matching panel for a patch and rivets of the same color at a building supply center. Measure the length and exposed width of the damaged panel and mark the patch to size; mark off excess width along the edge with the nailing flange. Wearing work gloves, cut the patch to length with tin snips *(page 120)*; to cut it to width, use a utility knife *(page 120)* to score repeatedly and heavily along the cutting line, then bend it back and forth along the scored line to snap off the excess. Use the tin snips to cut the raised edge off the lip of the patch *(above)*, leaving the other edge *(inset)*. If necessary, fit the patch at an obstruction *(page 111)*.

2 **Applying sealant.** If necessary, use a mallet to flatten any protruding section of the damaged panel; wash it off with water and a soft cloth or sponge and let it dry. Wearing work gloves, apply sealant *(page 115)* along the length of the damaged panel, working first back and forth across it and then along its edges *(above)*.

REPAIRING AN ALUMINUM SIDING PANEL (continued)

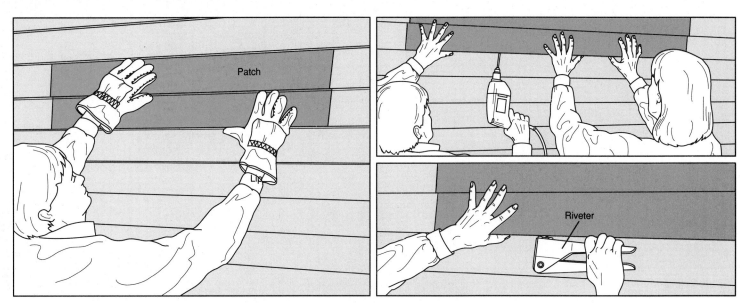

3 **Installing the patch.** Wearing work gloves, position the patch on top of the damaged panel and press it down firmly to bond it to the sealant *(above, left)*; to fit it snugly, hold a wood block against its lip and tap with a mallet, if necessary. Having a helper support the patch in place, drill *(page 121)* a hole for a rivet every 24 inches along its lip *(above right, top)*; use a bit equal in diameter to a rivet. Using a riveter *(page 122)*, install a rivet in each hole *(above right, bottom)*. Use the same procedure to drill holes and install rivets along the edge of the patch opposite the lip. If necessary, also drill a hole and install a rivet in the center at each end of the patch to flatten it. Using a soft cloth, wipe off any extruded sealant.

REPLACING AN ALUMINUM SIDING PANEL

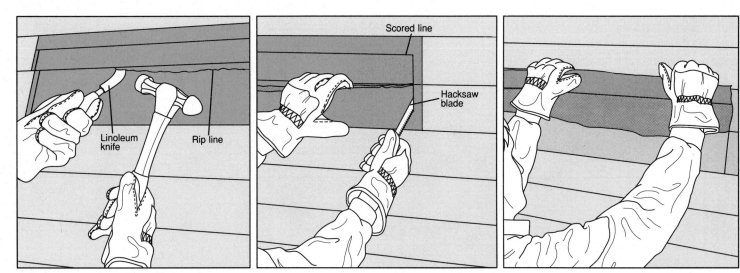

1 **Removing the damaged panel.** Prepare to work safely along the siding *(page 24)*, having a helper on hand. If the panel is not damaged extensively, patch it *(page 107)*; otherwise, replace it. To remove the damaged panel, mark a cutting line across its width 1 inch from each end and along its length 2 1/2 inches from the panel, trim channel, J channel or corner post overlapping it. Wearing work gloves, use a utility knife *(page 120)* to score repeatedly and heavily along each cutting line. Drill *(page 121)* a hole at the center of the panel and fit the tip of a linoleum knife into it. Using a ball-peen hammer to hit the blade of the knife, rip the panel along its length to the scored line across its width at each end *(above, left)*. Then, cut along each scored line across the width of the panel using a fine-toothed hacksaw blade *(above, center)*. To remove the ripped half of the panel overlapped by a panel, trim channel, J channel or corner post, lift out its edge *(above, right)* and bend it back and forth along the scored line to snap it off; have your helper support one end, if necessary. To remove the other ripped half of the panel, push on it to unlock it from the panel or starter strip it overlaps. Replace any damaged furring strip *(page 100)* and starter strip *(page 109)*. Repair any damaged building paper *(page 117)*.

REPLACING AN ALUMINUM SIDING PANEL (continued)

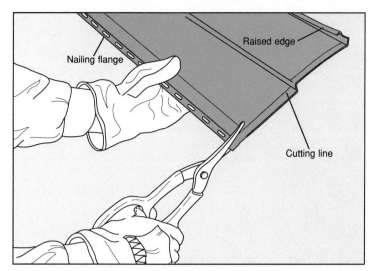

2 **Fitting a replacement panel.** Buy a replacement panel and rivets of the same color at a building supply center. Mark the new panel to size, 2 inches longer than the opening and 2 1/2 inches wider than it; mark off excess width along the edge of the new panel with the nailing flange. Wearing work gloves, cut the new panel to length *(above)* with tin snips *(page 120)*; to cut it to width, use a utility knife *(page 120)* to score repeatedly and heavily along the cutting line, then bend it back and forth along the scored line to snap off the excess. If the lip of the new panel is not notched 1 inch at each end, use the tin snips to cut 1 inch off the raised edge of it. If necessary, fit the new panel at an obstruction *(page 111)*. Wash off the remaining damaged panel with water and a soft cloth or sponge and let it dry.

3 **Installing the replacement panel.** Wearing rubber gloves, apply sealant *(page 115)* along the length of the remaining damaged panel. Working with a helper, wear work gloves and position the new panel *(above)*, ensuring an overlap of 1 inch at each end. Press firmly on the new panel to lock it onto the panel or starter strip it overlaps and bond it to the sealant; to fit it snugly, hold a wood block against its lip and tap with a mallet, if necessary. Drill *(page 121)* a hole for a rivet every 16 inches along the edge of the panel overlapped by a panel, trim channel, J channel or corner post; use a bit equal in diameter to a rivet. Using a riveter *(page 122)*, install a rivet in each hole *(inset)*. If necessary, also drill a hole and install a rivet in the center at each end of the new panel to flatten it. Using a soft cloth, wipe off any extruded sealant.

REPLACING A STARTER STRIP

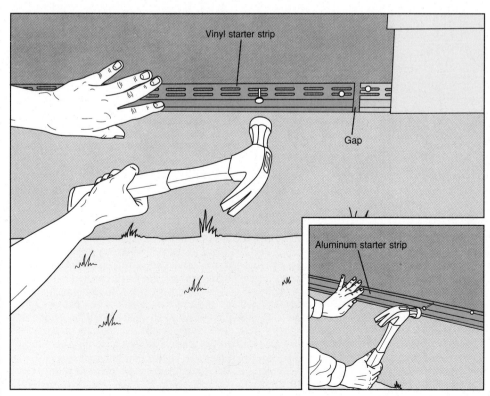

Removing and installing a starter strip.
To remove a damaged section of starter strip, pull out its nails using a pry bar. Wearing work gloves, cut off each end of the damaged section using tin snips *(page 120)* or a utility knife *(page 120)*. Buy a replacement starter strip at a building supply center and use the tin snips to cut it to fit the opening; if the starter strip is vinyl, allow for a gap of 1/4 to 1/2 inch at each end. Position the new starter strip and drive a nail *(page 121)* every 8 to 10 inches along it into the nailing flange; also nail any unnailed end of a starter strip adjacent to it. If the starter strip is vinyl, drive each nail through the center of a hole *(left)* until its head just touches the flange; if the starter strip is aluminum, drive each nail through the top of the flange *(inset)*. Fit and install the vinyl *(page 105)* or aluminum *(steps above)* panel overlapping the starter strip.

REPAIRING A CORNER POST

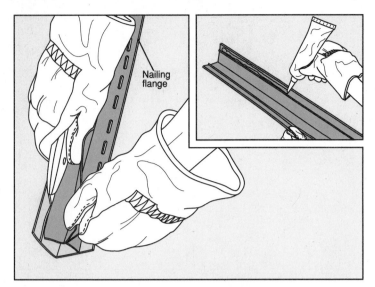

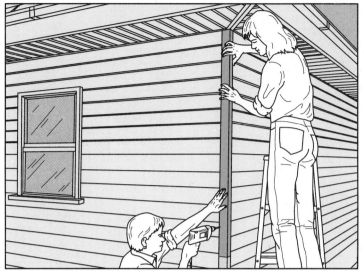

1 **Preparing a patch.** Prepare to work safely on the siding *(page 24)*. If the corner post is damaged extensively, call for a professional evaluation; otherwise, patch it. Buy a matching corner post for a patch and rivets of the same color at a building supply center. Wearing work gloves, use a hacksaw *(page 120)* with a fine-toothed blade to cut the patch equal in length to the damaged corner post. Using a utility knife *(page 120)*, cut each nailing flange off the patch, scoring heavily and repeatedly along it *(above);* if the patch is aluminum, bend it back and forth along the scored line to snap off the excess. Apply sealant *(page 115)* on the back of the patch along its edges *(inset)*.

2 **Installing the patch.** If necessary, use a mallet to flatten any protruding section of the damaged corner post; wash it off with water and a soft cloth or sponge and let it dry. Wearing work gloves, position the patch on top of the damaged corner post and press it down firmly. Having a helper support the patch in place, drill *(page 121)* a hole for a rivet every 24 inches along each edge of it *(above);* use a bit equal in diameter to a rivet. Using a riveter *(page 122)*, install a rivet in each hole. If necessary, also drill a hole and install a rivet in the center at each end of the patch to flatten it. Using a soft cloth, wipe off any extruded sealant.

REPLACING AN ALUMINUM CORNER CAP

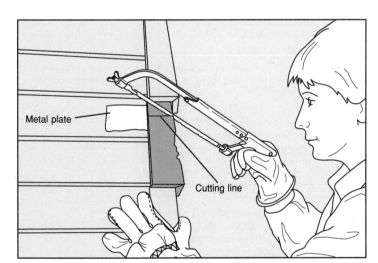

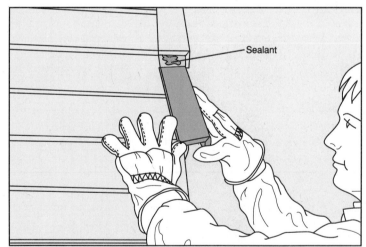

1 **Removing the damaged corner cap.** Prepare to work safely on the siding *(page 24)*. To remove the damaged corner cap, slide a thin metal plate behind the top of it on each side of the corner to protect the siding. Using a carpenter's square *(page 117)*, mark a cutting line across each side of the damaged corner cap, 2 1/2 inches below the corner cap above it. Wearing work gloves, use a hacksaw *(page 120)* with a fine-toothed blade to cut through the damaged corner cap along the cutting line *(above);* work carefully to avoid damaging the siding. Pull out the damaged corner cap, working it off the corner cap below it. Use a mallet to flatten any protruding section of the remaining damaged corner post; trim any ragged edges with tin snips *(page 120)*.

2 **Installing a replacement corner cap.** Buy a replacement corner cap and rivets of the same color at a building supply center. Wearing work gloves, use tin snips *(page 120)* to cut the new corner cap 1 inch longer than the opening; cut the excess off the top of it. Wearing rubber gloves, apply sealant *(page 115)* along each edge of the remaining damaged corner cap. Then, slide the new corner cap into place *(above)*, fitting it onto the panel on each side of the corner; to fit it snugly, hold a wood block against its lip and tap with a mallet, if necessary. Drill *(page 121)* a hole for a rivet at the top on each side of the new corner cap; use a bit equal in diameter to a rivet. Using a riveter *(page 122)*, install a rivet in each hole. Wipe off any extruded sealant with a soft cloth.

FITTING SIDING AT AN OBSTRUCTION

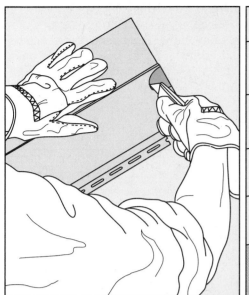

Fitting a panel at a fixture. To fit the panel at a fixture such as a faucet, outlet or vent, use the old panel as a template, if possible; otherwise, measure and mark it *(page 117)* using a compass or by eye for a curve, for example. Cut the panel *(page 118)*, using a utility knife *(above, left)* or tin snips for tight or awkward angles and shapes. First, cut the panel slightly larger than the cutting lines, test fit it and, if necessary, adjust the cutting lines; then, cut it to size. Slide the panel into position *(above, center)*, installing it as you would to fit and install another vinyl panel *(page 105)* at a trim channel *(page 107)* or an aluminum patch *(page 108)* or panel *(page 109)*. Apply sealant *(page 115)* along the joint around the fixture, using a caulking gun *(above, right)*.

Fitting a panel at a window or door. To fit the panel at a window or door, use the old siding as a template, if possible; otherwise, measure and mark it *(page 117)*, holding the new panel at the window or door and marking it by eye *(above, left)* or using a carpenter's square or a try square to measure and transfer a 90-degree angle, for example. Cut the panel *(page 118)*, using a utility knife or tin snips for tight or awkward angles and shapes. First, cut the siding slightly larger than the cutting lines, test fit it and, if necessary, adjust the cutting lines; then, cut it to size. Working with a helper, if necessary, slide the panel into position *(above, right)*, installing it as you would to fit and install another vinyl panel *(page 105)* at a trim channel *(page 107)* or an aluminum patch *(page 108)* or panel *(page 109)*. Apply sealant *(page 115)* along the joint around the window or door.

TOOLS & TECHNIQUES

This section introduces tools and techniques used in repairing roofing and siding, such as applying sealants and adhesives *(page 115)*, patching rotted wood *(page 116)* and damaged building paper *(page 117)*, installing fasteners *(page 121)* and applying finishes *(page 124)*. Charts on sealants and adhesives, fasteners and finishes are designed for easy reference. For instructions on setting up and using ladders and scaffolding, refer to Working Safely at Heights *(page 24)*.

Most roofing and siding repairs require only the basic kit of tools and supplies shown below. Special equipment, such as a pump-up sprayer, a pressure washer or a paint sprayer, can be obtained at a tool rental agency. For the best results, always use the right tool for the job—and be sure to use the tool correctly. When shopping for new tools, purchase the highest-quality ones you can afford. You can purchase most tools and supplies at a building supply center; however, in

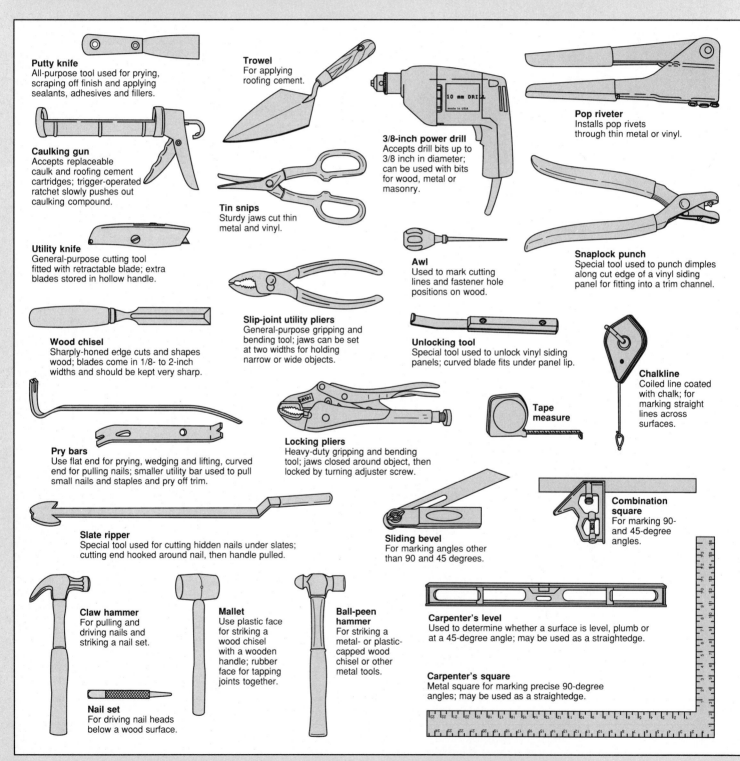

Putty knife
All-purpose tool used for prying, scraping off finish and applying sealants, adhesives and fillers.

Caulking gun
Accepts replaceable caulk and roofing cement cartridges; trigger-operated ratchet slowly pushes out caulking compound.

Utility knife
General-purpose cutting tool fitted with retractable blade; extra blades stored in hollow handle.

Wood chisel
Sharply-honed edge cuts and shapes wood; blades come in 1/8- to 2-inch widths and should be kept very sharp.

Pry bars
Use flat end for prying, wedging and lifting, curved end for pulling nails; smaller utility bar used to pull small nails and staples and pry off trim.

Slate ripper
Special tool used for cutting hidden nails under slates; cutting end hooked around nail, then handle pulled.

Claw hammer
For pulling and driving nails and striking a nail set.

Nail set
For driving nail heads below a wood surface.

Trowel
For applying roofing cement.

Tin snips
Sturdy jaws cut thin metal and vinyl.

Slip-joint utility pliers
General-purpose gripping and bending tool; jaws can be set at two widths for holding narrow or wide objects.

Locking pliers
Heavy-duty gripping and bending tool; jaws closed around object, then locked by turning adjuster screw.

Mallet
Use plastic face for striking a wood chisel with a wooden handle; rubber face for tapping joints together.

Ball-peen hammer
For striking a metal- or plastic-capped wood chisel or other metal tools.

3/8-inch power drill
Accepts drill bits up to 3/8 inch in diameter; can be used with bits for wood, metal or masonry.

Awl
Used to mark cutting lines and fastener hole positions on wood.

Unlocking tool
Special tool used to unlock vinyl siding panels; curved blade fits under panel lip.

Sliding bevel
For marking angles other than 90 and 45 degrees.

Carpenter's level
Used to determine whether a surface is level, plumb or at a 45-degree angle; may be used as a straightedge.

Carpenter's square
Metal square for marking precise 90-degree angles; may be used as a straightedge.

Pop riveter
Installs pop rivets through thin metal or vinyl.

Snaplock punch
Special tool used to punch dimples along cut edge of a vinyl siding panel for fitting into a trim channel.

Tape measure

Chalkline
Coiled line coated with chalk; for marking straight lines across surfaces.

Combination square
For marking 90- and 45-degree angles.

some instances, materials such as panels of vinyl or aluminum, tiles of clay or concrete and slates may be available only through a specialized dealer or the manufacturer.

Take the time to care for your tools properly. Avoid laying tools on the ground unprotected. Clean, sharpen and lubricate tools according to the manufacturer's instructions. Store tools on a shelf safely away from children, in a locked metal or plastic tool box, or hang them well out of reach.

Read and follow the safety information in the Emergency Guide (page 8). Wear the proper clothing and protective gear for the job. Set up a temporary barrier to keep others away from the work area. Exercise caution when using cleaning and refinishing products. Follow precautions when working outdoors with power tools (page 114). If you are ever in doubt about your ability to complete a repair, do not hesitate to consult a professional.

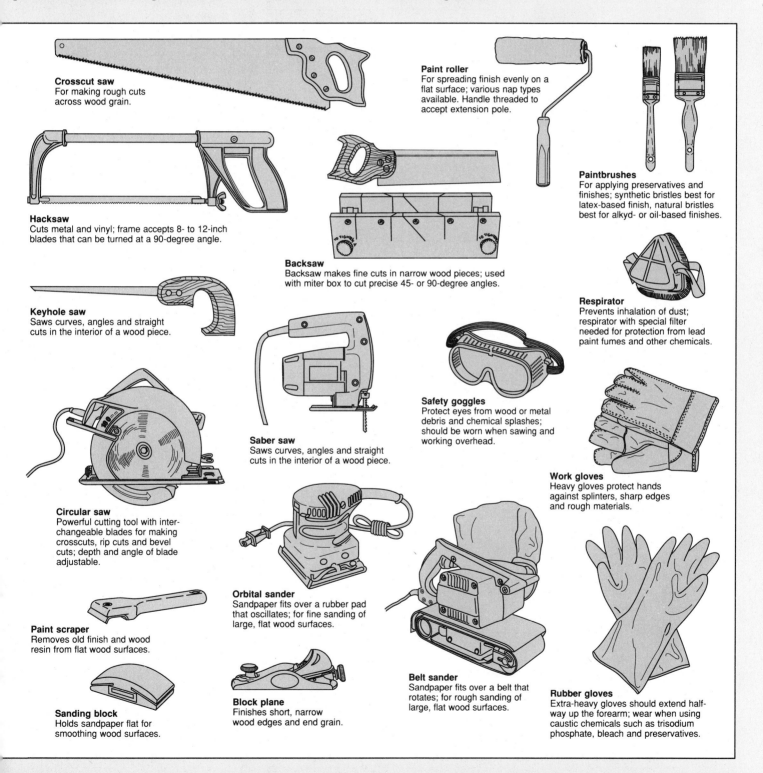

Crosscut saw
For making rough cuts across wood grain.

Hacksaw
Cuts metal and vinyl; frame accepts 8- to 12-inch blades that can be turned at a 90-degree angle.

Keyhole saw
Saws curves, angles and straight cuts in the interior of a wood piece.

Circular saw
Powerful cutting tool with interchangeable blades for making crosscuts, rip cuts and bevel cuts; depth and angle of blade adjustable.

Paint scraper
Removes old finish and wood resin from flat wood surfaces.

Sanding block
Holds sandpaper flat for smoothing wood surfaces.

Backsaw
Backsaw makes fine cuts in narrow wood pieces; used with miter box to cut precise 45- or 90-degree angles.

Saber saw
Saws curves, angles and straight cuts in the interior of a wood piece.

Orbital sander
Sandpaper fits over a rubber pad that oscillates; for fine sanding of large, flat wood surfaces.

Block plane
Finishes short, narrow wood edges and end grain.

Belt sander
Sandpaper fits over a belt that rotates; for rough sanding of large, flat wood surfaces.

Paint roller
For spreading finish evenly on a flat surface; various nap types available. Handle threaded to accept extension pole.

Paintbrushes
For applying preservatives and finishes; synthetic bristles best for latex-based finish, natural bristles best for alkyd- or oil-based finishes.

Respirator
Prevents inhalation of dust; respirator with special filter needed for protection from lead paint fumes and other chemicals.

Safety goggles
Protect eyes from wood or metal debris and chemical splashes; should be worn when sawing and working overhead.

Work gloves
Heavy gloves protect hands against splinters, sharp edges and rough materials.

Rubber gloves
Extra-heavy gloves should extend halfway up the forearm; wear when using caustic chemicals such as trisodium phosphate, bleach and preservatives.

USING POWER TOOLS OUTDOORS

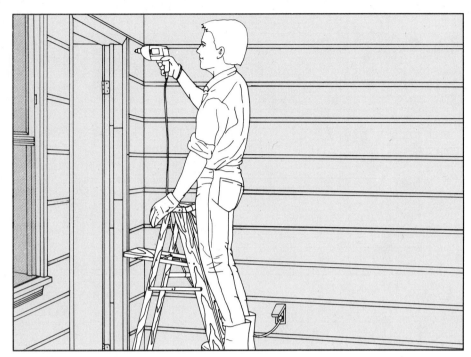

Working safely with electricity. Keep power tools dry; never use them outdoors in wet conditions. Before using a power tool, examine its power cord and any extension cord for signs of wear; if it is frayed or cracked, replace it with a new cord labeled for outdoor use. To prevent electrical shock, power tools should have a three-prong plug or be double insulated—with a plastic housing that isolates metal parts from contact with your hand. Plug power tools into grounded outlets only, and never cut off or bypass the third, or grounding, prong on a plug. Lay out power and extension cords carefully, untangling knots; keep them clear of ladder feet and scaffolding end frames.

Most electrical codes now require that new outdoor outlets be protected by a GFCI (ground-fault circuit interrupter). When working outdoors with a power tool, make sure its extension cord or the outlet is protected. As an added precaution, wear heavy rubber gloves when using power tools; stand on a board or rubber mat on the ground, or use a wooden ladder at heights *(left)*.

USING A PUMP-UP SPRAYER

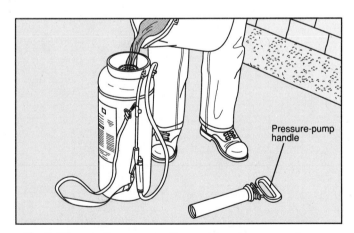

Pressure-pump handle

1 **Setting up the sprayer.** For applying cleaner on a large area of roofing or siding, use a pump-up sprayer, available at a tool rental agency or garden supply center. Wearing rubber gloves, safety goggles, and long sleeves, follow the manufacturer's instructions to remove the pressure-pump handle and mix the cleaner. If you are mixing dry ingredients with water, combine them first in a plastic bucket and then pour the solution into the canister *(above)*. To mix liquid ingredients, fill the canister with the water first and then add them. Close the canister tightly and shake it. To pressurize the canister, vigorously pump the pressure-pump handle. To apply the cleaner, aim the spray wand and squeeze the trigger.

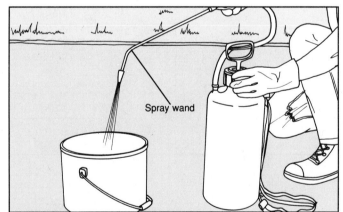

Spray wand

2 **Cleaning the pump-up sprayer.** To clean the pump-up sprayer, follow the manufacturer's instructions for releasing the pressure and remove the pressure-pump handle. Empty leftover cleaner into a sealable plastic container. Rinse the canister with water and empty it into a plastic bucket. Add more water to the canister, close it and pressurize it; then, pump the water into the bucket *(above)*. If the canister contained oxalic acid, follow the same procedure, washing it out first with a mixture of soapy water, and spraying until the water runs free of soap. When the sprayer is dry, follow the manufacturer's instructions to lubricate moving parts and seals, if necessary.

USING A PRESSURE WASHER

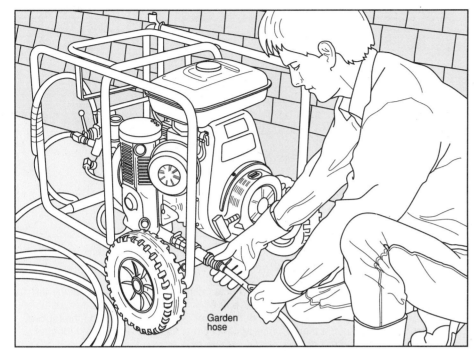

Garden hose

Pressure-washing wood roofing or siding.
To clean embedded dirt off wood roofing or siding, rent a gas-powered pressure washer rated 1000 to 1500 pounds per square inch (psi) at a tool rental center. If you are cleaning the siding, tape plastic sheeting over light fixtures, electrical outlets and vents, close windows and doors, and cover nearby vegetation. Following the manufacturer's instructions, connect a garden hose to the pressure washer's intake *(left)* and snap a small nozzle onto the end of its spray wand.

Wearing rubber gloves, safety goggles and rain gear, open the faucet. With the pressure washer turned off, point the spray wand at the ground and squeeze the trigger; when a steady stream of water flows, release it. Following the manufacturer's instructions, turn on the pressure washer. To clean, aim the spray wand at the surface, holding the nozzle about 18 inches from it, and squeeze the trigger. To rinse, use a large nozzle and repeat the procedure. After cleaning and rinsing, follow the manufacturer's instructions to turn off the pressure washer.

APPLYING SEALANTS, ADHESIVES AND FILLERS

Sealants	
Caulk	Used to seal open joints and small holes: acrylic-latex for wood joints; butyl rubber-, silicone- or styrene copolymer (synthetic rubber)-based for metal flashing and gutter joints; styrene copolymer (synthetic rubber)- or polyurethane-based for vinyl and aluminum siding joints. Available in squeeze tube and applied by hand or in cartridge and applied with caulking gun *(page 116)*
Asphalt paint	Black, asphalt-based liquid coating; sold as enamel or non-fibered roof coating. Used to seal non-visible surfaces of metal gutters or flashing, for example. Available in tins and applied with paintbrush *(page 124)*
Adhesives	
Roofing cement	Can be asphalt-, tar- or neoprene (rubber)-based. Used to bond roofing materials or seal nail heads and holes in roofing materials or metal flashings or gutters, for example. Neoprene-based used on all roofing; asphalt-based used on all roofing except tar; tar-based used only on tar built-up roofing. Available in tins and applied with trowel or putty knife *(page 116)* or in cartridge and applied with caulking gun *(page 116)*
Epoxy resin	Consists of resin and hardener which form strong, waterproof bond. Used to bond fiberglass repair tape on metal gutters or flashing, for example. Available in tin or tube; mix and apply with stick or putty knife *(page 116)*
Exterior wood glue	Resorcinol best for exterior use; consists of base powder and hardener which form strong, waterproof bond. Available in tin or tube; mix and apply with stick or putty knife *(page 116)*. Clamp bonded materials until glue sets
Wood fillers	
Wood putty	Pliable wood filler compound; used to cover nail heads or fill small holes and cracks. Available in tin and applied with putty knife *(page 116)* or as crayon in a variety of colors; apply crayon only on finished surface
Epoxy patching compound	Consists of base and hardener which form strong wood filler compound that holds its shape. Used to fill large holes or build up section of damaged or missing wood. Available in tin or tube; mix and apply with putty knife *(page 116)*.

Choosing a sealant, adhesive or filler.
Sealants, adhesives and fillers all have sealing, bonding and filling properties; however, a sealant is used primarily to provide a barrier, an adhesive is used primarily to bond materials and a filler is used primarily to fill in holes and gaps. Building supply centers carry sealants, adhesives and fillers that vary in flexibility and durability. Read the product's label carefully to ensure it can be used in your situation with your roofing or siding material. Always buy a high-quality product and check for an expiry date. Follow the manufacturer's instructions to prepare the surface and apply the product; wear rubber gloves and, if the product is toxic, safety goggles and a respirator. Allow the product to cure properly; curing times will vary with the temperature and humidity. Store any leftover product away safely.

APPLYING SEALANTS, ADHESIVES AND FILLERS (continued)

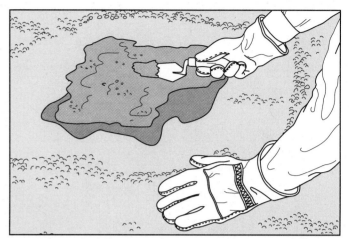

Using a caulking gun. To apply caulk or roofing cement from a cartridge, use a caulking gun. Remove old or loosened sealant or adhesive with a putty knife. Buy a cartridge of the sealant or adhesive *(page 115)* at a building supply center and load it into the caulking gun. Cut off the cartridge tip at a 45-degree angle with a utility knife; if caulking a joint, make an opening slightly narrower than the joint. Use a long nail or an awl to puncture the cartridge seal. Holding the caulking gun at a 45-degree angle to the surface, squeeze the trigger to eject a continuous bead of sealant *(above)*. If necessary, wear a rubber glove and run a wet finger along the bead to press it in place, smoothing and shaping it.

Using a trowel or a putty knife. To apply a sealant, adhesive or filler from a tin, use a trowel or a putty knife. For example, apply a large amount of roofing cement on roofing material with a trowel; apply a wood filler in a hole or crack with a putty knife. Buy a tin of the sealant, adhesive or filler *(page 115)* at a building supply center. Use the tip of the trowel or putty knife to scoop the product out of the tin, covering one third of its blade. Spread a thick coat of the product on the surface *(above)* or in the hole or crack, then use the edge of the trowel or putty knife to smooth it or level it with the surrounding surface. After applying the product, clean off the trowel or putty knife *(page 125)*.

REPAIRING ROTTED WOOD

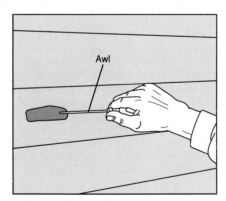

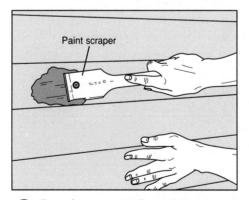

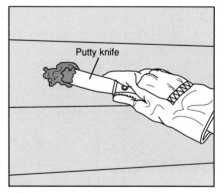

1 **Testing for rot.** Damaged finish and spongy or discolored wood may indicate rot or insect damage. If the wood is pitted, powdery, or riddled with tiny holes or tunnels, suspect insect damage and call a pest control professional. To test for rot, poke the wood with an awl as deeply as possible *(above)*. Soft wood that crumbles instead of splintering is rotted.

2 **Scraping out rotted wood.** If the wood is rotted all the way through, replace the damaged section or the entire board or panel. If the rotted area on a roof or wall is large, call for a professional evaluation. To repair a small area of surface rot, use a paint scraper, wire brush or putty knife to dig out all the soft, rotted wood *(above)* down to firm, healthy wood.

3 **Patching the surface.** Buy epoxy patching compound at a building supply center; prepare it following the manufacturer's instructions. Using a putty knife, pack compound into the damaged area *(above)* overfilling it slightly; then, level it with the surrounding surface, scraping off the excess. Allow the compound to dry, sand the surface *(page 123)* and refinish it *(page 124)*.

REPAIRING BUILDING PAPER

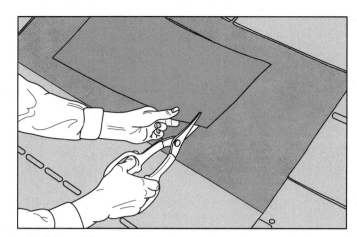

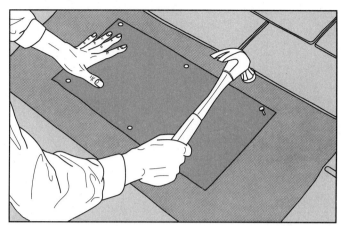

1 Preparing a patch. Patch damaged building paper before replacing the roofing or siding material. Since the "weight" of asphalt-saturated building paper may vary according to the type of roofing or siding, the location of the paper on the roof or wall, and local building codes, take a small sample with you to a building supply center and buy identical building paper. Using tin snips *(page 120)* or scissors, cut a patch *(above)* 6 inches longer and wider than the damaged area.

2 Installing the patch. Center the patch on the damaged area and use a hammer to drive a roofing nail *(page 121)* into it every 8 to 10 inches along its edges *(above)*. Using a trowel or a putty knife *(page 116)*, apply a small dab of roofing cement *(page 115)* on each nail head. Then, replace the roofing or siding material you removed.

MEASURING AND MARKING

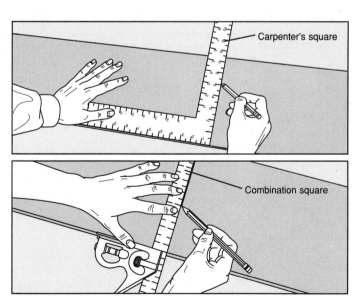

Carpenter's square

Combination square

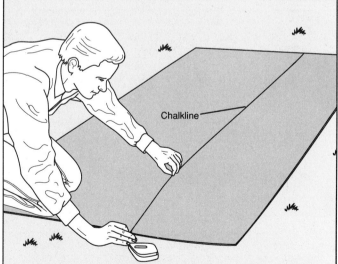

Chalkline

Measuring and marking straight lines and 90-degree angles. Accuracy in measuring and marking is essential. The standard tool for measuring length is a tape measure; be sure to add the case length when taking an inside measurement. Always measure both sides of an opening rather than presume corners are square. Use a sharp pencil or an awl for marking. To mark straight lines and 90-degree angles across a piece, use a carpenter's square *(above left, top)* or combination square *(above left, bottom)* or try square, holding it flat against the side of the piece. To mark long, straight lines, use a chalkline. Hook the line on a nail or edge at one end of the piece and stretch it tautly to the other end; holding the end of the line or case firmly, snap the line only once by lifting it straight up 3 to 4 inches *(above, right)* and letting it go.

MEASURING AND MARKING (continued)

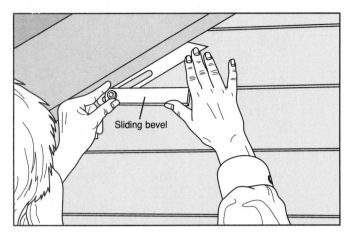

Measuring and marking other than 90-degree angles. To measure and transfer angles larger or smaller than 90 degrees, use a sliding bevel. Loosen the wing nut on the sliding bevel, adjust the sliding bevel to the angle being measured *(above)* and then tighten the wing nut. To transfer the angle, hold the bevel flat against the side of the piece to be marked and use a sharp pencil or an awl to mark the angle onto the piece.

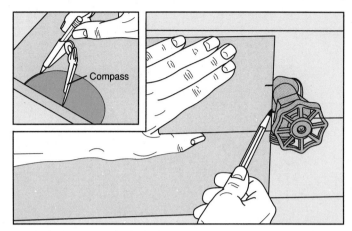

Marking curves and shapes. For a curve or odd shape, hold the piece as close as possible to its installed position and use a sharp pencil or an awl to mark it by eye *(above)*. An arc or a circle can be accurately marked with a compass; find the midpoint, open the compass to the radius and, holding the point of the compass on the midpoint, mark the arc *(inset)* or circle. First, cut the piece slightly larger than the cutting line; then, test fit it, adjust the cutting line, if necessary, and cut it to size.

CUTTING

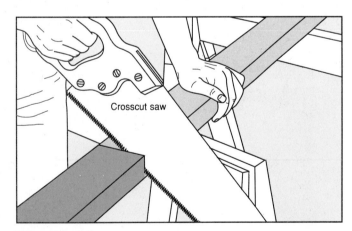

Using a crosscut saw. For quick, rough cuts across the wood grain of a board or for cutting hardboard or plywood, use a crosscut saw. Measure and mark the piece *(page 117)* and, if necessary, support it. To start the cut, hold the saw almost perpendicular to the piece, aligning your shoulder and arm with the cutting line, and draw the blade slowly toward you a few times. Lower the saw to a 45-degree angle and cut on the downstroke *(above)* until the blade is 1 inch from the end of the cut. To finish the cut, grip the waste end with one hand, hold the saw perpendicular to the piece, and cut using short up-and-down strokes. Preserve or finish the piece before installing it *(page 124)*.

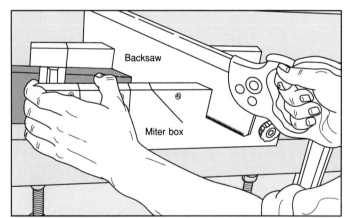

Using a backsaw and miter box. For fine wood cuts, especially joints in small boards, use a backsaw. To saw a small piece at a 90- or 45-degree angle, use a miter box. Measure and mark the piece *(page 117)* and, if necessary, support it. If using a miter box, protect the interior with a wood block and clamp it to the work surface. Align the cutting line on the piece with the appropriate angled slot and clamp the piece in the miter box. Fit the saw blade into the slot. To start the cut, hold the saw level and draw the blade slowly toward you a few times. Applying light pressure, use long, smooth back-and-forth strokes to cut through the piece *(above)*. Preserve or finish the piece before installing it *(page 124)*.

CUTTING (continued)

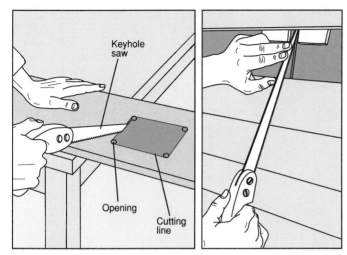

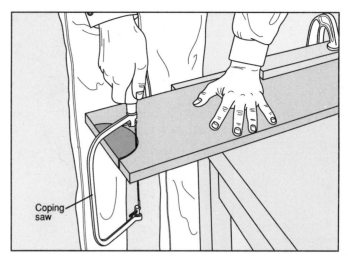

Using a keyhole saw. For wood cuts within the interior of a piece, in a tight corner or at an awkward angle, use a keyhole saw. Measure and mark the piece *(page 117)* and, if necessary, support it. If starting in the interior of a piece, bore *(page 121)* openings for the saw blade. To start the cut, insert the toe of the blade, hold the saw almost perpendicular to the piece, and draw the blade slowly toward you a few times. Lower the saw to a 45-degree angle and cut on the downstroke *(above, left)*; use long, even strokes to keep the blade from buckling. In a tight corner or at an awkward angle, cut with the toe *(above, right)* or heel of the blade using short strokes. Preserve or finish the piece before installing it *(page 124).*

Using a coping saw. For irregular or curved wood cuts at the edge of a piece, use a coping saw. Measure and mark the piece *(page 117)* and, if necessary, support it overhanging the edge of a bench. With the blade set in line with the handle, start the cut by holding the saw almost perpendicular to the piece and drawing it towards you a few times. Cut through the piece on the upstroke; use long, even strokes to keep the blade from twisting and snapping. If the blade begins to bind, stop sawing, remove the saw and reset the blade angle in the direction of the cut; then, continue cutting *(above).* Preserve or finish the piece before installing it *(page 124).*

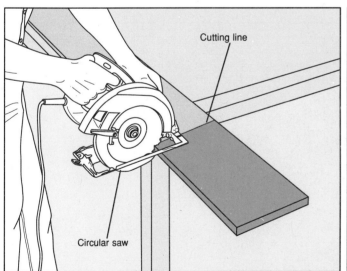

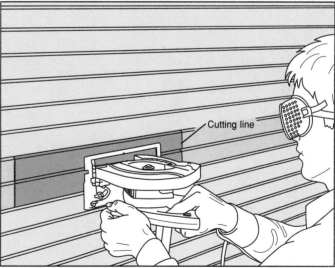

Using a circular saw. For crosscuts, across wood grain, and rip cuts, along wood grain, use a circular saw with a combination blade. Measure and mark the piece *(page 117)* and, if necessary, support it. Set the blade depth: for a standard cut, about 1/2 inch more than the wood thickness; for a plunge cut, equal to the wood thickness. Set the baseplate to the cutting angle desired; for a plunge cut, always 90 degrees. Wear safety goggles. For a standard cut, align the baseplate notch with the cutting line on the piece, turn on the saw and push it forward *(above, left)*. For a plunge cut, lift the saw at an angle to the piece and rest the baseplate farther along the cutting line. Turn on the saw, raise the guard and slowly lower the blade; then, if necessary, push the saw along the cutting line *(above, right)*. To make a saw guide, temporarily nail or clamp a straight-edged board along the outer edge of the baseplate. Preserve or finish the piece before installing it *(page 124).*

CUTTING (continued)

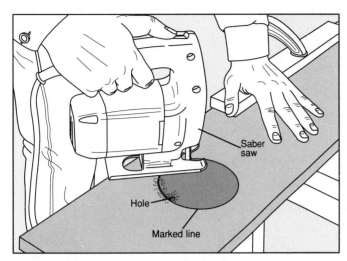

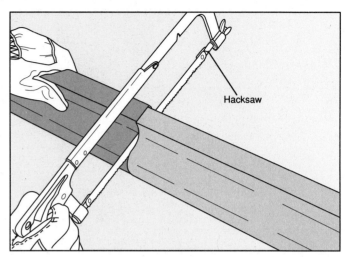

Using a saber saw. For wood cuts in the interior of a piece, or at tight or awkward angles, use a saber saw. Measure and mark the piece *(page 117)* and, if necessary, support it. Wear safety goggles. For a standard cut, align the blade with the cutting line, turn on the saw and push it forward. For cuts in the interior of a piece, bore *(page 121)* an opening, insert the blade, turn on the saw and push forward along the cutting line *(above)*. For a plunge cut, hold the saw at an angle above the piece and rest the baseplate farther along the cutting line; turn on the saw and slowly lower the blade into the piece. For a bevel cut, set the baseplate at the angle desired and follow the standard procedure. Preserve or finish the piece before installing it *(page 124)*.

Using a hacksaw. To cut metal or vinyl, use a hacksaw; for aluminum or steel, use a blade with 32 teeth per inch. Measure and mark the piece *(page 117)* and, if necessary, support it. Wear work gloves and safety goggles. To start the cut, position the blade on the cutting line and push it slowly away from you a few times. Cut the piece on long push strokes using light, even pressure *(above)*. To finish the cut, grip the waste end with one hand and cut using short strokes. File any burrs off the cut edge *(page 123)*. If necessary, finish the piece before installing it *(page 124)*. Use a hacksaw blade alone to saw off fasteners hidden under roofing or behind siding; position the teeth on the metal and cut using short push strokes.

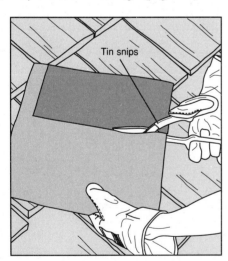

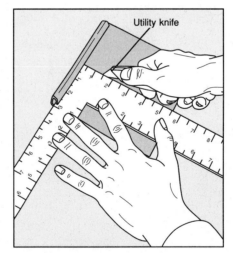

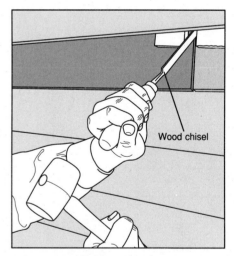

Using tin snips. To cut metal or vinyl, use tin snips. Measure and mark the piece *(page 117)*. Wear work gloves. Unlock any safety catch on the tin snips, open the jaws and slide the piece between the blades. Close the jaws and cut along the cutting line with a smooth scissors-like motion *(above)*; hold the piece firmly with your hand and avoid closing the jaws completely to prevent cutting a ragged edge. File any burrs off the cut edge *(page 123)*.

Using a utility knife. To score metal or vinyl, use a utility knife. Measure and mark the piece *(page 117)*. Position the tip of the blade at the end of the cutting line farthest from you, then firmly draw the blade along the line toward you, using a carpenter's square as a guide *(above)*. Repeat, pushing the blade deeper with each pass, until the piece is cut; or, bend the piece back and forth along the scored line to snap off the excess. Dispose of dull blades.

Using a wood chisel. To cut through or shape and smooth a wood piece, use a chisel. Point the cutting edge away from you. To make a deep cut, hold the chisel at a 90-degree angle to the piece with the bevel facing the waste and strike the handle: with a mallet, if it is wooden *(above)*; with a ball-peen hammer, if it is plastic- or metal-capped. To shape or smooth the surface, turn the chisel bevel up, holding it almost horizontal; make light, even strokes using only hand pressure.

DRILLING

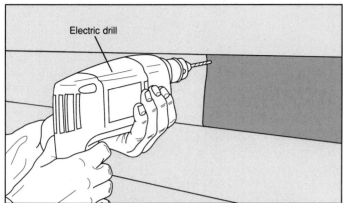

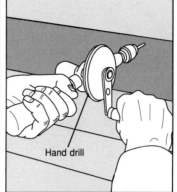

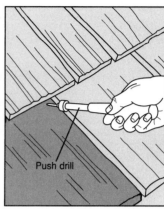

Using a drill. For boring into wood and drilling into metal or masonry, use a power drill. A power drill is sized by the largest diameter bit its chuck can hold. For most drilling purposes, use a 3/8-inch drill; into metal, use a variable speed drill. Cordless electric drills are useful at locations far from outlets, such as the roof. Bits are available for boring into wood or drilling into metal or masonry; always use the proper bit for the job. Unplug the drill when loading or unloading a bit. When drilling a hole, the bit size to use depends on the diameter and type of hole required. Bore or drill a pilot hole equal in depth to the fastener length, using a bit slightly narrower than the fastener. Bore or drill a clearance hole using a bit of the same diameter as the fastener. To mark the hole depth, if necessary, wrap tape around the bit. Punch a starter hole for the bit using an awl. Wear safety goggles. Position the bit at the starter hole, pull the trigger and push the bit into the piece *(above, left)*. When withdrawing the bit, keep the drill running. For boring or drilling into thin materials, use a hand or push drill. With a hand drill, position the bit and, applying light pressure, turn the handle counterclockwise a turn or two to start the hole; then, turn it clockwise to bore or drill the hole *(above, center)*. For a push drill, push forward firmly on the handle to bore or drill the hole *(above, right)*.

CHOOSING A FASTENER

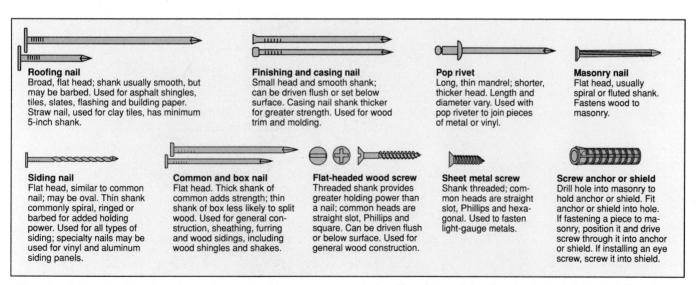

Roofing nail
Broad, flat head; shank usually smooth, but may be barbed. Used for asphalt shingles, tiles, slates, flashing and building paper. Straw nail, used for clay tiles, has minimum 5-inch shank.

Finishing and casing nail
Small head and smooth shank; can be driven flush or set below surface. Casing nail shank thicker for greater strength. Used for wood trim and molding.

Pop rivet
Long, thin mandrel; shorter, thicker head. Length and diameter vary. Used with pop riveter to join pieces of metal or vinyl.

Masonry nail
Flat head, usually spiral or fluted shank. Fastens wood to masonry.

Siding nail
Flat head, similar to common nail; may be oval. Thin shank commonly spiral, ringed or barbed for added holding power. Used for all types of siding; specialty nails may be used for vinyl and aluminum siding panels.

Common and box nail
Flat head. Thick shank of common adds strength; thin shank of box less likely to split wood. Used for general construction, sheathing, furring and wood sidings, including wood shingles and shakes.

Flat-headed wood screw
Threaded shank provides greater holding power than a nail; common heads are straight slot, Phillips and square. Can be driven flush or below surface. Used for general wood construction.

Sheet metal screw
Shank threaded; common heads are straight slot, Phillips and hexagonal. Used to fasten light-gauge metals.

Screw anchor or shield
Drill hole into masonry to hold anchor or shield. Fit anchor or shield into hole. If fastening a piece to masonry, position it and drive screw through it into anchor or shield. If installing an eye screw, screw it into shield.

Choosing fasteners. The chart above shows typical fasteners used on roofing and siding. Follow your roofing or siding manufacturer's recommendations for fasteners, or take an old fastener to a building supply center and buy an exact replacement. Fasteners must be compatible with the type of material they are being driven into; unless otherwise indicated, buy hot-dipped galvanized (HDG) types for corrosion resistance. You may need to buy nails of brass or copper for tiles; of copper, bronze or stainless steel for slates. For treated wood siding, ask which corrosion-resistant fastener material is compatible.

INSTALLING FASTENERS (continued)

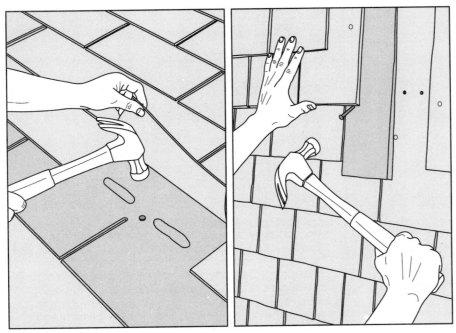

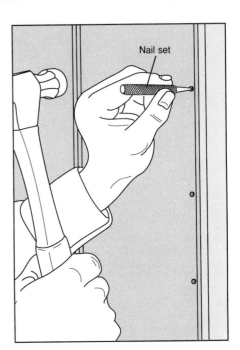

Driving in nails. Choose an appropriate type of nail *(page 121)*. To keep a nail from splitting wood, make a starter hole with an awl or bore a pilot hole *(page 121)*. To nail through one piece of material into a parallel piece of material, drive in each nail straight—a technique called face-nailing *(above, left)*. To drive in a nail at an angle through one piece of material and into another piece of material is called skew-nailing *(above, right)*. Tap the nail lightly to get it started, then drive it until its head is flush with the surface. If necessary, set the nail head *(step right)*.

Setting nail heads. To drive a nail head below the surface, use a nail set with a tip slightly smaller than the head. Position the tip of the nail set on the center of the head and tap sharply on the top of the nail set with a hammer *(above)*, driving the head about 1/16 inch below the surface. Fill the hole above the set nail head with wood putty *(page 115)*.

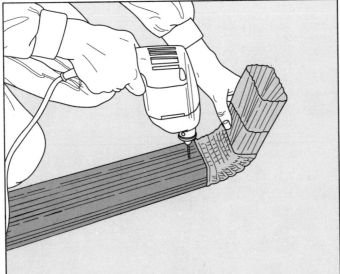

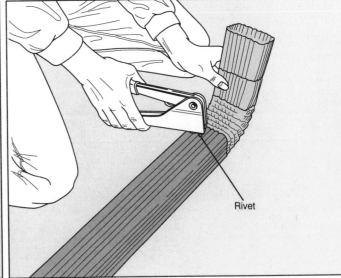

Riveting. To join two thin pieces of metal or vinyl, install pop rivets *(page 121)* using a pop riveter. Wear safety goggles. Align the two pieces of material to be joined, then drill *(page 121)* a hole equal in diameter to the rivet head through the pieces *(above, left)*. Open the handles of the riveter and insert the mandrel of a rivet. Hold the riveter in position, pushing the head of the rivet into the hole *(above, right)*; pressing firmly, squeeze the handles tightly to seat the rivet. Continue squeezing tightly until the mandrel of the rivet breaks off.

SMOOTHING SURFACES

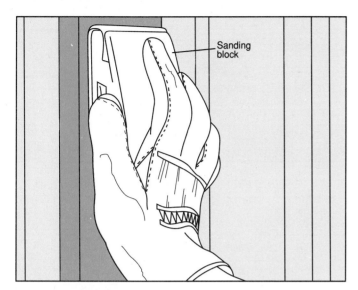

Using a sanding block. Use sandpaper and a sanding block to smooth small, flat surfaces. Wear a dust mask and work gloves. Using scissors or a utility knife *(page 120)*, cut a sheet of sandpaper to fit the sanding block. Work along the grain as much as possible, applying even, moderate pressure *(above)*. Replace the sandpaper when it clogs and cannot be cleared by tapping the sanding block on a hard surface. Use a whisk to brush off dust. Before applying a finish, wipe off the surface with a clean cloth.

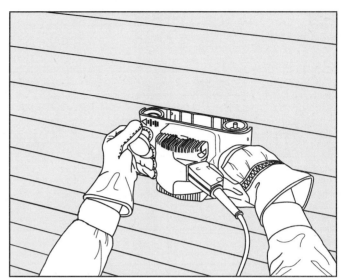

Using a power sander. Use a belt or orbital sander to smooth large, flat surfaces; use a belt sander to remove paint or smooth rough surfaces and use an orbital sander for final smoothing or on unfinished surfaces. Wear a dust mask, work gloves and safety goggles. Using scissors or a utility knife *(page 120)*, cut a sheet of sandpaper to fit the sander. Applying even, moderate pressure, work along the grain with a belt sander *(above)*; with an orbital sander keep it moving smoothly. Replace clogged or ripped sandpaper. Use a whisk to brush off dust. Wipe off the surface with a clean cloth before applying a finish.

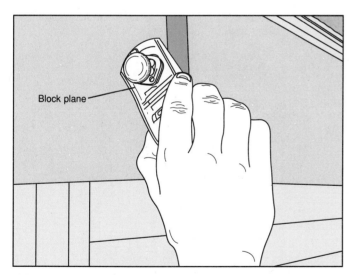

Using a block plane. Use a block plane to smooth or trim a piece of wood across its end grain. To adjust the blade, or iron, hold the plane upside down. Turn the depth-adjustment nut until the iron barely protrudes from the mouth; push the lateral-adjustment lever from side to side until the iron is aligned squarely within the mouth. Test the plane on scrap wood and readjust the iron until the plane provides the desired cutting depth. To use the plane, work across the wood grain. Hold the plane in one hand, with the heel of the lever cap resting in your palm, and push the plane forward, applying even pressure *(above)*; transfer pressure to the heel to raise the plane from the surface in a smooth motion.

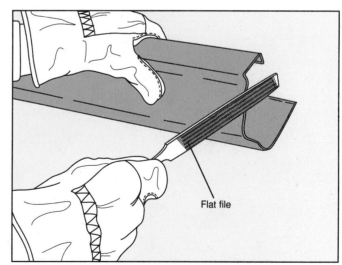

Using a file. Use a flat file to smooth rough edges on metal or vinyl, and to take burrs off metal—especially after cutting it. Wear work gloves. Support the piece to be filed firmly against a surface or clamp it in place. Holding the handle of the file with one hand, apply light, even pressure and slowly push the blade in a straight line across the edge of the piece *(above)*; lift the blade off the edge of the piece on the return stroke. Continue the procedure until all sharp edges and burrs are smoothed.

APPLYING PRESERVATIVES AND FINISHES

FINISH	CHARACTERISTICS	REMARKS
Water-repellent preservative	May contain inorganic arsenic, fungicides, wax, solvents; may contain pigment or may temporarily darken wood; eventually weathers to natural color	Apply to bare wood; dip or brush on; can be used under finish in place of primer or for treating end grain on pressure-treated wood; reapply or touch up every 1-2 years
Semi-transparent penetrating stain	Alkyd-based; may contain water repellents, fungicides and mildewcides; contains pigment that tints wood but does not obscure wood grain; penetrates wood	Brush, roll or spray on; must be applied to bare wood or over similar stain; stir frequently to distribute pigment; reapply or touch up every 2-3 years
Opaque stain	Latex- or alkyd-based; colors but does not completely obscure wood grain; forms a thin film on wood surface	Brush, roll or spray on; reapply or touch up every 4-5 years
Exterior-grade alkyd paint	Contains synthetic resins; may contain fungicides and mildewcides; forms a film on wood surface	Brush, roll or spray on; apply alkyd primer, then one or two top coats; reapply or touch up every 4-6 years
Exterior-grade latex paint	Contains acrylic or vinyl resins; may contain fungicides and mildewcides; forms a film on wood surface	Brush, roll or spray on; apply latex or alkyd primer, then one or two top coats; reapply or touch up every 4-6 years
Metal paint	Alkyd- or latex-based; contains a rust inhibitor or requires a rust-inhibiting primer; galvanized metal primer available	Brush, roll or spray on; reapply every 5-6 years, touch up rust spots immediately

Choosing a finish. Consult the chart above to select a finish; before applying it, sand the surface *(page 123)*. Follow the manufacturer's instructions for surface preparation, priming, application and safety. Use drop cloths or tarps and masking tape to protect nearby surfaces and vegetation. Wear rubber gloves, long pants and long sleeves. Apply a small test patch on an inconspicuous surface to check its effect before starting work. Keep product labels for reference when a touch-up or a new finish is necessary. Before installing new wood, preserve or finish it; use a paintbrush *(below)* or dip the piece in a container of preservative or finish.

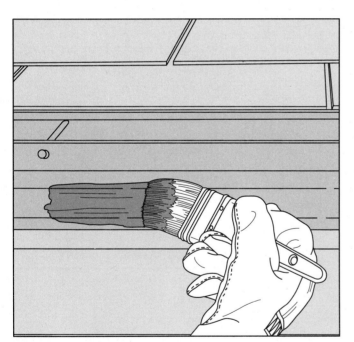

Using a paintbrush. To preserve or finish most surfaces, use a paintbrush; a synthetic, flag-bristled type is usually recommended. Before using a latex-based finish, dampen the brush with water; for alkyd- or oil-based finishes, dampen it with mineral spirits. Wipe off excess with a clean cloth. To use a paintbrush, load one third to one half the bristle length, then gently slap the bristles against the inside of the pail or can to remove excess paint. Work top to bottom, first coating surfaces hard to reach. Work along the surface, using short and then long strokes to spread the finish evenly; ensure that any end grain is well covered. Sand the surface between coats *(page 123)*. Clean the brush *(page 125)* when finished.

Using a roller. To finish large, flat surfaces, use a roller; one with a short nap of synthetic fiber is recommended. If necessary, attach an extension pole. Before using a latex-based finish, dampen the roller with water; for alkyd- or oil-based finishes, dampen it with mineral spirits. Wipe off excess with a clean cloth. Pour 1 inch of finish into a roller pan; use the flat ridged end to work finish into the roller, without overloading it. Roll on the finish evenly, one small area at a time, pushing and pulling the roller *(above)*. To spread a stain or penetrating finish evenly, backbrush the edges with a dry paintbrush. Sand the surface between coats *(page 123)*. Clean the roller *(page 125)* when finished.

Using a sprayer. To apply finish to large, irregular surfaces, use a paint sprayer, available at a tool rental agency. Work only on a calm day and wear work gloves, safety goggles and a respirator. Following the manufacturer's instructions, pour about 8 ounces of finish into the reservoir of the sprayer; if applying paint, first filter out lumps through a doubled layer of cheese cloth. Screw the reservoir tightly onto the gun. Test the sprayer on a scrap piece; if necessary, adjust the nozzle until the sprayer produces an even coating of finish. Working top to bottom, hold the sprayer nozzle 10 to 12 inches from the surface and pull the trigger *(above)*; move the sprayer slowly from side to side. Sand the surface between coats *(page 123)*.

Using a commercial airless sprayer. To apply finish on the entire roofing or siding, use a commercial airless spayer, available at a tool rental agency. Following the manufacturer's instructions, fill the hopper of the sprayer with finish; otherwise, fill a separate container and insert the suction hose into it. If necessary, fit a nozzle onto the spray wand. Wear work gloves, safety goggles and a respirator. Turn on the machine. To start, aim the spray wand at the roofing or siding with the nozzle 12 inches from the surface and pull the trigger. To stop, release the trigger; when finished, turn off the machine. Sand the surface between coats *(page 123)*.

CLEANING TOOLS

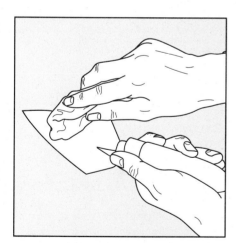

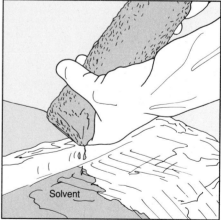

Cleaning a trowel or putty knife. Clean off a trowel or putty knife with mineral spirits immediately after using it to prevent a sealant, adhesive or filler from hardening on it. Following the manufacturer's instructions, work in a well-ventilated area and wear rubber gloves. Dampen a clean rag with the mineral spirits, then vigorously rub the blade of the trowel *(above)* or putty knife to clean it off; avoid applying mineral spirits on the handle.

Cleaning a paintbrush or roller. Remove excess finish from a paintbrush or roller by applying it onto newspaper. To clean off remaining latex-based finish, hold the brush or roller under running water and rub it with your fingers until the water runs clear. Apply a drop of household detergent, work it in by hand and rinse. Shake off excess water. To clean off alkyd- or oil-based finish, use a solvent (either paint thinner, mineral spirits or turpentine). Wear rubber gloves and work in a ventilated area. For a brush, fill a container with solvent, agitate the brush in it until it clouds, then pour it out; repeat with clean solvent until it no longer clouds. Pour clean solvent onto the bristles and work it in by hand *(above, left)*. Hang the brush to dry. Clean a roller in a paint tray *(above, right)* following the same procedure, then stand it on end to dry. Pour used solvent into a sealed container for disposal.

INDEX

Page references in *italics* indicate an illustration of the subject mentioned. Page references in **bold** indicate a Troubleshooting Guide for the subject mentioned.

A

Adhesives, 115
  Removal from tools, *125*
Aluminum siding, **103**, *102-103*
  Cleaning, *104*
  Corner caps, *110*
  Repair, *107-108*
    surface damage, *104*
  Replacement, *108-111*
  Starter strips, *109*
Asphalt shingles, **50**-*51*
  Popped nails, *52*
  Replacement, *54-56*
    chimneys, *60*
    eaves, *58*
    rakes, *59*
    ridges and hips, *59-60*
    valleys, *56-58*
    vents, *61*
  Tabs, *53-54*
Attics, *10*, 16
Augers, *36*

B

Blisters:
  Plywood siding, *98*
  Tar and gravel roofing, *73*
Boards and battens, *96*
Building paper, *117*
Built-up roofing. *See* Tar and gravel roofing

C

Cap and pan tiles, *66-67*
Ceilings:
  Leaks, *11*
Cement tiles. *See* Tile roofs
Chimneys:
  Asphalt shingles, *60*
  Wood shingles and shakes, *84*
Chisels, *120*
Clay tiles. *See* Tile roofs
Concrete tiles. *See* Tile roofs
Corner boards:
  Wood siding, *101*
Corner caps:
  Aluminum and vinyl siding, *110*
  Wood siding, *95*
Corner posts, *110*

D

Doors:
  Aluminum and vinyl siding, *111*
  Wood shingles and shakes, *84*
  Wood siding, *101*
Downspouts, **34**-*35*
  Cleaning, *36*
  Metal, *37*, *44-45*
  Screening, *37*
  Vinyl, *45*
Drain cages, *71*
Drills, *121*
Drip edges, *40*

E

Eaves:
  Asphalt shingles, *58-59*
  Icicles, *12*
Electrical circuits, *10*
Electrical shock, 8, *13*
Emergency procedures, **9**, 8
  Electrical, *10*
  First aid, *12-13*
  Leaks, 8, *10-11*
  See also Safety precautions

F

Fascias, **46**, 39
  Aluminum and vinyl, 46, *48-49*
  Wood, 46, *47*
Fasteners, *121-122*
Files, *123*
Finishes, *124-125*
  Wood shingles and shakes, *79*
  Wood siding, *90*
First aid, *12-13*
Flashings, 14, *18-21*
Flat roofs. *See* Tar and gravel roofing
Furring strips, *100*

G

Gables:
  Vents, *23*
Gravel. *See* Tar and gravel roofing
Gutters, **34**-*35*
  Cleaning, *36*
  Drip edges, *40*
  Hangers, *39-40*
  Metal, *37-38*, *41-43*
  Screening, *37*
  Vinyl, *43-44*

H

Hips:
  Asphalt shingles, *59-60*
  Wood shingles and shakes, *85*

I

Ice, 8, 11
  Icicles, *12*
Interlocking tiles, *64-65*

L

Ladders, 24, *26-29*
  Extension, *27-28*
Leaf guards and strainers, *36-37*
Leaks, 8, *10-11*

M-N-O

Miter boxes, *118*
Nails, *122*
Oxalic acid, 78, 89, 90, 104

P

Painting tools, *124-125*
Paints, *124-125*
Plywood:
  Blister repair, *98*
Power tools, *114*
  Circular saws, *119*
  Drills, 11, *121*
  Pressure washers, *115*
  Safety precautions, 8, 11
  Sanders, *123*
  Sprayers, *125*
Preservatives, *124-125*
  Wood shingles and shakes, *79*
Pressure washing, *77-78*, 115
Professional repairs:
  Aluminum and vinyl siding, 102, 110
  Asphalt shingles, 55, 58, 59
  Chimney flashing, 60
  Fascias and soffits, 46
  Gutter hangers, 39
  Rafters, 47
  Slate roofs, 63, 68, 69
  Sloped roofs, 24, 26
  Tar and gravel roofing, 73
  Tile and slate roofs, 24
  Tile roofs, 63, 64, 65, 66, 67
  Wood shingles and shakes, 74
  Wood siding, 87

R

Repair techniques, *117-125*
Ridges:
  Asphalt shingles, *59-60*
  Wood shingles and shakes, *85*
Rivets, *122*
Roofs, **16-17**, *14-17*
  See also Downspouts; Fascias; Gutters;
  Shingles; Slate
    roofs; Tile roofs

S

S-shaped tiles, *65-66*
Safety harnesses, *30-31*
Safety precautions, 8, *24-25*, *29-30*
  Electrical circuits, 10, *11*
  Ice and snow, 8, 11, *12*
  Ladders, 24, *26-29*
  Oxalic acid, 78, 89, 90, 104
  Safety harnesses, *30-31*
  Scaffolding, 24, *31-33*
  See also Emergency procedures
Sanders, *123*
Saws:
  Backsaws, *118*
  Circular, *119*
  Coping, *119*
  Crosscut, *118*
  Hacksaws, *120*
  Keyhole, *119*
  Saber, *120*
Scaffolding, 24, *31-33*
Sealants, 115
  Removal from tools, *125*
Service panels, *10*
Shakes, **76**, *74-75*
  Cleaning, 74, *77-79*
  Replacement, *81, 83-85*
Shingles. *See* Asphalt shingles; Shakes;
Wood shingles
Shiplap board siding, *9798*
Sidings, **16-17**, *14-17*
  See also Aluminum siding; Vinyl siding;
  Wood siding, See
Slate rippers, 63
Slate roofs, **63**, 24, *62-63, 68-69*
Sloped roofs, 24
  Measurement, *26*
Snow, 8, 11

Soffits, *46*
  Vents, *22*
Spikes and ferrules, *39, 40*
Sprayers, *114, 125*
Stains:
  Wood shingles and shakes, *78-79*
  Wood siding, *89-90*
Starter shingles:
  Asphalts, *58-59*
Starter strips:
  Aluminum and vinyl siding, *109*
  Wood siding, *95*

T

Tar and gravel roofing, **70**-*71*
  Blisters, *73*
  Patching, *72-73*
Tile roofs, **63**, 24, *62-63*
  Cap and pan tiles, *66-67*
  Interlocking tiles, *64-65*
  S-shaped tiles, *65-66*
Tin snips, *120*
Tongue and groove siding, *97-98*
Tools, *112-113*
  Augers, *36*
  Cleaning, *125*
  Drills, *121*
  Files, *123*
  Ladders, 24, *26-29*
  Miter boxes, *118*
  Paintbrushes and rollers, *124-125*
  Safety harnesses, *30-31*
  Sanders, *123*
  Saws, *118-120*
  Scaffolding, 24, *31-33*
  Slate rippers, 63
  Sprayers, *114, 125*
  Tin snips, *120*
  Utility knives, *120*
  Vinyl siding, 103
  Wood chisels, *120*
Trim channels:
  Vinyl siding, *106-107*
Troubleshooting Guides:
  Asphalt shingles, 50
  Emergency guide, 9
  Fascias, 46
  Gutters and downspouts, 34
  Tar and gravel roofing, 70
  Tile and slate roofing, 63
  Vinyl and aluminum siding, 103
  Wood shingles and shakes, 76
  Wood siding, 87
  Your roofing and siding, 16-17
Turbine vents, 23

U-V

Utility knives, *120*
Vents:
  Asphalt shingles, *61*
  Gables, *23*
  Soffits, *22*
  Turbine, *23*
  Wood shingles and shakes, *84*
Vinyl siding, **103**, *102-103*
  Replacement, *105-107, 110, 111*
  Starter strips, *109*
  Surface damage, *104*

W

Windows:
  Aluminum and vinyl siding, *111*
  Wood shingles and shakes, *84*
  Wood siding, *101*
Wood shingles, **76**, *74-75*
  Cleaning, 74, *77-79*
  Finishing, *79*
  Replacement, *80-81, 82, 83-85*
  ridges and hips, *85*
Wood siding, **87**, *86-87*
  Cleaning, *89-90*
  Furring strips, *100*
  Horizontal lapped board
    repairing, *91-94*
    replacement, *94-95*
  Nail patterns, *88*
  Panels, *99*
  Plywood, *98*
  Refinishing, *90*
  Replacement, *101*
  Tongue and groove / shiplap board, *97-98*
  Trim boards, *100*
  Vertical board and batten, *96*
Woven corners
  Wood shingles and shakes, *84*

ACKNOWLEDGMENTS

The editors wish to thank the following:
Roland Bélanger, Multi-Ventilation Inc., Montreal, Que.; Steven Boots, Stinson Manufacturing Co., Spokane, Wash.; BPCO Inc., Lachine, Que.; Brian Buchanan, Texas Forest Service, Lufkin, Tex.; Cedar Shake and Shingle Bureau, Bellevue, Wash.; Construction Safety Association of Ontario, Toronto, Ont.; Domtar Construction Materials, Roofing and Insulation Division, Montreal, Que.; Dick Fricklas, The Roofing Industry Educational Institute, Englewood, Colo.; Jean-Paul Grenier, Cargil Gérance (1980) Ltd., Boucherville, Que.; GSW Building Products Company, Hamilton, Ont.; John Gurniak, P.E., American Architectural Manufacturers Association, Des Plaines, Ill.; Rick Kelly, Roofing Wholesale Co., Inc., San Marcos, Calif.; Pete Kent, Western Wood Products Association, Portland, Oreg.; Alan D. Kline, Lynn Ladder and Scaffolding Co., Inc., West Lynn, Mass.; Rich Kotowski, Allendorfer Roofing, Chicago, Ill.; Robert LaCosse, National Roofing Contractors Association, Rosemont, Ill.; Raymond Loomis, Evergreen Slate Co., Granville, N.Y.; MacMillan Bloedel Building Materials, Montreal, Que.; Karl Marcuse Reg'd, Montreal, Que.; Marley Roof Tiles Ltd., Milton, Ont.; Jim Meszaros, Alcan Building Products, Scarborough, Ont.; Tom ("The Tank") O'Brien, Clark Roofing, Chicago, Ill.; The technical advisors of Primeau Metal Inc., Montreal, Que.; Walter Pruter, National Tile Manufacturers Association, Los Angeles, Calif.; Bradford S. Raleigh, The Roofing Industry Educational Institute, Englewood, Colo.; Michael Reinmueller, Montreal, Que.; Normand Renaud, Scaffold Fast Montreal Inc., Montreal, Que.; Reynolds Extrusion Co., Richmond Hill, Ont.; H.E. Saint-Amour, Canadian Roofing Contractors' Association, Ottawa, Ont.; Sashco Sealants, Commerce City, Colo.; Robert Seaman, Benton Roof Co., San Diego, Calif.; Jim Sexton, Fallbrook, Calif.; Douglas Sheldon, Vermont Structural Slate Co., Fairhaven, Vt.; Thomas Lee Smith, National Roofing Contractors Association, Rosemont, Ill.; Richard D. Snyder, Asphalt Roofing Manufacturers Association, Rockville, Md.; Luc Thériault, Alcan Building Products, Montreal, Que.; James R. Thomson, Sully-Jones Roofing Co., Lemon Grove, Cal.; Seth Warfield, The Roof Center Inc., Washington, D.C.; Lori Williams, Genova Products, Davison, Mich.

The following persons also assisted in the preparation of this book:
Daniel Bazinet, Patrick J. Gordon, Line Roberge